THE BLACK SASH

THE BLACK SASH

Women for Justice and Peace

Mary Ingouville Burton

For Steve,
With all good wishes,
Mary.

First published by Jacana Media (Pty) Ltd in 2015

10 Orange Street
Sunnyside
Auckland Park 2092
South Africa
+2711 628 3200
www.jacana.co.za

ISBN 978-1-4314-2228-9

Set in Minion Pro 11/16pt
Printed and bound by Shumani Mills, Cape Town
Job no. 002534

Also available in as an e-book
d-PDF ISBN 978-1-4314-2290-6
ePUB ISBN 978-1-4314-2291-3
mobi file ISBN 978-1-4314-2292-0

See a complete list of Jacana titles at www.jacana.co.za

To the women of South Africa, present and future,
who in a myriad ways will carry our still-fractured country
towards justice and peace

CONTENTS

PREFACE

Gathering material for this book has been a wonderful experience, spread over about a dozen years. Interviews and conversations with Black Sash colleagues have revived memories and clarified my understanding. The remarkable amount of books and documents available is a treasure trove of information and offers many more opportunities for exploration. A full history of the Black Sash and the period in which it was formed and developed was my original goal.

Yet, as I considered what contribution the Sash had made, it seemed more important to tell its story in a way that could convey the spirit of resistance to injustice, of seeking to overcome a heritage of racism and oppression. My intention has been to write an honest book, one that tells a part of a real experience, about women, privileged women, working for a better society, seeking knowledge and understanding about how to build it, learning about themselves and others. I have tried to give a glimpse of what it was like to be part of this organisation and, thereby, part of South Africa's history.

The people who have contributed to this book make a lengthy list. Some of them are no longer alive, and they are greatly missed. There are many others, too many to name individually – the thousands who made the Sash what it was and those whose own lives were intertwined with it. It is my hope that even if they do not find their names in these pages, they will recognise the work that they did and the value it had. My first thanks, therefore, go to my Black Sash colleagues over 50 years, those wonderful, intelligent, dedicated women, who could also be quirky, controversial, argumentative, inspiring and challenging. They and the organisation itself provided opportunities for all of us to grow in understanding, to encounter new experiences, to serve South Africa and its people in many different ways, and sometimes to be stretched beyond imagining. Thanks also to the trustees of the 'new' Black Sash, carrying the responsibility for its growth and development, and to the staff who keep it in active service.

All those who shared their memories with me have enriched my understanding of the Black Sash and its achievements, but not all of them are cited in the text. I am grateful to Di Andrews, Rosemary Meny-Gibert, Beva Runciman, Val Rose-Christie, Margie Probyn, Mary Grice, Sarah Burns, Patty Geerdts, Jayne Beaumont, Thisbe Clegg, and the group who met in Grahamstown: Rosemary Smith, Catherine Letcher, Dorothy Holder, Lynette Paterson, Priscilla Hall, Maggy Clarke, Gus Macdonald, Shirley Maclennan, Peggy McCoy and Margie Laing. Hearing them talk about their experiences was one of the most rewarding aspects of preparing for this book. I wish I could have reached more members still. In writing about all of them, I have used first names after an initial mention of their surnames, and trust that they will accept this informal approach.

There have been several books and theses written about the Black Sash, which are listed in the bibliography. I have welcomed with great pleasure two books published recently which shed extra light on the organisation. Annemarie Hendrikz's biography of Sheena Duncan is a fine portrayal, revealing Sheena as a multifaceted person who made an indelible impact on the Sash. The carefully documented *Standing on Street Corners*, by Mary Kleinenberg and Christopher Merrett, records its history in the Midlands of KwaZulu-Natal. Both books are notable for their acknowledgement of the members and staff who carried out the work of the organisation and the people who were interviewed. The authors were generous in sharing with me some of the content of the interviews they conducted.

I wish to pay tribute to archivists and librarians and all those who protect memory and make history accessible. I am grateful to Michele Pickover and her team at the Historical Papers Research Archive, William Cullen Library, University of the Witwatersrand, and I have spent countless days in the Jagger Reading Room of the University of Cape Town, relying on the assistance and knowledge of all the Special Collections staff. Many of us in the Black Sash in Cape Town are indebted to Lesley Hart, retired head of UCT's Manuscripts and Archives section, for her assistance and her knowledge of the archive. We express our thanks, too, to the Andrew Mellon Foundation, for its support for UCT Libraries' project of creating a guide to the various repositories where Black Sash collections are held, thus enabling researchers to access material more efficiently.

It was my good fortune to have been granted the luxury of an office in the Centre for African Studies at UCT for several years, thanks to Brenda Cooper, the director of the centre, and to her successor, Harry Garuba. It was Brenda who advised me to apply to become an honorary research associate, which made this possible, and gave me the opportunity to work through an accumulation of many years of documents and publications, and to benefit from the stimulus of staff and students at the centre. I am grateful to them all.

Others have also provided fruitful places for writing, reading and thinking: Paul and Kari, Alan and Marcelle, Keith and Belinda. In Kleinmond the wonderful group of Grail Writers shared inspiration and encouragement, particularly Anne Schuster and Annemarie Hendrikz, as well as my companions along the journey, Carmel Rickard and Chantal Stewart.

Kylie Thomas gave wise editorial suggestions. Candy Malherbe, Judy Chalmers, Jenny de Tolly and Di Oliver read early versions of the book and made useful comments. Ann Field helped for weeks to sort through an accumulation of documents in my cluttered study.

Russell Martin of Jacana has steered me carefully to publication and helped me to believe the book would finally appear. I am immensely grateful for his guidance.

My family and friends have been patient and generous supporters of this book-writing process for much longer than they had anticipated. My sons, my daughters-in-law and my grandchildren have wondered if it would ever come to an end. Nowethu Ntlutha has taken care of my house and kept my silver gleaming. My husband Geoff, most of all, has given me companionship and support, practical help and unfaltering faith in the project. I could not have done it without them.

Mary Burton
Cape Town

INTRODUCTION

In May 2015 the Black Sash marked its 60th anniversary, tracing its history back to six founding members, who rallied thousands of South African women to public action. They were a part of widespread opposition to the National Party government's determination in the mid-1950s to alter the original constitution of the Union of South Africa, and they formed the Women's Defence of the Constitution League, wearing black sashes in their protest demonstrations. Although at the time the government succeeded in its plan, the core of the women's organisation embarked on the greater task of opposing the injustices of apartheid itself. It took on the name of the Black Sash (often informally abbreviated to 'Sash') and developed over the years into an organisation that would make a real difference to the lives of thousands of South Africans caught in the iron web of apartheid laws. Its protest activities, the in-depth knowledge gained through its advice office work, and its meticulous publications and reports gained it a remarkably wide degree of credibility and respect in both South Africa and abroad.

When I joined the Black Sash in 1965, I was fascinated by its history. Newly settled in South Africa, newly married, trying not to condemn too hastily but shaken by the cruelty of the Group Areas Act and the pass laws, I was full of questions. A friend had been invited to a meeting by Moira Henderson, a leading Cape Town member of the Sash and its regional chair at the time, and we agreed we would both join. We found ourselves in the Rondebosch branch with quite a few other new members, and were encouraged and inspired by those with longer experience. Mary Birt took us to hearings of the Group Areas Board, then imposing residential segregation on Cape Town as elsewhere. Joan Dichmont shepherded us into our first protest stands. Interesting speakers shed new light on legislation, on socio-economic issues, justice and equal rights, and we were privileged to meet some of the leading thinkers of the time, such as Leo and Nell Marquard.[1] We accompanied Noël Robb to inspect the hostels in Langa on the outskirts of Cape Town where migrant workers were obliged to live. We persuaded Peggy Roberts to give us answers to the hostile questions often tossed at us at dinner parties, so that we would be better equipped. Doors were opened to us that we could not have envisaged, such as being invited through Eulalie Stott (also a founding member of the Sash and one of its early national presidents) to meet Imam Abdullah Haron – an encounter which made his arrest and death in detention in 1969 even more of a shock.

These experiences were much the same all over the country. Memories bubbled up when a group of Sashers met in Johannesburg in 2010 to talk about the ways they had been drawn into the organisation.[2] Several claimed to have been inveigled into action by Jill Wentzel or by Audrey Coleman. 'She just told me to organise the fete.' 'She would draw people into tasks and show them that she believed in them, which gave them confidence.' Laura Pollecutt joined through links made in the Progressive Party: 'I did not have the same social standing and education as some of the leaders; when Jill brought me in to coordinate the morning market, I had to attend the regional council meeting to report on progress, but was only allowed to stay in the meeting for that item, not for the whole agenda.' She was soon drawn into many more aspects of the work, and says what she really valued in the Black Sash was the knowledge she gained. 'It was a real revelation and a wonderful experience', she said, and recounted how she and others were mandated to represent the Sash in campaigns with other civil society organisations and how this expanded their awareness, gave them insight and a broader understanding of politics.

Other members remarked: 'The Sash was a place in a very hostile world, where you could say what you felt. You joined because you wanted to do something – we were all desperate for social justice. The sharing, and the learning, that is what kept me around. We used to get together to make the placards, and the discussions would whirl around that.' Ethel Walt, who had brought the group together in her apartment in 2010, added, 'Those poster stands were so wonderful. A man once came and stood right by me, and I felt anxious, but he said, "You women are doing what we men are too cowardly to do."' Others remembered more unpleasant responses, having cars swerve at them, or objects and insults hurled at them. Especially when protest stands in groups were banned in 1976, as were all outdoor gatherings, it took courage for individual women to stand in public with a lone placard.

Taking part in demonstrations sometimes resulted in being arrested, and even this had its intriguing aspects, illustrating the parts played by women in resistance to apartheid. In August 1989, a Sash protest stand outside the Methodist Church in Cape Town's Greenmarket Square led to the arrest of some of us, and our being transported to Caledon Square police station in a rather smart police bus. A few days later, many of the same group participated in a march of over 200 women to the British Embassy, and were all arrested and taken to Caledon Square, where the situation was very different.[3] This time we were there for hours, each one being photographed and fingerprinted, and in the meantime we sang, danced and formed a long chain in which each massaged the shoulders of the person in front of her. Once again, different strategies were evident: some women were defiant, even aggressively angry towards the police; others tried to engage them in conversation. Leah Tutu was among us, and we heard later that a phone call had gone to Bishopscourt to tell Archbishop Tutu the news. By chance my husband was at a meeting there, and the two of them came to Caledon Square to intervene. Leah and I were not willing to leave until everyone had been released, so the processing continued. One of the senior police officers, who had been involved in both events, said sorrowfully to me, 'We tried to treat you so nicely, but then you go and do this now.'

This book is a contribution to understanding the place of the Black Sash in our history. It tries to answer the questions we are often asked: What brought the Black Sash into being? Even more interesting, what kept it alive for so many decades? How did an organisation of mainly white, mostly middle-class, privileged women create and sustain a viable structure that eventually made its contribution to the collapse of apartheid and the development of a democratic society? What was it like to be involved in it? And, more recently, what can we learn from its history that will teach us to be activists again?

So who were these hundreds of women who formed the Black Sash over its first 40 years? They were educationists and teachers, poets and writers, artists and musicians, respected academics, lawyers and doctors, elected public representatives, counsellors and councillors, activists and campaigners. Some were brave and forthright, some 'the timidest titmouse'.[4] Some were highly intelligent and politically sophisticated. Some were artistic and creative, some deeply spiritual. Some were moved by anger, some by pity, some by guilt. All shared a profound awareness of the injustice of their society.

We recognised the ambivalent place of white women in apartheid society, from which we could not help deriving some benefits, but yet chose to oppose the system. We understood that we could use our very privilege and protection to exert pressure for change. Far from being unwitting tools in the hands of the liberation movements, as some of our critics claimed,[5] we were fully aware that although our contribution was limited, it was still a part of the whole. We were realistic about what we might be able to achieve, and we had the ability to laugh at ourselves, but without abandoning our right to a voice and a role. All of us had a willingness to learn, to engage, to participate in debate, and the ability to grow, to change our minds if presented with good arguments, to find new ways of existing in a complex, changing society.

The Sash was politically astute in choosing where best to place its energies and skills. All of us longed for a society in which the law would not be based on race, the levels of poverty and inequality would be reduced, every citizen would have equal rights, and violent conflict would be replaced with peace and stability.

Joining the Black Sash influenced the course of my life. Its leaders were an inspiring example and its members became friends and colleagues. It prompted me to join other organisations committed to the same ideals, and to study more about South Africa and its history. It was owing to the Black Sash that many of us were offered opportunities to serve the new society being created after 1990, working for the democratic elections, contributing to the new Constitution, taking part in the Truth and Reconciliation Commission, or participating in the new government structures.

We all had many tasks in the organisation. I was schooled into the Cape Western regional council first as treasurer, later as secretary and chairperson. When the Black Sash headquarters moved to Cape Town in 1986, I served as the national president until 1990, following Sheena Duncan and being followed by Jenny de Tolly. I have seen the organisation change and develop, and been privileged to know some of the people who devoted their lives to bringing about justice in South Africa, many of whom continue to do so.

Now in 2015 the Black Sash Trust has sought new ways to focus on the socio-economic rights guaranteed in South Africa's Constitution but still inaccessible to millions of its inhabitants. It has replaced its individual advice-giving function within its regional offices with a wider outreach to all nine provinces, working with a network of partner organisations with the goal of 'making all voices count'. Modern technology makes possible a telephone help-line, a website and other resources for keeping a widespread community of activists in communication. These are the eyes and ears of those who monitor conditions at local level throughout the country. Gathering and disseminating information, and using it to exert pressure for change, is still essential in working for social justice. The Black Sash continues to strive to make human rights real for all the people of South Africa.

1

WHITE SKIRT AT DAWN

Half-hidden among the scrubby bushes in the sand dunes on the outskirts of Cape Town, the two of us sat in the car. Lights switched off, we waited for the starry night sky to pale. We kept an apprehensive watch for any sign of a police vehicle, but all was quiet. We could just make out twenty or thirty rounded tent-like shapes about a hundred metres away.

One by one candles and torches began to illuminate small groups of people taking down their shelters of black plastic sheeting stretched over poles and bushes. Bedding and clothing were stuffed into bags and parcels. Washing which had been stretched out to dry was gathered in. Children were roused and helped to wash and dress. Where could these families get water? we wondered. In one group near us, a grandmother sat in the centre of a mattress, creating a secure nest for the smallest children until all the other work was done, and all other belongings packed away. Then they too were gathered up so that no trace of their overnight presence remained.

The dawn brought more light to the scene, and now we could see the site almost cleared, and people beginning to move away, carrying their possessions. One last pole held a washing-line anchored to a tree, with a white skirt still fluttering in the wind. Suddenly the roar of large vehicles – police Casspirs [armoured vehicles] and flatbed trucks – drowned out all other sounds, and the people ran in every direction over the dunes, pursued by the police. Scattered belongings left behind were confiscated, shouts and threats filled the quiet air. A police official came across to our car and warned us to leave the area.

We drove slowly away, silent with sadness and anger, back to the warmth and shelter of our own homes. The images lingered in our minds. For me, it was that white skirt: how could someone living in such conditions sustain the effort of wearing anything so delicate? The white skirt had waved like a flag of courage, signalling a determination to resist the forces of discrimination and oppression.

What did we think we were achieving by being at KTC, between the townships of Gugulethu and Nyanga, that early winter morning in 1984? We were Sash members in the Cape Town region, and our goal was to see and record the conditions under which so many people lived in apartheid South Africa. This small community had asked for our presence, to witness part of their desperate quest to live in a city where their breadwinners could find work, yet where their presence was forbidden by legislation. As the Black Sash, we sought to speak from first-hand knowledge, and to use that knowledge to condemn and oppose the laws and practices which prevented black South Africans from exercising their rights of citizenship: to be treated equally, to move freely about their country, to have access to the same benefits as all other citizens.

A few weeks later the *Cape Times* published Candy Malherbe's letter describing what had taken place.[1] The English-language press of the time was often generous with space to the Black Sash, and provided one of the means through which we could attempt to influence public perceptions. Writing letters to the press, publishing articles and pamphlets, holding public protests and marches, and organising public debates had all formed part of the Sash's activities since the very beginning.

It all began in May 1955 with the formation of the Women's Defence of the Constitution League, in a spirit of outrage against a government plan to tamper with the constitution enshrined in the South Africa Act, which established the Union of South Africa in 1910. It included two clauses (section 35 and section 137) which could only be amended by a two-thirds majority in a joint session of both Houses of Parliament.[2] Section 35 protected the right of the franchise for men classified as 'coloured'. In 1948 the National Party had come to power, and had embarked on the process to remove this right, but its initial efforts had been thwarted by the courts. In 1955 it found a way around the legal obstacles: first by enacting a bill to enlarge Parliament's upper chamber, the Senate; then by packing it with National Party members. The enlarged Senate and the House of Assembly, voting together, would provide the two-thirds majority required to amend the entrenched clause.

Protest and outrage had already been aroused by the government's racial programme known as apartheid: the Population Registration Act to classify people by 'race', the Group Areas legislation to enforce residential separation, and the infringements of civil liberties under the Suppression of Communism Act. The Senate Bill was fought by opposition MPs, by coloured men (coloured women were not included in 1930 when white women were enfranchised), by civic organisations and concerned individuals – some of whom would come together to form the Women's Defence of the Constitution League.

'On 19th May, six Johannesburg women met to take tea. These women were not only good friends, with a liking for each other and a trust founded on common ideals, but they shared a mutual temper in the steel of their principles.'[3] They were Ruth Foley, Jean Sinclair, Jean Bosazza, Helen Newton Thompson, Tercia Pybus and Elizabeth MacLaren. Their exploits over the next weeks have been recounted with pride by their successors. 'We can't sit still and do nothing', said Foley. 'I don't know what we *can* do, but we must do it. We must act. There must be thousands like us and we must get together.'

They used their contacts to create a telephone cell system, and within 24 hours hundreds of women gathered for action. The next few days were filled with activity, and not only by the women. They called on the mayor of Johannesburg to hold a public meeting – which he did. University leaders issued statements. At least 30 separate petitions were drawn up, and between them they collected thousands of signatures. Major newspapers covered the stories, and announced that on 25 May 1955 the women of the Witwatersrand would march through Johannesburg – 'the first move in a sustained campaign by women of the Rand against the Senate Bill'.

The women issued a manifesto: 'We are the ones who have borne the children of today who are the South Africans of tomorrow, and who will have to bear the brunt of the sins of their fathers.

'We cannot stand by doing nothing. This Government has stated that it will listen to no protests. As mothers and grandmothers, as wives and sweethearts, career-women and professional women, as young women looking forward to a peaceful South Africa we are uniting to take common action.

'As women we intend to bring this Government to its senses. We therefore call on all women, English- or Afrikaans-speaking, to join us in this march. Let all women who value liberty and freedom heed this call to action.'[4]

Some two or three thousand women marched in Johannesburg that day, and were then joined by thousands of others in a mass protest meeting outside the City Hall. Within days support spread to other parts of the country, and the fledgling organisation grew rapidly, with what has been described as a 'slight framework' of a structure and a basic constitution. Branches were formed in all regions, bringing women together and organising public meetings, attracting considerable attention.

By the weekend of 4 June, with 'relays of eight to ten women working through the nights' in Jean Sinclair's home, over 30,000 petition forms were prepared for dispatch all over the country. Within ten days, more than 100,000 women had signed the petitions, and the processes of collecting the signatures and then counting them were recorded by international film media. The petitions were addressed to the governor-general and were delivered to him in Cape Town on 20 June – in vain, for only two days later he 'assented on behalf of the Queen to the Senate Act'.[5]

Although they were disappointed, the women continued with the collection of signatures for a further petition, calling on the prime minister, J.G. Strijdom, to resign. On 28 June 1955 a large number of women gathered in the frosty early morning to travel from Johannesburg to Pretoria to present it. They were not received by the prime minister, but by the minister of transport, Ben Schoeman, who had been deputed to represent him. About 80 of them kept a 48-hour vigil in the grounds of the seat of government, the Union Buildings. They then returned to a warm welcome by a crowd of supporters on the steps of the Johannesburg City Hall. By now their black sashes, symbol of mourning for the loss of constitutional rights, were becoming a familiar sight.

The petitions may have failed to stop the process, but the work went on. The optimistic upsurge of protest by so many women with common purpose was profoundly inspiring, and many of the speeches and articles of the time are deeply moving. The language is dramatic and emotional, often spiritual, and the stories told are of courage and determination. A dedication was adopted, written for the organisation by Alan Paton: 'In pride and humbleness we declare our devotion to the land of South Africa; we dedicate ourselves to the service of our country; we re-affirm our loyalty to the contract of Union which brought us together. We pledge ourselves to uphold the ideals by which our Union was inspired, of mutual trust and forbearance, of sanctity of word, of courage for the future, and of peace and justice for all persons and peoples. We pledge ourselves to resist any diminishment of these, confident that this duty is required of us, and that history and our children will defend us. So help us God, in Whose strength we trust.'

The women in the leadership positions were generally well educated, committed to liberal principles, and sufficiently well established to be able to contribute their time and efforts on a voluntary basis. They contributed the necessary financial resources too, with assistance from a circle of supporters. They were all white, since only white women had the vote, and the original goal had been to mobilise women voters. It was not until 1963 that membership of the Black Sash became open to all South African women and all women permanently resident in South Africa.

They included English- and Afrikaans-speaking women. Their first newsletter, called *The Black Sash / Die Swart Serp*, published in January 1956, included items in both languages. The women were a product of their history and their class: some were descendants of signatories of the Union constitution, and one of the banners carried in their march to Parliament in Cape Town in 1956 read, 'Our forebears signed the Act of Union'. Although they would not have defined themselves as such, they were early feminists, arguing that the Black Sash was 'a natural outcome of the anger of thinking women in South Africa at the stupidity shown by a group of men since their election to office in 1948 … The women were sick of a growing spirit of hate … They had long waited for men to give them a lead; but the men, it seemed to them, merely argued on the sidelines, all but a few avoiding the main issues … Every woman in South Africa today, Nationalist and non-Nationalist, career woman, mother and grandmother has now to make her choice.'[6]

Those early members of the Black Sash had made their choice. They were inspired, brave and efficient. Undaunted by their inability to prevent the passing of the Senate Act, they prepared for a second phase of protest. On 18 July 1955 they embarked on a vigil at the ministers' entrance to the Union Buildings, to be maintained on every working day until Parliament should convene in Cape Town in January 1956, and continued until December 1957. It was said that a thousand women had taken part, and spent 18,600 hours there.[7]

The next day they began the practice of 'Black Sashing' or 'haunting', appearing in silent demonstrations, wearing the black sashes, at any place where government ministers were to arrive.[8] Sash members appeared 'at dedications of hospitals, bridges and schools, turning what were to have been festive and even triumphant occasions for the ministers and their families into tense, embarrassing affairs'.[9] Week after week their numbers grew and so did the demonstrations. By mid-1956 the number of regions and branches had reached 161.[10]

November 1955 saw widespread protests in many towns against the dissolution of the old Senate and the election of the new. The protest action that attracted the most interest and that was recalled the most vividly by those who took part was the convoy of cars which drove from Johannesburg to Cape Town in preparation for the parliamentary debate in February 1956. Contemporary accounts and the memories of those who took part testify to the excitement and energy that went into the event.[11] Members converged from all over the country in twin convoys from the Transvaal–Natal regions and from the Eastern Cape. The newspapers listed their towns of origin, and described meetings held along the way in Bloemfontein, George, Knysna and many others. They came from Pretoria, Johannesburg, Welkom, Port Shepstone, Umzimbi, Botha's Hill, Winburg and Beaufort West, and their numbers included well-known citizens from many parts. Stories were told about the hotel keepers or garage owners who offered help and hospitality (and of those who refused). Some 300 women and 86 cars reached Stellenbosch on 'D-Day-minus-one' and 'revived swiftly in the deep shade of its famous oaks'.[12]

On 13 February 1956 the convoy, now consisting of about 150 cars, made its way through the centre of Cape Town towards Parliament, led by Jessie Power's green Morris Minor carrying a sash-draped replica of a book, symbolic of the constitution. They were met by thousands of applauding spectators and a shower of 'ticker tape'. Simultaneously, a large group of 'Sashers' took up their silent stand outside the Houses of Parliament to begin a 48-hour vigil. The next day, within the House itself, a group of Black Sash members in the public gallery had their sashes confiscated by an official. Undaunted, they donned black roses, which were also confiscated but returned after objections. They gleefully recounted how some of them wore long black gloves, and held an arm to their shoulders, creating the impression of a sash. Everywhere, the members wore their badges, designed by Bob Connolly, cartoonist for the *Rand Daily Mail*, inspired by the image of the sash-draped constitution.

The support the women received from the general public, and the considerable interest from the press, gave them some encouragement. Newspaper articles appeared in papers not only from around South Africa, but also from Great Britain, India, British Guiana, Canada, New Zealand, Iraq, Trinidad, Australia, the United States, Kenya, Rhodesia and other countries in Africa.

When their protests and petitions failed to stop the offending legislation, the harsh truth of defeat was not easy to bear. The high price of hard work and sacrifice became too much for many of the women, and over the next few years their numbers dwindled. The realities of South African governance were far harsher than simply the issue of tampering with the Union constitution. Racial discrimination had been a factor for decades, and was to become more and more deeply embedded in the years to come. For some members of the Black Sash, confronting this was too great a challenge, and they drifted away.

The question still remains, how were they so successful, how did they gather thousands of signatures to their petitions, bring crowds out on the streets of Johannesburg to protest, muster the numbers to hold a 48-hour vigil in the grounds of the Union Buildings, organise a convoy from all over the country to drive to Cape Town to protest outside Parliament? All women, in 1955, all within a few short weeks?

I look at the photographs, read everything I can – their magnificent rhetoric, their invocations of a glorious past, their certainty in the rightness of their cause. There are wonderful stories about the enormous amount of work they did, copying and checking the petitions until all hours, creating the organisation the Women's Defence of the Constitution League, communicating its message far and wide in a time of fairly labour-intensive technology. But still, how did they pull it off?

Why did they attract the support of thousands of women, and also the respect of men and the attention of the press? The constitution was by no means a just and democratic one, but rather a compromise from which some precious things had been salvaged, such as the entrenched clauses. Was it really worthy of all that defence?

I try to put myself into that time. During the previous decade the country had decided by a narrow parliamentary majority to enter the Second World War. Idealistic South Africans had stepped forward to volunteer to serve, and many had been wounded, captured or killed. Those who returned from the confrontation with racist ideology in Europe were dismayed to have to confront it in their own country. Pride in South Africa's role in the establishment of the United Nations was offended by the overt racism of National Party policy, and many Afrikaans-speaking people shared this concern. A number of those military veterans formed the Torch Commando. They shared the convictions of the women wearing the black sashes and encouraged their participation, even if they were somewhat bemused at the way in which the campaign escalated. It was a specific moment in South Africa's history, and the united opposition did not last.

The reality is that while some of the leaders of the Sash were committed to a democratic society and opposed to racism, the majority of supporters were motivated more by a general anxiety about the growing power of the National Party and its authoritarianism. After the initial excitement, and even the belief that they might be able to stop the Senate Act, the women were obliged to recognise that they had lost that battle. Bravely, some of them committed themselves to the longer-term task of opposing discrimination 'against any section of the population, no matter what race, colour or creed', in Jean Sinclair's words.[13] Much of the membership, however, was not ready for such a challenge, and within a short time the numbers dropped dramatically.

Those who remained began the work of building the organisation. The first national congress of the 'Black Sash League' was held on 29 November 1955 at a private house in Port Elizabeth (probably that of Di

Davis, mentioned below).[14] The following year the first formal annual national conference was held in the Clarendon Hall, Bloemfontein, on 26 April 1956.[15]

A newsletter was already in place, and was to be the forerunner of regular publications until 1994. These early issues record the establishment of regions and branches: 22 local branches in Johannesburg, 16 in Cape Town with a further 4 'country branches'; Port Elizabeth with over 500 branch members and 13 outside branches, East London and Middelburg (Cape), Kimberley with branch membership of 170 and plans to form country branches, Bloemfontein with 6 good branches, Durban, Pietermaritzburg, the Lowveld region, Witbank, Magoebaskloof, Klerksdorp, Pretoria.

It is true that the founders of the Black Sash were brave, intelligent and dedicated. Yet when I look back, 60 years later, I feel disappointment that they did not embrace opportunities for action on a non-racial basis. The African National Congress (ANC) and the Pan Africanist Congress (PAC) were building strength during that decade. In June 1955, at the very time when the Black Sash was being formed, the ANC was holding its Congress of the People at Kliptown, at which the Freedom Charter was adopted. There is almost no reference to it in the contemporary publications or statements of the Black Sash. Their manifesto announced, 'Let all women … heed this call', but they excluded those who were not classified white.

The original decision in 1955 that membership would be open to 'all women voters' meant that only white women, who had obtained the vote as recently as 1930, could belong to the Black Sash. The argument for this restriction was that it was the electorate that bore responsibility for the government and, therefore, it also bore the responsibility for challenging unjust laws: 'it seemed reasonable and proper to most of our members … they saw themselves as the conscience of the White electorate, whom they held primarily responsible for the state of affairs.'[16] It was not until 1963 that membership was opened to all women over the age of 18 who were South African citizens or permanent residents.

By the mid-1950s other women were becoming more and more militant. The African National Congress Women's League (ANCWL) had been protesting against the pass laws for a considerable time. These influx control regulations, which had governed the movement of African men, and restricted their rights to live and work in urban areas, were increasingly being extended to women too. On 17 April 1954 the Federation of South African Women (FSAW) was founded after more than a year of preparations. It adopted a Women's Charter, setting out its broad aims: 'This organization is formed for the purpose of uniting all women in common action for the removal of all political, legal, economic and social disabilities.' The ANCWL was a strong participant, as were women members of the Transvaal Indian Congress and the Natal Indian Congress, as well as the (white) Congress of Democrats. Other affiliates included the Cape Housewives League, the South African Coloured People's Organisation, the League of Non-European Women (Cape), and the Food and Canning Workers' Union.[17]

Records in the Helen Joseph collection show that in Johannesburg Miriam Heppner and Muriel Fisher were among the women who signed the FSAW inaugural launch invitation, and Cape Town signatories included Nancy Dick and Jean Bernadt.[18] All four were members of the Black Sash, but would have signed in their personal capacity.

On 9 August 1956 FSAW in their turn held a march to the Union Buildings, bringing many thousands of women from all over the country to protest against the pass laws. Forty years later, 9 August became South Africa's Women's Day – a national holiday. Sophie Williams de Bruyn, one of the four leaders who presented their petitions on that day, said, 'We were inspired by the women of the Black Sash to organise the march, as they had done. They had not invited us to join their march, but we invited them to join ours.'[19] The white women who did take part in that march in August were mainly members of the left-wing Congress of Democrats, though some of them were also members of the Black Sash.

Minutes of a Black Sash central executive meeting held on 3 August

1956 record that a letter had been received from Helen Joseph, secretary of FSAW, Transvaal region, asking for Black Sash support of the African women in their protest against the government's attempt to force passes upon them. It was agreed:

(a) That according to the Bloemfontein Conference the Black Sash could only co-operate with other protest movements if the protest were organised by the Black Sash.

(b) That any individuals who wished to join the protest of the African women should be encouraged to do so. Office bearers should not be prevented from attending, as individuals.

(c) That the members at the Southern Transvaal general meeting should be interested in the appeal.

(d) That Mrs Green would inform Mrs Joseph of the decision and point out that as a movement we do not propose to go into the demonstration, but that many individuals would be attending.[20]

At the next meeting, on 10 August 1956, Mrs Dey reported that very few 'European' (white) women had been present at the Union Buildings.[21] This ran counter to reports in *Die Transvaler*, a National Party-supporting newspaper, which had implied that the event had been organised by white women, with the intention of fuelling international criticism of South Africa. On the day of the protest, its front-page article referred to the example set by the Black Sash march to the Union Buildings the previous year.[22] The next day, together with its report on the FSAW protest, it published a photograph of three women observing the event. The caption read 'Members of the Black Sash who yesterday morning remained sitting in a Johannesburg motor car before the demonstration of native women at the Union Buildings. When the photo was taken, one of them said, "Take off your sashes."'[23] The three women were not named in the caption, but the Sash meeting confirmed that the one whose face could be seen was Tercia Pybus. *Die Transvaler*'s report also carried a photograph of Helen Joseph carrying a bundle of the petitions and described her as 'the brain' behind the protest. Ongoing references to 'white helpers who handed out protest letters' and 'other whites and members of the Liberal Party ... "and Sash Ladies"' continued to suggest that the demonstration had been orchestrated by white people, as though black women, bitterly opposed to the pass laws, would not have been able to organise such an event.

In a 40th anniversary publication of the *Sash*, Jo MacRobert commented, 'The hand of friendship that was extended to the Black Sash by the Federation of South African Women was rejected.'[24] A number of explanations can be found for this. The first lies in understanding the main reasons for the remarkable response to the Senate Act and the Separate Representation of Voters Act, which abolished the coloured vote. The outrage felt at the tampering with the Union constitution was based not only on the removal of the rights of male coloured voters, but also on the fear that the next step would be the denial of other rights, particularly the equal status of English with Afrikaans as a national language (which was protected by the other entrenched clause, section 137). In December 1956 the editorial in the Sash magazine lamented: 'Nothing is left of the work of our Founding Fathers but a worthless scrap of paper, for nobody believes that the present generation of Nationalists or subsequent generations will honour the one remaining Entrenched Clause a day longer than it suits them. The guarantee of the rights of the English language is worth nothing. The Nationalists dishonoured their pledges about the rights of the Coloured voters. Why should they bother about any other pledges?'[25]

The surge of support for the Black Sash came mainly from white English-speaking South Africans, together with Afrikaans speakers who did not support the National Party. It arose, too, from a horror of Nazism and fascism, and from anxiety about the increasing authoritarianism of the governing party. Some Sash supporters were opposed to racial discrimination, but not all. It was the shock of the government's brazen trampling on the constitution that galvanised so many into action, but not all were ready to support a universal franchise, or to take on the struggle for the rights of all South Africans.

Another reason that the Black Sash did not join the FSAW march was its opposition to communism. The national and international fear of communism was at its height during those years, and the Black Sash too demonstrated this attitude, at a time when the Suppression of Communism Act had already laid down severe penalties for anyone convicted of furthering the aims of communism (which was very broadly defined). The ANC had been leading a wave of opposition during the 1950s, and had been drawing in new members and allies, including the Congress of Democrats, which was largely made up of white people who had been supporters of the Communist Party until it was banned in 1950.

Although some of the women who joined the Black Sash from the start were also members of the Congress of Democrats, the majority of Sash members were much more conservative. The Sash's first national president, Ruth Foley, responded in November 1955 to a circular distributed by the Congress of Democrats which included a book draped in a sash, a symbol that the Sash considered its own: 'I wish to state that this emblem was used without the knowledge of our organisation … [and] to disclaim any association whatsoever with the South African Congress of Democrats.'[26]

Many of the founding members of the organisation were eminently respectable and socially well-connected supporters of the official opposition party, the United Party, and some were not opposed to segregation. Added to this was the social reality that few of them had worked closely with women of other groups – informal segregation and centuries of slavery and colonial rule had already created huge divisions in society. The Congress movement and the black community saw little prospect of building any association with such a conservative grouping.

Jo MacRobert wonders 'how the history of the Black Sash would have been written if the organisation had not taken the conservative decision in those early days to restrict membership to white female voters'.[27] Indeed, the American academic Gwendolen Carter considered that the Black Sash's greatest mistake was to remain aloof from FSAW. Jean Sinclair, the first president of the Sash, had responded that if this had been attempted 'there would have been no Black Sash' because agreement would never have been reached. Many Black Sash members at the time were timid politically, and in later years Jean Sinclair herself very honestly acknowledged her own early conservative standpoint, and her change of mind.[28]

Some of the members of the Black Sash and some leaders of FSAW continued to try to maintain a relationship, notably Helen Joseph herself and Ray Alexander in Cape Town. But over the next few years FSAW was itself under increasing pressure from the government, and by 1962, after the 1960 state of emergency when many of its leaders were banned, its activities were severely curtailed.

With hindsight it can be argued that if the Black Sash had joined FSAW and become engaged in its activities, it might also have been banned or restricted at that time, and an opportunity would have been lost to mobilise the group of women who gradually learned to find ways of opposing apartheid. Much later, through meeting Helen Joseph and reading her autobiography, I learned that she and others had recognised this, and retained personal links with some of the Black Sash women. She spoke warmly, for example, of the role played by Sash members in a 24-hour vigil held in St Mary's Cathedral in Johannesburg in June 1977: 'the night passed very slowly in complete silence ... the gallant team of Black Sash women ... in continuous vigil in front of the candle, below which were the names of those who had died in 1976, those in detention, and those known to be banned or banished'.[29] In 1971, after having been banned and silenced for almost ten years, Helen Joseph spoke at a student meeting in the Great Hall at the University of the Witwatersrand to protest against the banning of Father Cosmas Desmond. Her brave words and the response of a standing ovation brought many to tears: 'I saw that Jean Sinclair, President of the Black Sash, standing close to me, was wiping her eyes.'[30]

Even without the challenge of deciding whether to work with FSAW, differences of opinion began to surface. Some of the members demonstrated their growing awareness of the acute problems arising from government policies. Others were not prepared to move beyond the original objectives of the Black Sash. The rural branches dwindled first. Far from the centres that provided mutual support, their members faced criticism from their own communities, and found Black Sash work hard to sustain. By 1958 the Barkly East branch decided to disband, despite the commitment which had led their 'seven women from outlying farms and two town members' to participate in a public stand for over two hours outside their local hotel (where a cabinet minister was attending a meeting in 1955), to create their own Black Sash library, and to contribute generously to fundraising projects. Although they could not sustain a branch, 'They are all willing to be called upon as loyal women ... the Black Sash owes them a deep debt of gratitude.'[31] Many years later, on a visit to a farm in the area, I encountered women who spoke with pride of their early involvement in the Sash.

The general election of 1958 drew much of the membership energy back into the United Party, the official opposition in Parliament, and its defeat at the polls caused considerable soul-searching in the Black Sash. Its May 1958 magazine's front page was headed 'Picking up the pieces' and commented, 'the United Party campaigned almost entirely on economic or bread-and-butter issues. Little was said about the betrayal of the spirit of Union, the broken pledges to the Coloured People, the trickery of the Senate Act, or the farce of the High Court of Parliament ... the memory of the public is short and of politicians even shorter – when it suits them.' Sturdily, it continues, 'The moral basis of the Movement remains as strong as ever ... there is a moral purpose in politics and a nation that ignores it is on the way to self-destruction.'[32]

At the same time, Black Sash members were taking up other issues, and discussing for example the serious housing shortages for African people in the Johannesburg area, aggravated by Group Areas legislation and the forced removal of the residents of Sophiatown. An article in the Sash magazine described the appalling situation in Dube and Orlando and 'the enormity of the problem'. Yet it also reflected the views of its more conservative members: 'If a vote were taken it is probable that the vast majority of both Europeans and Non-Europeans would agree that residential segregation is desirable.'[33]

As early as 1957 Jean Sinclair, by then the organisation's national president, spoke against 'entirely unjust, discriminatory, unscrupulous, immoral and cruel' laws that affected 'the rights and civil liberties of the Non-European'.[34] Leading articles in the magazine pointed to 'major blots on our Statute Book' and in 1958 it criticised the United Party, the only remaining parliamentary opposition, as being 'stuck in a rut ... Since the election the United Party has so far shown no stirrings of intellectual effort.'[35] This was strong talk, and demonstrated the growing commitment of some of the organisation's leaders to move onto the 'new venture' of which they spoke, of working for a new constitution that would safeguard the civil liberties of all sections of the population. Yet the bulk of the membership would not follow them. Ruth Foley, who had been the first national president in 1956 and had been much admired as an inspirational speaker, resigned from the Sash in 1959,[36] unwilling to move away from the original impulse that had formed the organisation. Many more followed, and the initial membership dropped to below 2,000 and never again grew beyond that in the remaining decades.

Though many of the first members were fairly conservative, there were strong individuals pressing for more progressive policies in most of the regions. In the Western Cape, regional council members included Moira Henderson, Eulalie Stott and Barbara Willis, who were members of the Liberal Party, and Peggy Roberts of the South African Labour Party. Others were Molly Petersen, Noël Robb and Hildegard Spottiswoode. They had links with a number of black leaders in Cape

Town and had worked together with them on issues of the Group Areas Act and other apartheid legislation. They were able to draw multiracial attendance at public meetings, most visibly at the mass meeting held on the Parade in Cape Town on the evening of the Black Sash convoy's arrival in Cape Town in February 1956.

Jo MacRobert asserts, 'There is no doubt that the leadership of the Sash in the Western Cape was to the left of the organisation as a whole.' She records the way in which the region raised controversial issues for consideration by the second national conference in May 1957. One of these called for the Black Sash to support the Universal Declaration of Human Rights, a proposal that was also advocated by the Eastern Cape Border region. However, this was deemed too controversial, and was withdrawn before the conference; the decision to accept the tenets of the Universal Declaration did not come until 1960.[37] The Declaration, adopted by the United Nations in 1948, upheld the right to universal suffrage, but this issue was seldom mentioned in the Sash until much later. In 1978, after considerable debate within all the regions, a resolution was carried 'that justice cannot be achieved without a universal adult franchise'.

The Cape Western region's ability to work in alliances with the organisations representing black and coloured communities kept its members engaged and committed. Where other regions were reporting widespread apathy and despondency, as well as dwindling membership after the 1958 elections, the Cape Western region still numbered 1,303, though it had lost 400 of its founding members. At the end of 1958 the headquarters of the organisation was transferred to Cape Town, with Molly Petersen as national president, followed the next year by Eulalie Stott.[38]

The Western Cape in general was often regarded as having a rather more liberal political outlook than the rest of the country. Although numbers were dwindling everywhere, there was still considerable support for the local branches of organisations opposed to apartheid such as the South African Institute of Race Relations (SAIRR), the

Civil Rights League, the National Council of Women, and the National Union of South African Students (NUSAS). Occasionally these all worked together on joint campaigns, and were mutually supportive. The early members of the Black Sash could look to these links for support, information and advice. But the 'liberal establishment' at the time was small, isolated and under threat. 'The fact that the liberal organisations are so few that they can be easily listed and described, demonstrates how limited the liberal movement in South Africa has become. The unanimity of voices indicates how embattled they are – how little they can afford the luxury of disagreement among themselves … With the political opposition in eclipse, the protest movement has, to a large degree, turned into an extra-parliamentary force.'[39]

In 1958 the Black Sash in Cape Town took the decision to start an advice office, which was to have a vital impact on the whole organis-ation. Its original goal had been to provide a bail fund for black people, particularly women, arrested in terms of the pass laws, and from this work grew an awareness of how the system functioned to deny rights and services to all black South Africans. As the knowledge grew, so did the organisation's protest work. The black sashes worn in mourning for constitutional rights were now brought out for protests against more and more unjust laws. The silent demonstrations, known as 'stands', with their trademark placards, were coupled with press statements and articles, letters to the press, and speeches at public meetings. Every vehicle the members could think of was used to convey a message, especially directed towards the white electorate, trying to effect a change of heart. 'Brains trusts', or panel discussions, were arranged to try to arouse public interest and debate, although the organisation's early dream of influencing white voters was fading.

The Sash headquarters moved back to Johannesburg at the end of 1960 and Jean Sinclair was national president until 1975, through 15 difficult years. At the same time, the backlash grew. The white electorate did not wish to hear the message that the Black Sash was conveying. The apartheid policy played all too well on the fears of white South

Africans – fears of communism, fears of being swamped electorally by the larger number of black citizens, fears of losing the comfortable lifestyle they enjoyed, fears of the prosperous economy suffering drastic changes. Hostility towards the Black Sash showed itself in attacks on the poster demonstrations, anonymous threats to individuals, attacks on the premises of the advice offices, and critical comments in the media. Security police attention was evident at the stands, with plainclothes officers taking photographs without any subtlety, clearly intending to intimidate.

Working for the Black Sash in its first two decades was a lonely task. Although some of its members had good working relationships with leaders of the various black political organisations, it was not part of the broad Congress movement, and not regarded as having the potential to bring about change. Neither did it have the support of the white population, where the prevailing view was largely supportive of the government's policy. In the early years it used to be said that English-speaking whites voted for the United Party, but thanked God for the Nationalists, and there was more than a grain of truth in this. Nevertheless, there was a breakaway from the United Party when the Progressive Party was formed in 1959. A few years later the Prohibition of Improper Political Interference Act forbade political organisations to have members of different race groups. This led to the closure of the Liberal Party and forced the Progressive Party to become all-white.

At much the same time, and despite the legislation, the Black Sash took the decision in 1963 to open its membership to all women, but it was too late. Tentative steps out of white isolation had been made more difficult by the banning of the ANC and PAC, and by the proclamation of a state of emergency in 1960. Although FSAW was not banned, many of its leaders were arrested, and the federation was thrown into considerable disarray. The Black Sash never succeeded in shedding its image of being an organisation of white, middle-class women, and very few black women ever joined.

In spite of this, some valued links had been established with leading black political movements and individuals, through campaigns against the pass laws and through jointly organised public meetings, as well as by private contacts. In 1960, when nationwide protests against the pass laws were met by the killings in Sharpeville near Johannesburg and led to a dramatic march from Langa into the centre of Cape Town, the Black Sash was jolted into greater action. In almost every region members initiated or participated in committees established to provide food and support for the families of the hundreds of detainees.

Chief Albert Luthuli, president of the ANC, had addressed a meeting in Noël Robb's house in 1959. When he was banned, the Black Sash protested strongly and featured articles about him in the Sash magazine. In Port Elizabeth, Govan Mbeki had addressed the Eastern Cape regional conference of the Black Sash.[40] Members of the Liberal Party in Cape Town had a good relationship with the PAC, and Black Sash members too were inspired by its leader, Robert Sobukwe. Leaders of organisations broadly identified as 'coloured' joined in meetings with the Black Sash and contributed articles to the magazine. Imam Abdullah Haron was associated with the organisation Defence and Aid, which had been founded in 1956 to provide legal assistance to political prisoners and support for their families. He worked closely in that body with Moira Henderson and was also friendly with Eulalie Stott, who introduced him to several of us new members. Our sorrow and anger at his death in detention on 27 September 1969 was all the greater for those who had been guests in his house.

As more and more of the black leadership was tried, imprisoned, or forced underground or into exile, these encounters became more difficult. This deepened the sense of isolation of the Black Sash. It became difficult to believe in the possibility of change.

It might have been tempting to give up the struggle against a seemingly invincible government, but by then the advice offices were an important element of the Black Sash work. The daily contact with those who were most vulnerable to the impact of apartheid policies would have obliged it to continue. It was not only a sense of duty.

The knowledge being gained by advice office workers was a richness that fed the entire organisation. Few white people could have the same exposure to their black fellow citizens, as cities became increasingly segregated, and contacts were often limited to employer–employee relationships. Those who worked in the advice offices became knowledgeable about the law and skilled in dealing with officials, while sharing the anger and frustration of the people they were seeking to assist. The wider membership had the benefit of regular reports from the offices, enhancing their knowledge and understanding too, and were often drawn into experiences related to that work. Attendance at the commissioner's courts where pass law trials were held, and keeping records of the way cases were handled, all helped to swell the body of knowledge, and to expose members to new experiences.

In addition to the advice office work, individual members developed a range of interests, in education, housing, health care and labour-related issues. All of these were distorted by apartheid policies, and Black Sash study groups sought to understand the issues at stake, and to consider alternatives.

During the first ten years of its existence, the Sash had struggled to establish and clarify its objectives, but by the mid-1960s it had built a structure that would sustain it for another 30 years, and had defined its goals more clearly: to pursue peace and justice, and to protest against infringements of people's rights. Its trademark became the monitoring of apartheid injustice, through the advice offices and by the experience and witness of its members, and the translation of that knowledge into pressure for change. It continued to protest, to scrutinise the laws, to organise and attend meetings, to build alliances and support communities. This fusion of service and advocacy was the essential element of the Black Sash. The women who belonged to it could be involved in one aspect or another, but it was the combined strength of the two that ensured its survival – and not only survival, but the quality of its work.

Twenty years later, observing the dawn demolition of a small community's temporary shelters in KTC was just one way of putting into practice the Sash belief that first-hand knowledge was important in building credibility, and that a personal presence demonstrated solidarity with those who experienced the harsh implementation of apartheid.

2

NOT AFRAID TO BE ABSURD

'Black Sash ladies, not afraid to be absurd, not afraid to
be emotional, have won back some part of White dignity.'
– Angus Wilson, *Sunday Telegraph*, 1961

*Wendy walks into the kitchen at the end of a hot and humid morning and
drops the shopping bags on the floor in astonishment and outrage. Mr G.,
the Bantu Affairs Administration Board inspector whom she had seen in
his office yesterday, is lounging nonchalantly at the kitchen table with his
junior side-kick opposite him. Dora is standing between them, her hands
wrapping themselves in a tea-towel, looking miserable and scared. The
men are not acting aggressive or threatening – on the contrary, they look
as if they are enjoying themselves – but the effect they have on Dora is to
terrify her. Her pass book lies on the table. So do the men's caps and the
inspector's briefcase.*

*The effect they have on Wendy is to infuriate her. How dare they come
into her house in her absence and sit there looking as if nothing is wrong?
The pot of soup is simmering gently on the stove, the baby is starting to
fret slightly as he wakes in his carry-cot in the corner, the hot breeze is
stirring the curtains – everything looks so normal, but it is definitely not.*

*This is nothing but intimidation, she thinks. It all comes from her
having gone to the administration office yesterday to ask why Mr Xolisiwe*

Guma had been detained for questioning and then released with a warning. The inspector had responded politely enough, and made it clear that he knew all about the newly-opened advice office in the church hall. Why should he now think he can come into her house like this?

She asks what the problem is and what they are doing here. The inspector gets up without haste and says he was just checking up. 'You wouldn't want to find you were employing someone illegally, would you?' he smiles. 'A beautiful woman like you wouldn't want to get into trouble when it could so easily be avoided.'

She says they must go and they slowly gather their caps and briefcase and head towards the door. 'You should just know that the security people know what you are doing, and that I have to keep a watch and report to them,' says the inspector. 'I know that you just want to be nice to these people you are helping, but you will just have trouble if you go on with this Black Sash business. You've got a nice home and family, and a baby to look after, and the Black Sash won't be able to help you if you get into trouble. I wonder what your husband thinks? Does he even know what you do? Doesn't he mind that you spend all that time with the young minister at the church? I would mind if I were your husband.'

His insolent words make her shake with rage, but she tries to stay calm and walks them out of the kitchen and to the gate without any reply. When they say goodbye she murmurs some response and heads back to soothe Dora. She finds that in spite of her anger, she is shaken too. They are so certain of their power. What can she do in the face of it? Had she been unwise to go to confront them yesterday? Could her action bring harm to the church or to the Black Sash?

Wendy Jackson was instrumental in opening an advice office in East London with other Black Sash members and the help of the Rev. Rob Robertson, a Presbyterian minister who had in 1962 initiated a multiracial congregation in the North End area.[1] She wrote to Jean Sinclair in 1963 after the incident described above, asking for advice.[2] She was by no means the only Sash member to encounter a patronising attitude and veiled threats from officials of the apartheid government.

East London's Border region was also not the only one of the smaller regions of the Black Sash to turn often to the national office-bearers for advice and support. Their numbers were smaller and the Eastern Cape was a particularly hostile environment. When they were confronted by the authorities, when they planned a new kind of activity, when their members were detained or their offices raided, a telephone call to headquarters would bring encouragement and assistance.

By 1963 the foundation members had acquired plenty of knowledge and experience. They were serious and determined, and brought together a remarkable array of talent and energy. Jenny de Tolly, who joined the Sash in 1983 and became its national president in 1990, has described them as the ancestors of the next generations, and they left a legacy of values still relevant in the 21st century. I have asked dozens of them what prompted them, have read about others, worked with them, heard stories about them, cherished them as friends and colleagues. Were they, as Angus Wilson said, not afraid to be absurd and emotional? The answers are as rich and varied as the women themselves.

They were certainly not afraid or, if they were, they did not allow fear to prevent them from acting. The ones who started it all, the legendary first six, were strong and articulate, well informed about public affairs, firmly committed to particular sets of principles inspired by their faiths or their political affiliations. They moved in influential circles, were successful and well connected, and some were married to important men in commerce, industry or politics. They had endured in disbelief and apprehension the victory of the National Party in 1948 and witnessed its determination to stamp its authority on all aspects of society and to advance only the interests of its supporters. The attempts to remove one of the entrenched clauses in the Union constitution being too much to endure, they swung into action.

The emotions that stirred them ranged from anger to sorrow and despair, and they were not afraid to act on them. During Jean Sinclair's

15 years as national president she was known for her telephone calls to the regions, which always seemed to start 'I'm furious!' before proposing some new campaign. When she was interviewed for the film *The Early Years*, she remembered, 'I was always furious.' Joyce Harris believed it was this anger that drove her: 'She cannot abide injustice, feels totally compelled to take action against it, and inspires others to follow.'[3]

A sense of theatre was not lacking. The protest strategies, particularly the 'haunting' of cabinet ministers, could be described as absurd, especially by those they were targeting, but they guaranteed attention. Those lines of silent women, eminently respectable, eminently accusatory, were a dramatic reproach. The black sashes were instantly recognisable, and provided opportunities for cartoonists to portray the ridiculous extremes to which cabinet ministers would resort to avoid encountering them. The long vigils, even overnight outside the Union Buildings, the posters and banners, and the marches to the beat of a muffled drum, all created strong images.

The women who made up the founding generation of the Black Sash were influenced not only by the political situation, which spurred them into action, but also by their own socio-economic position in a highly stratified society. In the South Africa of the 1950s white women, particularly English-speakers, were better educated and financially better placed than their counterparts who were not white. They had had the vote since 1930, and they had opportunities to pursue careers. The Sash counted among its members doctors, lawyers, university lecturers and professors, teachers, nurses and women in business. However, social custom strongly favoured middle-class married women remaining at home or working outside their homes only part-time; even the taxation system served to encourage this attitude, as the income of married couples was jointly taxed until 1988.[4] Many women discovered in the Black Sash that their skills and knowledge were useful and valued, and their confidence and fulfilment consequently grew. Noël Robb, whose leadership was important to the Cape Western region for decades, and who had been a science teacher, wrote: 'All I know about politics, administration of government policy, about people of other race groups and other levels of society, I learnt in the Black Sash ... If I had never joined ... I would have been playing tennis, making clothes for the children, and bringing them up – without the knowledge of how to do so. I am eternally grateful to the Black Sash for digging me out of my suburban existence ... for enlarging my vision and stirring my conscience.'[5]

They were women from a varied cross-section of white South Africa, some of whom already had considerable leadership experience in politics, or who played leading roles in society. They came from Afrikaans families, as well as those of English descent, but as the years went by it became increasingly difficult for Afrikaans-speaking women to be publicly identified as Black Sash members – and, it has to be said, the organisation's own efforts to be inclusive of this sector dwindled. Anna Marais, an active member in the founding generation, encouraged the use of Afrikaans in many Sash publications, but this became less frequent over the years.

The women were mildly amused by descriptions of some members as being of the bluest blood and the highest society; they were equally amused by different perceptions in other places, where being a member of the Black Sash was seen as not quite 'the thing' by the socialites.[6]

The Black Sash was a privileged organisation, led by women who could afford to work as unpaid volunteers and had the freedom to pursue their ideals. It is true that many of them had the benefit of bourgeois lives, free of many domestic duties, secure in their financial situation and not dependent on being employed. Others were employed but could still afford some time for engagement with the issues which the Sash took on. Their greatest privilege arose from the benefit of having time to think, to debate, to explore, to speak and act without the constraints even of a political party, which needs to conform to the views of its members, financial supporters and voters. That freedom is what enabled the Black Sash to be well ahead of the rest of the white population in its understanding and acceptance of the changes that had to be made if South Africa was ever to become a democracy.

An item in the Sash magazine of August 1956 gives a glimpse of the household of the indomitable Jean Sinclair. It describes 'Abraham, the grey-haired old aristocrat who presides over the tea tables when we have meetings at her house', and recounts 'what a stalwart he proved to be' when he accompanied the convoy to Parliament in Cape Town. The BBC photographer was dashing alongside the cars, and 'there, just behind him, hurried Abraham … after three gruelling days, immaculate in his neat khaki suit, laden with all the photographer's heavy gear, and with an expression on his face in which exhaustion and anxiety strove for mastery'.[7]

Some of the early members of the Black Sash were accustomed to travelling in style, and there is a note in the minutes of the national conference held in Cape Town in 1960 indicating that the delegation from Natal Coastal region would be arriving a day late because their ship was delayed. A leisurely cruise would have been a good way to prepare for and recover from a busy three-day conference. (Of course, the reason could have been that it was quicker than the long rambling train journey between Durban and Cape Town.) A generation later, delegates from Cape Town to Johannesburg for the national conference would be issued with second-class rail tickets, and we thoroughly enjoyed sharing a six-berth compartment and discussing the conference agenda all the way. (I remember, too, on that journey being given firm advice by Noël Robb about how to bring up children, get fretful babies to 'go down', and how to keep husbands from complaining at our absence.)

By no means all of the members were affluent. Many who were in full-time or part-time employment had little spare time to give to the organisation, but welcomed the possibility of supporting it in a variety of ways. Others who lived on small pensions dedicated many hours to the advice offices or the multiple tasks needed in a busy regional office.

Enid Robertson was a founder member of the Black Sash and remained loyal to it throughout her life, which had never been an easy one. Born into the Roux family, of farmer stock, and with a fiercely political father, she was one of six children, and particularly devoted to her brother Eddie Roux, dedicated socialist and author of the radical history of South Africa entitled *Time Longer than Rope*. She was deeply saddened by his early death. She was twice widowed, and her son, unsurprisingly an active opponent of apartheid, left South Africa at an early age. She did not let lack of money or transport prevent her from taking part in meetings and protests. She compiled and kept up to date an index of the Black Sash magazine. Jill Wentzel remembered her 'dogged gallantry … the example she set, of living each day in an organised, interested and involved way'.[8]

Mary Livingstone lived widowed and alone in Cape Town, in very straitened circumstances, in the last years of her life. She had been among the founding members of the Liberal Party, had spent years with her husband in Lesotho at Roma University, and never lost the academic rigour with which she wrote, studied legislation, scrutinised the *Government Gazette*, and worked in the advice office. She held clear and strong principles, which were vital in regional council discussions.

Suzanne Stephen, a founder member of the Sash in the Transvaal, was active on its committees, but is particularly known for her outstanding contribution to the education of people in prison. Starting in 1960 in response to an appeal from two prisoners in the Komati Dam Prison, she began coaching them by correspondence. When they were transferred to Witbank Prison, which was a rehabilitation centre, many of their fellow convicts asked to be included. The numbers grew rapidly, and she was obliged to draw in some assistance, but the commissioner for prisons insisted that all the work should be routed through her hands. She also had to supply books and stationery, and 'became the world's best scrounger, haunting second-hand book shops' and appealing through the press for support. She received moving letters from what one prisoner referred to as her 'bunch of jolly students', and also from the people who helped with the coaching.[9]

All three of these women are a humbling testimony to what can be achieved by one person's dedication. They, and others like them, brought depth and richness to the whole organisation.

There was plenty of scope from the very beginning for those who had public speaking skills, or who quickly acquired them. Ruth Foley and Jean Sinclair were in demand all over the country to address meetings, and others followed. Of Ruth Foley it was said, 'She was perhaps the most effective speaker in the Sash. Her shining sincerity, her mastery of facts and figures and her political experience in the United Party, made her a natural leader.'[10] She was widely respected, and in April 1957 she was invited to the Bloemfontein mayoral garden party to celebrate the 100th birthday of Mrs Sophie Leviseur, one of the founding Black Sash members in the Orange Free State, who partook in all the demonstrations, even in a wheelchair.

Jean Sinclair may not have seen herself as a gifted orator, and colleagues have spoken of her innate shyness, which caused her to have to 'gird her loins' for any public address. Yet she was known for her forceful and thought-provoking speeches, and her presidential addresses over 15 years are a remarkable record of the organisation's progress through the tightening web of apartheid.

Professional women who did not have the time to participate in activities still valued the information they received through the Sash publications and newsletters, and they were often willing to be called upon for their specific skills. Dr Frances Ames, for example, well-known neurologist in Cape Town, did not hesitate to take on the case of Siphiwo Mthimkulu, a leader in the Congress of South African Students (COSAS), when he was brought to her from Port Elizabeth by Sash members in 1981. It was she who revealed that he had been poisoned with thallium while in the hands of the security police. Stories were also told of a doctor in the Eastern Cape, never named, who used to treat patients who were in hiding and were brought to her kitchen at night, where she would extract bullets or treat wounds, with all the curtains drawn. She provided a safe place for activists on the run in the 1980s who could not risk going to the state hospitals, where the police kept watch in an effort to identify and detain suspects.

Women who were active in other organisations gave their support to the Sash, including Ellen Hellman and Hansi Pollak of the Institute of Race Relations, the anthropologist Monica Wilson, and Barbara Grieve and Else Schreiner of the National Council of Women. Even when they did not participate actively, they provided a network of like-minded people and access to information and resources. Prominent politicians such as Margaret Ballinger and Helen Suzman were always accessible for information and ideas, and in turn received detailed and reliable reports and statistics that could strengthen their arguments in Parliament. Other well-known women became fully engaged in the Black Sash. Several had been mayors, deputy mayors or city councillors. Eleanor Russell, convener of the first Sash meeting in Pietermaritzburg in 1955, was the retired headmistress of Girls' Collegiate School. She had been the first woman mayor of Pietermaritzburg, and was active as well in the National Council of Women and the Institute of Race Relations. She was elected vice-chairman at the first meeting, and, with plenty of experience in meetings and committees, she is said to have had a major impact on early conferences of the Black Sash.

Although the Black Sash was often regarded as a fairly conservative group of women, it also attracted a more diverse membership, including those with more progressive beliefs and different lifestyles. At the same time as Eleanor Russell was vice-chair in Pietermaritzburg, the regional chairperson was Maimie Corrigall, who is remembered as 'a real tough leftie – actually a communist'.[11] Like Ruth Foley, Eleanor Russell resigned when the membership was opened to all South African women and permanent residents, but Maimie Corrigall led the region for a number of years and served on the regional committee until the end of her life in 1981.

In a time when so few white women were ready to face the challenge of opposing the government, differences in the Sash over party political alignments gradually took second place. In Johannesburg there were influential members who were staunch members of the United Party, while others were Liberals or had been members of the Communist Party of South Africa (CPSA) until it was banned, or were members of the Congress of Democrats. Yet when Sonia Bunting, a listed communist, applied for membership in Cape Town, her application to join the Sash, and her appeal to headquarters, were turned down. Others who had been members or supporters of the CPSA and were subsequently 'listed',[12] and therefore obliged to tender their resignations, found themselves supported in principle, but somewhat abandoned in practice. The Black Sash wrote to the minister of justice protesting against such action taken against its members, who included Jean Hill (Durban) and Jean Bernadt (Cape Town), and issued public statements not only in their cases but also about others who were not its members. A strong statement was made against the banishment in 1959 of Elizabeth Mafekeng, a founding member of FSAW, from her home town of Paarl to far-flung Kuruman, and in Cape Town the Sash held a protest stand. Principled opposition to these measures did not overcome the Black Sash's antipathy towards communism.

Dot Cleminshaw remembered that the Cape Town Sash had 'drawn its skirts aside from Jean Bernadt', who had been lonely and isolated after her banning.[13] Jean was one of several women who were detained by the government in the 1960 state of emergency. She is described by Myrna Blumberg as 'radiant in her mid-forties' and active in projects for the care of African children.[14] In her book Blumberg provides a glimpse into the prison conditions, the attitudes of the police and the security police, and the relationships that grew among the women detained in 1960. Among them were Amy Rietstein (later, Thornton), who had been a member of the Communist Party, and the Black Sash members Nancy Dick and Sarah Carneson.[15] Sonia Bunting is not mentioned by name by Blumberg, but Dot Cleminshaw thought that she was one of the detainees, and also identified 'Granny Annie' as Annie Goldberg, mother of Denis Goldberg. Denis was also in prison, together with Fred Carneson.[16]

Women with different viewpoints joined the Sash in the expectation of finding a place where they could work towards real change. Divergent political positions were reflected in most of the regions, and although this sometimes gave rise to tensions, there was usually sufficient agreement about the need to oppose the pass laws and other apartheid legislation to enable the work to continue. The regional councils included not only the more fiery members, but also women who are still remembered and esteemed for their wisdom and tolerance, women who had a gentle regard for each colleague and would seek to bring consensus.

Several issues of *Sash* magazine, from as early as 1960, published answers from members who were asked why they had joined. Their replies include:

'The policy of apartheid is at the root of our country's misery and dissension … the remedy lies in the slow process of changing people's minds … [to] stir a nation's conscience.' (Olive Rowe, foundation member, Cape Town)

'I believe in Parliamentary democracy, but it cannot work without a strong, healthy, critical opposition … The official opposition appears to have forgotten this … its feeble antics so infuriated me that I was prepared to join the Black Sash almost before it started.' (Mary Stoy)

'I returned from the first big meeting in Cape Town impressed by the sincerity and straight thinking of the Sash. Members discussed politics without sentimentality or bias. What made some of them prepared to go 500 miles to talk to a branch – or to stand in the street and be spat at; or to work until they dropped from exhaustion; or to neglect their husbands, children and homes? … Our struggle is only a part of an age-long battle against evil.' (Anna Pearce)

'The feelings of horror, despair and frustration that used to surge in me have now been directed into a course that has meaning and hope. Every effort, every voice spoken in protest, every action, however small, in support of the deprived and the oppressed is a little more on the scale.' (Sheila Newman)

Similar phrases were repeated: 'until we have honesty and decency in public life'; 'that justice may prevail'; 'The Black Sash was non-party political'; 'Even if our protest fails it's a good thing to have protested, to have cared.'[17]

There was even a page in the magazine on 'why I didn't join the Sash': from an 'ex-Communist' who felt that even if she no longer supported communism, the political label could do harm to the early efforts of the Black Sash to win recruits and recognition. Another could not support a 'whites-only' organisation and had preferred to join the Liberal Party. A 'sympathiser' wrote that among her acquaintance there were several who said their husbands would not allow them to join, for fear of antagonising business connections, some who thought it a waste of time, and some who were too involved in charitable work, while she herself had simply run out of faith and enthusiasm, and felt it better to keep her bitter defeatism away from those who still had energy and commitment.[18]

From the early days the organisation relied on a team of dedicated staff, most of whom were women. Office secretaries, advice office case-workers and interpreters, many remained with the Sash for decades. Some of them were Sash members, some preferred not to join. All were dedicated to the work of the regions and the advice offices, and their knowledge and experience were invaluable. The number of employees grew in the 1980s and included fieldworkers and coordinators, both women and men, who greatly strengthened the capacity of the organisation.

For younger women joining the Sash in the 1960s, the leadership of the senior women was a particular attraction. In a time when women in public life were still very much in the minority, these determined, well-informed and articulate leaders were an encouragement and source of hope. From the earliest days there was a sense of pride in demonstrating efficiency and good organisational skills. Marie Dyer (Natal Midlands) speaks of having been intrigued by the efficient way the Black Sash had been started, 'how quickly people joined, how much people were doing and all of these huge marches ... that it was all women and the press was commenting "these women are so well organized", because we were. We filed nicely in little lines, and people felt good ... and proud."[19] The photographs of the time show disciplined marches, massed demonstrations, impressive vigils and ceremonies.

The women also took pride in the recognition those leaders, and the organisation itself, received nationally and internationally. Jessie Power attended the July 1957 conference in Geneva of the International Alliance of Women.[20] Anna Marais and Marjorie Juta, as well as Jessie Power, were in England during the northern summer of 1958, where they were interviewed by the BBC, laid a wreath on the occasion of the Emmeline Pankhurst centenary, and reported back on the British media's interest in the Black Sash.[21]

Newer members valued the opportunity for self-education: groups were formed to learn Afrikaans or African languages; study groups and discussions provided deeper understanding of history and politics; the magazine covered a variety of subjects; a Black Sash Summer School in Johannesburg offered a three-day course on 'Parliamentary government, Pressure Groups and Elections'. Members burnished skills such as taking minutes, organising conferences, presiding over meetings, writing reports, taking affidavits and developing general organisational techniques.

Other opportunities for learning and self-development included a workshop held in Cape Town in August 1989, led by Sandy Lazarus of the University of the Western Cape, to enhance chairing skills. The work was done in small groups, and Sandy's summary of the points was made available for wider use.[22] A training session for public speaking was offered by the Communications Department of the University of Cape Town.

The branch structure, which was established in most of the regions, was instrumental in maintaining interest and support. Here women found intellectual stimulus and formed strong friendships. Tasks were not too onerous, the telephone 'grapevine' kept members informed of activities, and opportunities arose for greater involvement. Patsy

Wells McIntosh, who was a member of the Rondebosch branch in Cape Town, described what it meant to her. She started by quoting Aung San Suu Kyi: 'You shouldn't stop doing something just because it's too small. After all, all the drops make up the ocean.' She continued, 'I lived in Cape Town from 1968 until 1973 and was a member of Black Sash ... At my London Sunday School we used to hear a lot about the parish links with a church in South Africa. As a teenager I read Trevor Huddleston and Alan Paton. Later I became aware of the repressive legislation being passed, so I'd always known a bit about South Africa.

'In my early 20s I married a South African, and a year or two later we came to live in Cape Town. Through my husband I met Mary Birt who was active in all sorts of things, including the Sash. I was very interested and she took me to a few meetings. My South African relations were not pleased and thought I shouldn't be involved – that it might be dangerous.

'I only did a very limited amount; it was quite clear to me that something had to be done to oppose the dreadful things the government were doing. I went to meetings and took part in stands when I could. We had the annual fund-raising morning market and a group of us from my Branch met weekly to make soft toys and other items to sell. We discussed politics, planned our activities, and we often wondered if we were making any difference to the situation. I remember that the regime seemed solid, brutal, repressive and immovable at the time. I'm sure I too wondered if we could make a difference but I do remember saying: "I don't know what the effects are of what we do. What is happening is very wrong, someone has to say so and I want to be on the side of people who are speaking out. We can't know what effect we may be having, but we have to do something." I also helped with a bursary scheme for African school students.'

Patsy quoted a friend from that time, Mary Olowin, who remembered, 'Mary Birt explained to me that the things we were making for the morning market were intended to convey to the public that we are ordinary women, not some kind of scary monsters.'

'Belonging to the Black Sash was important to me personally; it politicised me, allowed me to declare myself as an activist. Ever since then I have used the lessons and skills I learned through Sash ... I learned that it is good campaigning strategy to start by putting arguments in terms the "opposition" understands.

'What else did I learn? I chaired my first big meeting (we took it in turns). I *was* terrified but survived (a good preparation for teaching and lecturing).

'With Sash I went on a visit to a township and was shocked by the poverty – I felt a terrible wimp – paralysed and overwhelmed by the conditions there. (Do we ever learn to confront the pain of the world with equanimity?) Later I taught about the effects of gender, race, class and disability on schooling. I'd become an active and campaigning feminist (this I'm sure built on my experience with Sash). My students would ask what they could do about such injustice. "Inform yourself," I used to say. "Find out all you can. Then join an organisation. Even having your name on their list and your money puts them in a stronger position. Get together with others and campaign."

'Through the Sash I had an early experience of making friends through shared activism, of the special quality of relationship that gives, of all one can take for granted. I also learned the thrill of a "successful" protest – that "high" one gets from making a stand – literally in our case.

'I learned to work with other people, later to encourage people each to do what they are good at and want to do. I learned that by involving people in a campaigning group they come to feel it belongs to them, and they feel loyal to and responsible for it. I am still very proud to have been a small part for a short time of the work of Black Sash.'[23]

While the first members of the Black Sash signed up in the great wave of enthusiasm in 1955, later the procedures were more formal. Becoming a member required an applicant to complete a form in which she accepted the aims and the constitution of the Black Sash, and was obliged to furnish the names of two existing members who would support her membership. This was justified as providing protection against infiltration by both government informers and potential agents provocateurs, but numerous incidents over the years demonstrated that it did not succeed completely in doing either. Some informers were exposed and no doubt there were others who were never identified. Anyone who joined with the ulterior motive of promoting illegal or violent actions would have found the policy-making procedures insurmountable. But the requirement of sponsorship for membership also meant that a number of willing applicants who did not know any existing members found it difficult to be accepted, and some were seriously offended. Anne Greenwell, for example, who was to become a core member of the monitoring group, remembers that when she first applied she was made to feel like a spy because, since she had not lived in Cape Town for long, she knew no members.[24]

The Black Sash was always aware that there were likely to be spies in its midst. Some of them were discovered and asked to resign. There were occasional reports from members that they had been approached and asked to give information to the security police. It was likely that others had been similarly approached and might have agreed. One or two were identified, such as Stephanie van Heerden, who in 1971 gave evidence for the state in the prosecution of the Anglican dean of Johannesburg, the Very Rev. Gonville ffrench-Beytagh. He was accused in terms of the Terrorism Act of inciting or encouraging an audience of the Black Sash (in Sheena Duncan's house) to 'support and prepare for a violent revolution'.[25] He was convicted and sentenced to five years' imprisonment, but was acquitted on appeal, and eventually expelled from South Africa. Stephanie van Heerden resigned from the Black Sash. Much later it was revealed that Vanessa Brereton, a trusted Grahamstown lawyer who handled many cases referred to her by the Black Sash, had also been giving information to the security police. Although these incidents caused rifts and disillusionment, we knew that while we needed to be watchful, we could never protect ourselves completely from infiltration by informers, and should not allow this to obstruct our work or deter us from the course we were pursuing.

Members were aware that their activities were watched by the security forces, and their mail and telephone conversations monitored. In general they tried to make light of this, but harassment could take various forms, and began early in all regions. 'We have heard recently [1956] of two cases of women victimised because they were members of our organisation. The first was a school teacher dismissed from her post, because she was seen handing out our leaflets. She found a post in a non-government school. Three months later the head of that school received a letter from the Education Department threatening the withdrawal of the Government grant unless the new teacher was dismissed. The family is thinking of leaving South Africa. The second victim was wearing a Black Sash badge when she went to draw her pension. The official commented on this and said she had better resign from the Black Sash, or her pension would be suspended. She replied that all her papers were in order and that they could not do anything to her. "Papers can be lost" was the dry reply.'[26]

'At the National Congress in Pretoria [1957] the banner held by Black Sash women was torn down by hooligans, and one of our members was hit in the face. "The satisfying aspect of the whole incident", writes my correspondent, "was that a young policeman who was on duty and witnessed the act, asked us whether we wished to lay a charge." The unsatisfactory aspect of the whole incident was that (a) it could occur at all, and (b) that my correspondent should find it amazing that a policeman should attempt to keep the peace. We are supposed to be a civilized people.'[27] In the same issue of the magazine there is an account of Black Sash women attacked by Nasionale Jeugbond [the National Party youth group], 'sashes cut off with knives ... placards torn up ... police standing nearby eating ice creams and laughing.'

If members were anxious about demonstrating, mutual support and a variety of strategies helped to allay fears. Ann van der Riet, who was part of the Cape Town Media Group, which created posters and drafted pamphlets, says, 'My memories of the Black Sash are mostly of the wonderful camaraderie in the organisation. I joined the Sash for very serious reasons – objecting in as many ways as possible to the dreadful apartheid legislation and behaviour of the previous government. The stands were a particular way of showing our disapproval of these laws as well as commemorating and bringing to the public's attention the various atrocities. I was involved in these stands from when I joined the Sash in 1973/74, as well as making the posters for them from the mid-'80s. I will never forget Anne Finsen's contribution of getting certified copies of the City Council permission to stand. She would take the original, and as many copies as were needed, to the Wynberg police station where they would stamp each copy as certified. These were stuck onto the back of each poster (about 15 altogether) to show that we had Council permission when confronted – mostly by the police. I do have to confess though that when we first started the individual stands, my heart would hammer away for about five minutes or so. It would start again if I saw a police van approaching. When I showed them the letter of permission and innocently said, "Look, we have permission", they would see the police stamp and immediately back off! This small victory always made me feel we had won a battle.'[28]

Inevitably, members witnessed a great deal of hardship, and from time to time proposals were made that the organisation should embark on welfare activities. It was argued that this would provide an outlet for members' energies, and attract more women who wanted to do something useful. Instead, they were urged to take on charitable work through other organisations, where they would also be able to influence the political views of a wider circle. The Sash was to remain a political organisation, working for justice as its primary goal. There was also a legal imperative – welfare work required registration as a recognised charitable organisation, and advice office work could not be seen as welfare.

The Sash offered scope for a variety of skills and energies which kept members involved. Not only could they work in the advice offices and in the monitoring groups, as well as participate in protest stands.

Fundraising projects kept many creative hands busy; women with particular interests in other fields, such as education, transport or public health, were able to bring their expertise into discussions at meetings and into the organisation's publications; poets, artists and writers found inspiration and outlets for their work; group activities, whether they consisted of drawing up placards for demonstrations or producing goods for sale, also included discussion and information. Many members have testified to the fact that these personal experiences were important to them in a society where people did not, in general, share their views.

Their abilities were sometimes stretched beyond anything they might have expected. Prue Crosoer reflected on how, confronted with the evil around them, they learned to respond to suffering, and how this helped them in other circumstances. When one of their own group experienced tragedy, 'we had the courage to face up to personal agony and find a way to deal with it'.[29]

The frustration and despair created by living in such an unjust society, with little real hope of effecting any change, could be countered by laughter, comradeship and the sharing of skills. Baking cakes, making artificial flowers, creating vibrant patterns on cloth with batik work, offering vegetarian cooking classes, all could be interchanged with writing speeches or putting up street posters. The sense of learning more, understanding more, devising successful strategies, receiving encouragement and support, all contributed to making membership worthwhile.

There were many times when it might have seemed that the task was too great, that Sash members were too few, and that all the hard work would not bring about any change. Yet those were precisely the times when there were enough voices to say that it was essential to keep working, to believe that a better society was possible, and that women striving together could make it so.

It was one thing to be a member in the cities, where there were others who provided support, companionship and encouragement.

It was quite another matter to have the courage to stand out in a conservative community of farmers or a mining town. Those who did are deserving of special respect. Di Davis (secretary of Cape Eastern region, Port Elizabeth) wrote about 'rural' members as 'the very fabric of the Sash: their only satisfaction comes from devotion to a cause … branches of nine women here, fifteen there, with their town 20 miles away, and their neighbour equally far … who never receive praise to revive them … By their membership alone they light a small flame that flickers in the consciences of their detractors.'[30]

Many of these lone members, or members of small branches, speak of the support and comfort they derived from the existence of the Black Sash and its advice offices and fieldworkers. They knew they could seek assistance when necessary, and felt the solidarity of being part of a community, even at a distance. An early country member said, 'When you live in the country, especially on a mine, you tend to lose heart. And to me, the fellowship of the League is like a candle set in a window at night, and I don't want it to burn out.'

For many of us who lived and worked in Cape Town, the 'country branches' were Elgin and Somerset West. Elgin was at the forefront of our awareness, partly because the members there would hold an annual picnic on one of the farms just after the apple harvest. We would set out from town, often in convoy, and descend on the farm – to spend a wonderful day walking, swimming, enjoying the delicious produce which would supplement our picnics or give us special treats to take home. Apartheid was forgotten for a day as we brought friends to share the delights. Foremost among the hosts were the sisters Patricia Denniston and Anne Browne, whose parents had moved from Natal to Elgin and established Elgin Orchards. Both devoted churchwomen, with strong social consciences, they worked with some other progressive farmers to transform the relationships with their farmworkers that were considered normal for the time, creating improved working conditions, starting a child-care centre so that the local women could work in the packing sheds, providing health care and educational opportunities, even a human resources manager to protect the rights of the workers.

Anne and her husband and children spent some time in England, while Patricia remained a formidable force in the area. She was particularly concerned about conditions in an informal settlement known as 'Newtown' where African seasonal workers had lived for over 20 years before being forced to leave in the 1960s, endorsed out to 'resettlement villages' in the Eastern Cape such as Sada.[31] They would never be allowed to acquire residential rights, nor seek other work in Elgin out of the fruit season, and could only be employed as contract workers by farmers, who had to apply for an annual quota. The Denniston–Browne family tried to maintain contact with these families and themselves went to see those bleak resettlement areas, and to take clothing, food and support. (Decades later, angry protests of seasonal farmworkers broke out in the Western Cape in 2013. Their complaints against their living and working conditions show that this is a problem that has not been resolved, even though the apartheid laws have gone.)

Patricia later settled in Canada, and I chanced to learn of her death in December 2012, which prompted me to seek out Anne, now living in Simonstown. I had not seen her for over 30 years, but would have recognised her immediately, her tall, elegant frame and lovely features unmistakable. Her daughter Rachel brought out an ancient photograph album and together they took us back to the group that made up that small branch: Molly Murray, Elspeth Donovan, Elly de Vries and many others.

Anne and Rachel recalled, too, that the wide network of contacts Patricia and Anne had established through the church as well as the Sash kept them in touch with many people who were working to oppose apartheid. Patricia's studio was a safe space where they were able to provide accommodation for an occasional guest hiding from the police – a fact they kept secret even from Anne's husband, so that when he, 'the Commander' as he was known, was visited by the police, he was able in complete honesty to dispatch them summarily off his property. They were not the only Black Sash people to offer shelter and a safe house, but probably provided the most beautiful and the safest place.[32]

Another farming member in the Western Cape was Jayne Beaumont, whose family's wine farm is in Bot River. Together with the Anglican Church, she started an advice office in Grabouw, which still exists today and seeks to assist people from all the surrounding areas.

There was also a small Sash branch in Knysna, and from 1987 until 2010 an advice office was sustained there. Lu Harding, a third-generation member, was particularly active in starting the Southern Cape branch and the advice office, and instrumental in drawing in staff members and the support of the lawyer Kobus Pienaar. She is remembered as 'a hero of the Black Sash'.[33] In conservative George, once the parliamentary seat of P.W. Botha, there was one lone member, Gill Dugmore, who attracted great hostility for her membership of the United Democratic Front as well as the Black Sash.[34] It took a particular courage and determination to speak out. In the 1980s the formation of a broader group, Southern Cape Against Removals (SCAR), provided an opportunity for mutual support and joint campaigns. It was a time when the security forces were particularly active, and there was constant surveillance and intimidation.

Sustaining the organisation depended on good management as well as inspiring leadership. The structures established in the first years, consisting of local branches, regional councils and a national executive, provided a clear system for policy-making while allowing a measure of regional autonomy. As a new member in 1965, I valued the well-organised meetings, fairly formal debates and stimulating conferences.

Every year delegates to national conferences would find a green paper among the first pages in the agenda folders. It was headed 'rules of procedure', and these were adopted by agreement at the very start of the meeting. We would laugh, because they were largely ignored thereafter, but they did provide an accepted mechanism which the presiding chairperson could use for managing debate if this became too heated.

Strong-willed women driven by high ideals were bound to differ at times, although in the earliest years the enthusiastic support of the members and their common determination to uphold constitutional principles formed a powerful bond. When challenges later arose, these could be a threat to the warm relationships that had been built. Women who were so united in their opposition to injustice could still be tormented by disagreements about policies and strategies. There were times when the Black Sash had to confront such conflicts, and even the possibility of being torn apart. Those who were at its centre, whose lives and identities had become closely bound up with the organisation, felt these divisions acutely.

Decisions made over the years were sometimes hard fought. Even a majority vote or the achievement of consensus could fail to satisfy those whose strongly felt views were not accommodated. If they remained in the organisation, there was a risk they would feel themselves to be a disregarded minority. If they left, close friendships could be broken.

Sometimes decisions were deferred for a year or longer, in the hope that consensus could be reached. An illustration of this is the Black Sash position on universal franchise. In 1960, responding to a far-sighted proposal submitted by Border region, the national conference agreed to support the Universal Declaration of Human Rights. The Declaration, adopted by the United Nations in 1948, upheld the right to universal suffrage. However, the issue was seldom mentioned within the Black Sash thereafter, remaining little more than a distant goal.

It was not until 1978 that the organisation faced up to the need to recognise the right of all citizens to an equal vote. By then, after the 1976 uprising of the youth in Soweto and the prevalence of discussions about black consciousness, many Sash members recognised, in the words of Moira Henderson, that 'things will never change until people have the vote'. Sheena Duncan proposed a resolution to be brought to the annual conference, and there were a number of meetings in all regions to discuss it. The general membership appeared not to have realised that they had already agreed to this in principle, in supporting the Universal Declaration of Human Rights, and a measure of anxiety and caution characterised the debates. The full text of the resolution recognised that political justice depended also on other factors such as an independent judiciary and the protection of human rights. The national conference of 1978 was able to adopt the measure, whose opening words were 'The Black Sash believes that justice cannot be achieved without a universal adult franchise'.[35] In doing so, it was ahead of all the political parties represented in Parliament at the time.

On a number of other issues, with wide social and political relevance, the Black Sash was also in the forefront of public opinion. The campaigns that were mounted on these issues helped broaden the organisation's focus and were often driven by a younger generation of members who entered the Black Sash from the 1970s, bringing with them new energy and ideas. They included capital punishment, military conscription and abortion legislation.

The Sash's concern for human life found expression in its campaign against capital punishment. Execution by hanging was a dark part of South Africa's judicial and penal system until it was finally abolished after the end of apartheid. Opposition to the practice was led by Professor Barend van Niekerk of the law faculty at the universities of Natal and the Witwatersrand, who launched the Society for the Abolition of Capital Punishment in South Africa in 1971. He had the support of senior professors of law and a number of judges.[36] Besides opposing the death penalty on principle, Van Niekerk also gathered an impressive array of statistics about the numbers of people executed and the discrepancies in the way the law was administered, including a racial bias: South Africa had the highest percentage of the total number of executions carried out throughout the world. He added that it had frequently happened that on one day six or seven condemned prisoners were executed simultaneously. An article in *Sash* magazine in 1967, entitled 'Here comes the hangman', concluded, 'No thinking person can condone something which has its true place beside the slave-galley and the rack.'[37]

During the next decade Black Sash members became increasingly aware of the numbers of hangings, and voiced their opposition to the death penalty itself. In April 1979 members of the Transvaal region participated in organising an all-night vigil at St Alban's Cathedral in Pretoria on the eve of the hanging of Solomon Mahlangu.[38] Mahlangu was a member of MK, Umkhonto we Sizwe, the ANC's armed wing, who was found guilty of killing two people in 1977 during a shootout with police in the middle of Johannesburg. He had been severely assaulted during his interrogation, and his assailant was subsequently granted amnesty by the Truth and Reconciliation Commission. Mahlangu is remembered today as a hero of the ANC.

Professor Van Niekerk died in 1981, but even before then public support for the Society for the Abolition of Capital Punishment had dwindled. In 1982 Jill Wentzel presented a paper at the Black Sash national conference, in which she outlined the position of Amnesty International on capital punishment, as well as the 1976 United Nations Covenant on Civil and Political Rights, and paid tribute to Dr Van Niekerk for his energy and commitment.[39] Members continued to gather information on executions in South Africa, and in 1988 the Sash published a detailed report titled *Inside South Africa's Death Factory*.[40]

The March 1988 national conference of the Sash focused attention on the subject, which it sustained throughout the year. At the conference Ann Colvin, Sheena Duncan and Jenny de Tolly described the growing public concern, partly because 164 people had been executed in 1987, and the 53 people on death row at the end of that year had been sentenced for actions arising directly out of the ongoing political conflict. They stressed that the Black Sash was opposed to the death penalty in all circumstances: 'We believe that the deliberate, planned killing of any human being is indefensible. It has a brutalising effect upon society as a whole; it debases those who carry out the execution, those who must witness it and all those who are members of societies which authorise it.' They listed what was known about the methods of executions at that time, and further questions to be raised; they outlined the campaign that was to follow; and once again tribute was paid to Barend van Niekerk.[41]

On 20 June 1988 the Sash national executive wrote to President P.W. Botha, proposing a moratorium on all executions pending an investigation, and arguing that 'If there is one single action which can immediately reduce levels of tension and anger in our society, elicit support from almost all groupings within the country and abroad, and also carry us a step forward towards the establishment of a just and benevolent society, that action is the abolition of the death penalty'.[42] This received a courteous reply, but no commitment.

In November 1988 a number of organisations, including legal bodies and the churches, decided to revive, with a new name, the Society for the Abolition of the Death Penalty (SADPSA). In the Cape Western region, the Black Sash had formed a Capital Punishment Interest Group, which took on much of the practical work of the launch, such as printing pamphlets and posters. The national executive of the new SADPSA included Beva Runciman (Black Sash regional chair) as its honorary secretary. Sheena Duncan was among its patrons.[43]

From then on, the Black Sash took up the death penalty as a major pillar of its work. Sash members attended trials, held protest stands (and were sometimes arrested for doing so), supported family members of those sentenced, and worked with other organisations involved, including the newly formed Family and Friends of People on Death Row.[44] Pretoria, being the city where the hangings all took place, became the focus of many vigils and protests. Sash members also supported the families who visited prisoners on death row. In particular, through public education and public protest the Sash addressed the way the 'doctrine of common purpose' was being used in the South African legal system. This was based on the argument that an instigator or accomplice, or someone who was part of a group of people involved, could be as guilty as the actual perpetrator of a crime. In the mid- to late 1980s attention centred on the death sentences imposed on the 'Sharpeville Six' and the 'Upington 26', where this principle had been taken 'to an unwarranted extreme'.[45] Six people were charged with the murder of the deputy mayor of Sharpeville township on 3 September 1984, during a protest by a large and angry crowd against rent increases. The six were sentenced to death. In Upington, in the northern Cape, 26 people were arrested after a municipal policeman was beaten and burnt to death by a protesting crowd on 13 November 1985. In May 1989, 14 of them were sentenced to be hanged. A long campaign of national and international pressure ended when the death sentences imposed on the Sharpeville Six were commuted to terms of imprisonment a matter of hours before their execution was due on 11 July 1988, while in May 1989 the Upington accused won their appeal against their sentences.[46]

While the death penalty was suspended after President De Klerk's announcement of the unbanning of the ANC and the PAC in February 1990, it was eventually a ruling of the new Constitutional Court that led to the abolition of capital punishment. On 6 June 1995, in its first action, the Constitutional Court ruled that capital punishment was contrary to the Bill of Rights, enshrined in the Interim Constitution, and ordered that all pending executions be halted while the appropriate legislation was drafted. This was duly enacted as part of the Criminal Law Amendment Act of 1997.[47]

In the same way as Jill Wentzel, Isie Pretorius and many more in the Black Sash put their energies in the campaign for the abolition of the death penalty, others became increasingly concerned about the growing militarisation of South Africa in the 1980s, and the numbers of young white men being drafted into the country's security forces.

As South Africa became more and more isolated from its neighbours, and the battle to defend apartheid led to increasing strife along its borders, the government's need to bolster its military resources grew. The system of military conscription, first introduced with the Defence Act of 1957, began to change. Young white men had been eligible for a 'draw' through which a certain number of them would be called up for military training. Many of them would have taken part in 'cadet' training at school, and might not have regarded military service as too much of a burden. Then the ballot system was withdrawn, and every white young man had to register, and would have to perform nine months (later one and then two years) of training and service unless he was found to be medically unfit or could provide good reason for religious exemption. From the 1970s conscripts were sent to 'the border', finding themselves at war with neighbouring countries. As the scale of internal resistance grew, there was a further demand to use the military within the country to help control the growing civil unrest.[48]

From the early 1970s the Black Sash, together with several other organisations, most notably the Civil Rights League, took a stance, first against the refusal of the government to recognise the objection of some young men to going into military service. A degree of provision for religious objectors did exist, especially for those who were members of faiths that were entirely pacifist, and those who would not carry weapons, to perform other tasks. There was no provision for those who opposed conscription on principle, either against war in general, or against the use of the military to enforce apartheid. Although the penalties were severe, a number of men proclaimed themselves publicly to be conscientious objectors. At the same time it became an offence, also carrying severe penalties, to encourage anyone to refuse military service.

Not all Sash members were pacifists, or opposed to military service in general. Many had sons or other male relatives who were confronted with hard decisions about what to do. A system of call-up for older men to form patrols in their local areas was also introduced, colloquially described as 'Dad's Army'. Among white people there was an increasingly military flavour to many conversations and activities. Serving in the South African Defence Force (SADF) was made to sound brave and glamorous, and many young men and women became caught up in enthusiastic patriotism. Songs, radio and television programmes, and stirring speeches contributed to the pressure to make the country safe from the 'total onslaught' of the liberation movements in league with the Soviet Union. It was a time when the deep divide between white young people and their black counterparts was greater than ever.

Although 'call-up' papers were usually received by boys still at school, it was possible to obtain deferment for a few years while embarking on university studies. Public opposition to military service was muted, although within the churches voices were raised about the morality of war in general and the South African situation in particular. Denis Hurley, Roman Catholic archbishop of Durban, was one of those who spoke out about the right to refuse. Another was the Rev. Rob Robertson, who became the convener of the South African Council of Churches (SACC) Commission on Violence and Non-Violence.[49] The Civil Rights League held a public meeting on conscientious objection to military service in Cape Town on 3 October 1970. Together with the SACC, it led the way in embarking on the study of theories about war, on what constitutes a 'just war', and on international statutes governing conscientious objection. The Cape Town home of Dot Cleminshaw, a dedicated member of the Civil Rights League and of the Black Sash, became a place where many troubled young men could meet to talk about the choices they faced. In the other regions too, Sash members actively supported the Conscientious Objector Support Groups.

Over the next few years those decisions had to be made, and the first conscientious objectors made national headlines from 1977 and 1979 when Anton Eberhard, Peter Moll and Richard Steele were tried and sentenced for refusing to serve in the SADF. Their long-considered willingness to perform national service in a non-military structure, and their principled reasons for their decisions, were ignored, and they served long sentences and cruel punishment. Peter Moll, for example, spent a total of 154 days in solitary confinement, and a few years later Charles Yeats had a similar experience.

Conscientious Objector Support Groups (COSGs) were set up in Johannesburg, Durban and Cape Town by 1978, as the number of objectors increased. In private and public meetings men declared their determination to refuse to serve in the military, and were joined by some who had already been conscripted, had served time in the army, and subsequently decided that their conscience would not allow them to continue. By 1982 there were 263 conscientious objectors serving sentences. The government faced a dilemma, and threatened harsh punishment, for objectors themselves, and for anyone who encouraged them.

Prohibited therefore by the law from advocating conscientious objection, the Sash was inspired by its president Sheena Duncan to chart a new path. There was no law against discussing conscription itself, and she brought a resolution to the national conference of March 1983 arguing for an end to conscription. Brett Myrdal, one of the COSG leaders, described its impact: 'That night a few of us chatting in a graveyard realised this resolution was the way to bypass the Defence Act, which prescribed a 10-year sentence for anyone who encouraged people to disobey their call-up.'[50] This opened the door for a new phase of opposition, and led to the formation of the End Conscription Campaign (ECC). The ECC took off dramatically with a series of innovative public events, and many Sash members gave their support.

One of them, Beva Runciman, was instrumental in arranging a meeting between some of the ECC leaders and Sir Richard Luyt, retired principal of the University of Cape Town, in the hope that he would support them. It was fascinating to see him listen closely to their arguments, and absorb ideas that were challenging to a man who had been in the British colonial service and used the army to quell local resistance while governor of British Guiana. It was greatly to his credit that he agreed to speak in support of the ECC at the Black Sash national conference in March 1985, and it was a tribute, too, to those who had enabled him to accept their point of view.[51]

Sash members sustained their links with the ECC members, in public and in private. Charles Yeats recalls how much he valued the monthly letters he received from Sheena while he was imprisoned, and many others also maintained contact with those serving sentences. In every region the Sash, and other women who were drawn in, took part in ECC activities, accepted invitations to speak at its meetings, and were inspired by the courage and determination of its members. In a society where violence was so widespread, working for peace instead of war was a sign of hope for the future.

Dot Cleminshaw, so active in the advocacy of conscientious objection, also played a part in shaping the attitude of the Black Sash to the question of women's health, particularly the right to birth control, sterilisation and abortion, another of the campaigns that the organisation took on. In general, the first founders of the Sash did not have women's rights as their main focus, but, later, feminist voices within the organisation came to have an impact on its policies. Dot's influence on the Black Sash and on other organisations illustrates the effect that one person can have to propel social change. Although she was restricted in her movements by a severe back injury, she campaigned throughout her life for civil and human rights for all, actively supporting a number of organisations and bringing issues to their attention, even when these were controversial. In the early 1970s she became aware of the concern among doctors and others about the extremely limited rights to legal abortion. This led to large numbers of women, many of them poor and black, faced with an unwanted pregnancy, resorting to illegal abortions, risking injury and death. The majority of the medical profession remained silent, but in 1971 the Cape Town feminist Dolly Maister and Dr Marj Dyer, a retired general practitioner whose husband was a gynaecologist, launched the Abortion Reform League (ARL). In the following year June Cope founded the Abortion Reform Action Group (ARAG) in Durban, after the trial and conviction of Professor Derek Crichton for having participated in illegal abortions. His testimony revealed the desperation of women who resorted to such illegal methods and subsequently had to be rescued from the consequences. He had previously spoken in support of abortion on demand, at a medical students' conference that was held at the University of Cape Town in 1971.[52]

For the majority of white women the subject of abortion appeared controversial and remote, and for the religious denominations it was generally too uncomfortable to confront. The National Party remained obdurate in opposing arguments in favour of clinical abortion. When establishing a parliamentary committee (all male) to consider draft legislation in the 1970s, a government spokesman commented, 'It is not necessary for a woman to serve on a committee if we wish to sound the conscience of the nation. If we wanted to abolish capital punishment, we would not appoint a bunch of murderers to go into the matter.'[53] In 1975 the Abortion and Sterilisation Act was passed, severely restricting a woman's right to decide when, where and by whom she might end a pregnancy.

June Cope illustrated the results of this law with some frightening statistics: 'Taking a two-year period from 1979 to 1980, a mere 770 women obtained legal abortions. Of them 535 were white and 235 were black.' She compared these figures with those of the 66,830 women hospitalised for 'the removal of the residue of a pregnancy' (often a euphemism for repairing the effects of an illegal abortion) in the same period. Of these, 15,555 were white and 51,275 were black. She added, 'These figures represent a fraction of the women who have resorted to backstreet abortion.'[54]

Concern over the law governing abortion took some time to gather strength in the Black Sash. For some years it was the work of a few individuals within it, and especially within the Civil Rights League, to support the campaign for legalisation of abortion. Jean Sinclair had signed an ARAG petition in 1973 but did so in her personal capacity. In 1981 the Natal Coastal region of the Black Sash stated that the matter of fertility control was a basic human right, and advocated safe and legal first-trimester abortion. The Black Sash adopted a resolution at the 1983 national conference urging the government 'to appoint a Commission of Enquiry under the chairmanship of a judge and including experts from various fields and women of all races to investigate the working and effects of the 1975 Abortion Act'.[55] This fell on deaf ears.

It was not until the late 1980s, with increasing focus on a wide spectrum of human rights, and with the formation of new women's groups such as the Western Cape Women's Alliance and the South African National Coalition of Women, that more women's voices were raised on the subject. Dot Cleminshaw, Marj Dyer and Dolly Maister wrote many letters to the press, spoke on radio and television, addressed meetings, especially of women's groups, and raised the issue wherever they could. They were instrumental in placing the subject of abortion in the October/November 1990 issue of *South African Outlook*, an ecumenical Christian journal edited by Professor Francis Wilson. They also held important discussions with religious leaders of different faiths.

In 1991 Dot was 'asked by Karin Chubb, Black Sash national Vice-President, and a feminist concerned about the oppression of all but especially black women', to write a paper for the annual national conference. The document, titled 'Women's human rights to informed choice on gender issues', included a section on the right of women to choose early, safe termination of pregnancy. It evoked considerable opposition at the conference, but Dot and those who supported her were not dissatisfied. 'A pebble had been dropped in the pond.'[56] Further articles in the *Sash* magazine, and proposals to adopt the 1979 UN Convention on the Elimination of All Forms of Discrimination against Women, were to follow.

In 1992, under the leadership of Jenny de Tolly, the Sash called for a commission to inquire into the workings of the 1975 law. In 1993 the national conference adopted a resolution calling for a freedom of choice bill.[57] The resolution acknowledged that some people had ethical or religious reservations, but it recognised the immense problems of women who suffered the most under the legislation proscribing abortion. It also gave attention to the concerns of medical practitioners who were confronted by these problems. It is testimony not only to the strategic skills of those who had worked so hard to bring the Black

Sash to that point, but also to the real care taken to respect divergent views and yet remain true to the essential protection of a woman's right to choose.

The Black Sash resolution of 1993 was used by Dot and others as a spur to discussion in many other spheres. She 'smiled inwardly recognising the positive influence the Black Sash and ARAG were exerting'. She was more than entitled to do so, having achieved so much. The tide of public opinion was changing dramatically, and the subject was taken up by organisations such as Lawyers for Human Rights, the National Association of Democratic Lawyers and the Black Lawyers Association, and by many ANC women recently returned to South Africa. A meeting arranged by the three legal associations on International Women's Day, 8 March 1993, was chaired by Sandy Liebenberg, a Black Sash member who was then a human rights lawyer from the University of the Western Cape.

Although some ANC members attended the meeting, the ANC itself was not at the time ready to take up the issue, and it was not until after the change of government in 1994 that the new minister of health, Dr Nkosazana Dlamini-Zuma, introduced a freedom of choice bill. The Choice on Termination of Pregnancy Act of 1996 finally became law in February 1997.

Reaching decisions on such major topics as conscription, capital punishment and abortion required a process of discussion, information and consultation. The Sash leadership valued the support of the members, and aimed at persuasion rather than dispute whenever possible. When the more radical members voiced strong opinions, often well in advance of general opinion, it was helpful to ask for a fact paper setting out the arguments, followed by a debate. If the matter was one requiring the organisation to take a position, branches and regions would be asked to consider it, and to report back to a plenary session. This provided a comfortable space for many of the women to express doubts and concerns, knowing that they would be heard.

When eventually a decision was taken, this process usually ensured that it was accepted.

The women of the Sash were not afraid to consider nettlesome issues, and to stand up for their beliefs, yet they sought to be tolerant of other opinions and to foster unity within the organisation. Denise Ackermann's research into the Black Sash for her doctoral thesis led her to speak of the 'liberating praxis' that derives from conscientisation, followed by action and reflection. She pointed out that 'the organisation is far less homogeneous' than first appears, but that 'a variety of different opinions, political persuasions, beliefs and ways of being are tolerated and accepted'.[58] It was this attitude of consultation and respect for divergence which gave the leadership of the Sash the ability to speak with confidence of its determination to oppose injustice and to work for change.

3

THE ADVICE OFFICES

'An advice office is a place where people are given information about various laws and the structures of administration in their area. To transfer information is to transfer power. An advice office is a place where people learn how to solve their own problems.'[1] When she wrote this introduction to a training programme for advice offices, Sheena Duncan had had more than 20 years of experience in the Johannesburg advice office. Many lessons had been learned since 1958, when the foundations for the first of the Sash's advice offices had been laid in Cape Town. At that time, its intention was much less ambitious: to administer a bail fund in order to assist women who had been arrested in terms of the pass laws, and enable them to return to their families until they were brought to court.

The immediate spur was the arrest, in March 1958, of 20 African women in Elsies River, Cape Town, for failing to produce their permits to be in the area. They spent several days in jail, some of them with their babies, because they could not afford to pay bail. Amy Thornton (then Rietstein), of the Congress of Democrats, asked Eulalie Stott for Black Sash help, which was provided in the form of money for bail, and for food, milk and nappies for the babies.[2] The connection between Amy and Eulalie arose through CATAPAW, the Cape Association to Abolish Passes for African Women, which was mainly led by members of the

ANC Women's League and the Federation of South African Women.[3]

The regional council of the Black Sash decided to establish a fund for the express purpose of providing bail in such circumstances. Shortly after, a 'Bail Fund office' was opened where people could seek help and the funds be administered, easing the burden on Sash members who had performed these services from their homes. That first office, located in Tigne Place off Klipfontein Road in the Cape Town suburb of Athlone, was small, cold and sparsely furnished. It was open three days a week from April 1959 and staffed by volunteers – at first including members of CATAPAW, but eventually these dwindled until only Boniswa Lettie Malindi remained. She used to say she had been 'seconded to the office by the ANC, to teach those white women about the pass laws'.[4] The Athlone advice office became known as a place where people could seek help. Shirley Parks was employed as its organiser and Lettie Malindi as interpreter, and a regular team of volunteers came forward.

The next practical step taken was to join forces with the Western Cape region of the South African Institute of Race Relations (SAIRR). 'Race Relations', as it was popularly known, had been concerned about the situation of African people under the influx control regulations for some time, well before the establishment of the Black Sash, and provided counselling at its Cape Town office, so this was a logical partnership. A number of people were members of both organisations, and this also facilitated the joint programme. Desirée Berman, editor of the Black Sash magazine for several years, was a volunteer in the SAIRR office. For a time, the Athlone advice office served mainly the requests for assistance from women, while men tended to go to the SAIRR office, then located in central Cape Town.[5] In 1962 the work was consolidated in the Athlone advice office, jointly financed and staffed by the two organisations.

For the majority of Black Sash members, the impulse to provide bail for African women arrested under the pass laws was first a charitable one, prompted by sympathy for their plight. The mass arrests of women who were refusing to apply for passes, or 'reference books' as they were officially called, and the nationwide campaign of FSAW resistance to the government's extension of passes to women in the 1950s, had aroused their concern. They heard accounts of women picked up in raids in the early hours of the morning, and taken away in vans without an opportunity to dress themselves or make arrangements for the care of their children. Their first reaction was to prevent such women from being held in jail.

It did not take long to identify the law itself as the problem. In order to oppose it, the women had to understand the law. This was the beginning of the expertise that would underpin the work in years to come. The leading members of the Black Sash had plenty of energy, as well as determination, to help those who suffered under unjust laws. Lettie Malindi, herself a political activist, was able to help the volunteers understand the impact of those laws, as well as undertake the necessary translation from Xhosa to English.

From the start, the advice and pro bono services of lawyers were of inestimable value. Donald Molteno, a prominent member of the Cape Bar and liberal politician, gave the founding members of the Black Sash his support and advice, and encouraged them in the formation of the advice office. A valued early supporter was the lawyer Ian Dichmont (husband of Joan Dichmont, a dedicated Black Sash member and advice office volunteer). He drew in a legal colleague, David Dallas (whose wife then joined the Sash), and over the years there were others who gave their services. Several legal firms agreed to make one of their staff available on a daily roster basis. Many newly qualified lawyers were thus exposed to the pass laws through this experience.

In Johannesburg too, several lawyers dedicated time and thought to the advice office work. One of them was Ruth Hayman Lazar, an attorney and one of the early Sash members. She gave legal assistance to many people accused of political offences, and defended women who had been arrested for their demonstrations in Johannesburg against the pass laws. When the advice office there opened in 1963, she gave generous advice, and when legal action was required for specific cases she acted for them *pro deo*. Jean Sinclair said, 'From the days of the Treason Trial in 1956 until she was served with a banning order and house arrested in 1966 she worked tirelessly to preserve the rule of law and to fight for justice in South Africa.'[6] Under house arrest, she was unable to practise, and she and her family left South Africa for London.

In later years a significant further number of lawyers became members and provided advice and support. They included Sarah Christie, Belinda van Heerden, Sandy Liebenberg and Kathy Satchwell, and some of them became judges and professors of law. Kathy Satchwell served her articles in the firm of Raymond Tucker, one of the Black Sash's most dedicated friends and legal advisers. In the 1990s she became a Constitutional Court judge. In Cape Town, Val West studied law and became an attorney after heading the advice office for several years.

The work of the Athlone advice office expanded rapidly, and a second caseworker and interpreter, David Viti, was introduced by Ian Dichmont, who had advertised for an interpreter for his own practice. David relates that when he applied, he was asked whether he knew anything about office work, and since he did not, he was sent to learn the ropes in the Black Sash advice office. 'I started on 5 September 1962, and the place was jam-packed with mothers and babies, and also men queuing. I worked with Mrs Malindi and three volunteers, under Shirley Parks. I learned interpreting from Mrs M and filing from Mrs Parks, and I would set out the tables and get everything ready in the mornings. In two weeks I got a grip on things. In the second month I could also work with my volunteers, usually Mrs Roper or Mrs Trewartha. By the end of the third month, when Mr Dichmont phoned to say he was ready to employ me, the Sash said no, he would have to go and find another David. And I stayed there for 39 years.'[7] David also enjoyed recounting how he was able to prepare the necessary documents for the lawyers on roster duty, and took pride in ensuring that they understood the significant arguments.

As they learned more about the law, and about ways of dealing with officialdom, advice office workers did battle with the authorities on behalf of the people who came for help. Noël Robb or Moira Henderson, for example, would have had no difficulty in securing the attention of an official or a clerk, and obtaining instant answers to their questions, whereas an African applicant might have been summarily turned away. In those days it did not seem possible to expect people to 'learn to solve their own problems'. The fact that many black women refused on principle to apply for a 'reference book', or 'dompas', was recognised, but there were others who opted to seek the legal status it could confer, and who welcomed any assistance.

While some Sash members acknowledged the criticism that this was merely 'band-aid' work, the visible evidence of injustice and hardship was a constant spur to action, and there was scant opportunity for self-examination. There was urgent work to be done, and the women learned all the time to do it better.

The early records, scribbled on pieces of paper or written into a notebook so that the next day's volunteer could follow up, make fascinating reading. The first formal annual report, typed and duplicated, which covered the period from 1 October 1962 to 30 September 1963, noted, 'In all the years we have been doing this work, bail has only been estreated three times.'[8] Advice office workers wrote letters to the authorities, went on a deputation to the Native Affairs Committee of the City Council, and submitted a memorandum to the Divisional Council – receiving at least an attentive response. They made referrals to welfare organisations, they intervened with employers, and they made contact with the magistrates or chief native affairs commissioners at those places where people were to be sent when 'endorsed out' – that is, denied their right to remain in the urban areas.

Most important of all, the volunteer caseworkers used the knowledge they were acquiring to inform the public and campaign for change. They gathered the statistics, reported to their own membership both regionally and nationally, addressed meetings of other organisations, organised protest demonstrations, wrote to the press, and lobbied politicians. The objective was to change the system. In November 1959 members held a three-day stand outside the Rondebosch town hall to protest against the first-time issue of 'reference books' to black women in the Cape Province.[9]

The nationwide resistance to the pass laws culminated in the massacre of protesters at Sharpeville in March 1960 and in mass demonstrations in Langa, Cape Town, followed by the proclamation of a state of emergency – with Lettie Malindi held, for a time, among the hundreds of detainees. As the political situation worsened, the African volunteers who had formed part of the first group working in the advice office were unable to sustain their involvement, and Lettie and David were fully occupied as interpreters. They translated not only the language, but also the essence of the experiences of those who came for assistance. Each person seeking advice would have the law carefully explained, and their options discussed. All too often the harshness of the law would mean that the choice could only be 'you will have to leave the area, or risk arrest'. The volunteers who worked in the advice office were instantly exposed to the effects of these harsh laws. They experienced profound distress, and sometimes felt that they could do little more than give people the courteous and sympathetic attention denied them by the authorities.

From the start it was made very clear that this was not a charity venture. The women who volunteered to work in the office were instructed that they were not to donate money or goods. If people seeking assistance were destitute, they were to be referred to welfare organisations within a reasonable distance. Day by day, bail was provided for people who had been arrested for being in an urban area without the right stamp in their pass book, or for not having the pass book on them. Advice office workers learned about the law, and they learned about the lives of the people who lived under that law. They heard about women who were trying to build a family life with their husbands and children; about youngsters who had come to town to find their migrant worker fathers; about people who had been born and

---

SECTION 10 of the Natives (Urban Areas) Consolidation Act of 1945 as amended in 1952

SECTION 10(1)

No Bantu shall remain for more than 72 hours in a prescribed area unless he produces proof in the manner prescribed that –

(a) He has since birth, resided continuously in such area; or

(b) He has worked continuously in such area for one employer for a period of not less than ten years or has lawfully resided continuously in such area for a period of not less than fifteen years, and has thereafter continued to reside in such area and is not employed outside such area and has not during either period or thereafter been sentenced to a fine exceeding one hundred rand or to imprisonment for a period exceeding six months; or

(c) Such Bantu is the wife, unmarried daughter or son under the age at which he would become liable for the payment of general tax under the Native Taxation and Development Act, of 1925 (Act No. 41 of 1925) of any Bantu mentioned in paragraphs (a) or (b) of this sub-section and after lawful entry into such prescribed area, ordinarily resides with that Bantu in such area ; or

(d) In the case of any other Bantu, permission to so remain has been granted by an officer appointed to manage a labour bureau in terms of the provisions of paragraph (a) of sub-section (6) of Section 21 ter of the Native Labour Regulation Act, 1911) (Act No. 15 of 1911), due regard being had to the availability of accommodation in a Bantu residential area.

(Memorandum on the Pass Laws, compiled by the Black Sash, 1966)

---

lived in the town all their lives but did not have the documentation to prove it. The law was the Natives (Urban Areas) Consolidation Act of 1945, as amended in 1952.[10]

Many of those volunteers dedicated one day a week for many years to this work, and found in it the satisfaction of making a contribution towards opposing injustice, as well as the intellectual stimulus of learning about the laws and regulations. In all the regions, they learned too about the way the law was administered: not through the judicial system, but by a network of commissioner's courts specially established to deal with this policy. As we shall see in the next chapter, Black Sash members began to attend the sittings of the courts in order to witness the proceedings.

Though the laws were administered harshly and efficiently, there were times when something could be done. The advice office workers became experts in identifying loopholes in the law, or seeing in a case history that someone might in fact qualify to remain in the urban area. When that happened, an attorney was found to represent them in court. As the workers in the advice offices acquired their considerable knowledge of the legislation, it often seemed to them as if they, the interpreters included, were guiding the lawyers who would argue the cases in the court. This later became most famously true of Sheena Duncan, acknowledged by many lawyers as having a better understanding than anyone else of these laws. It also applied to the dozens of advice office people all around the country who learned how to handle the cases, and seek for any loophole or interpretation which might benefit those who came for assistance. They would identify cases in which it seemed there might be a chance of an acquittal or of having the charges withdrawn. With legal representation, the entire process could be slowed down as arguments were allowed in defence or in mitigation, and occasionally a case might be won.

Taking a case through the courts required a great deal of patience and meticulous gathering of information and evidence. If the outcome was successful, not only did it transform the life of the individual family concerned, but it also established a legal precedent that could benefit many others. Noël Robb described as a 'sensational event' the final success in the case of Mr Gideon Mtima, after a six-year struggle through the courts.

'Mr Mtima first came to the Athlone Advice Office in March 1972 to complain that his wife had been refused extension to her permit to live with him at his home, which is his mother's house. She had lived with him lawfully from the time of her marriage to him in 1961 until 1968, when she was endorsed out.' She had nowhere else to live so she returned, and was endorsed out again, but eventually in 1972 was given a 'visiting permit', although permanent residential right was denied. 'As she had entered the area lawfully to join her lawful (under section 10(1)(b)) husband, at his lawful home, they were at this point referred to our attorneys, who claimed that her circumstances entitled her to section 10(1)(c) recognition.' Noël explained that this right had been established through an earlier successful advice office case, that of Christine Nqwandi in 1967.

'The authorities now brought a new and serious objection to bear on the case', claiming that Mr Mtima himself was not qualified as a permanent resident. He had come to Cape Town in 1953, and was allowed to remain and work, and had been with one employer for ten years and one month when the attorneys began to work on the case. This would seem to qualify him under section 10(1)(b), but the provisions governing section 10 of the Act had come into force in 1952, a year before he arrived in the city. A previous Supreme Court judgment had ruled that only people who could prove they had *already* achieved the qualifications by that date could qualify. If Mr Mtima was not qualified, his wife would certainly have no case.

It began to seem hopeless, and the advice office report for 1976 reported sadly, 'Adverse judgment was delivered in the Supreme Court case of Mr Gideon Mtima. His wife's claim was rejected on the grounds that his qualification was unacceptable … An appeal has been noted.' The appeal was finally heard in May 1977 and judgment delivered in September, ruling in favour of Mr Mtima. Once his qualification was established, the advice office and its supportive lawyers could take up the claim for Mrs Mtima's right to section 10(1)(c) status, which was finally recognised in May 1978. After six years of waiting, not only could the Mtima family live together legally in Cape Town, but a significant precedent had been established, and the advice office had at least a dozen similar cases in the pipeline.

Reading the reports, I am fascinated to note how even at the very early stages advice office workers were able to identify trends or patterns in government practice. In 1962/63, they encountered three cases of women who had worked in Cape Town for a number of years and who, on changing their employment, were given a form to be signed by their new employer in which a deposit was demanded, covering the cost of the train fare to their place of birth. This was an indication that when they left that employer, it was likely they would be 'endorsed out'. Noël Robb spoke in 1968 of the importance of observing, recording and disseminating such information: 'Often the first evidence of new regulations is a sudden increase in the number of cases, all of the same type ... Records are moreover made available to experts for university and other research projects. We have nearly 12,000 cases on our files.'[11]

As an early historian of the Sash remarked of the advice offices, 'their achievement has been remarkable ... By gathering and recording case histories of African victims of the pass laws, they have compiled an effective indictment of those laws. If the Black Sash hopes that "history and our children will vindicate us", as their protest placards have often proclaimed, their advice offices and the records they have compiled may provide the information out of which this vindication will be fashioned.'[12]

Deeper understanding of the impact of these ever-tightening regulations grew with each year of the Black Sash's experience. In 1967 Noël Robb described the impact on society of the contract labour system: as men were forbidden to come to Cape Town to look for work or accept work offered except on contract, and no women were allowed to come to Cape Town except for a short while, the 'proportion of contract workers to permanent ones is steadily increasing, as is the alarming increase in the ratio of men to women.'[13] In Langa at that time it was estimated that there were approximately

24,550 'bachelor' migrant workers – 68 per cent of whom were actually married men. Housing conditions were totally inadequate, and the men were obliged to live in overcrowded single-sex hostels. The proportion of men to women in Langa was approximately 10 to 1, and this raised anxiety about the social fabric of the township, which was estimated to have almost 4,500 children, probably half girls and some of them teenagers.

Dr Trudy Thomas, Sash member in East London, described in 1974 the physical and psychological impact of the influx control policy and the resultant damage to family lives. 'It is difficult not to become impassioned when considering the dehumanising and uncivilising effects which the disruption of their home life has on Africans, especially when they are blamed for becoming the inevitable products of inescapable circumstances.' She listed some manifestations of these effects: 'broken families and absent fathers; the burden imposed on the elderly, especially women, and neglect of their needs; abandonment of children; teenage pregnancies; deprivation and desperate poverty'.[14]

Seeking ways of overcoming this terrible damage became Trudy Thomas's major quest, most of it outside the Black Sash, some of it within the ANC and as provincial minister of health for some years, and eventually simply as a dedicated doctor and protector of people's rights and needs. Her legacy is as powerful as ever, and her understanding of the effects of migrant labour on the young population an essential tool for finding explanations and solutions to crime and violence and alienation in South Africa in the 21st century. Even now, 50 years since that time, the damage to healthy relationships between men and women, and problems arising in family lives, such as domestic violence, can be seen as having grown from seeds planted in the poisoned ground of influx control policy.

After 1958 the experience of the new advice office in Cape Town soon had an impact on the other regions, and advice offices were established in cities where there were sufficient Sash members to sustain them. There was some discussion about whether such offices constituted charitable work, but after a national conference decision of 1962 (to aid victims of unjust laws), it was agreed that this was an entirely appropriate venture for the organisation. The Johannesburg office opened on 11 February 1963.[15] Durban, Port Elizabeth, East London and Elgin started offices in 1964, and others followed later. From that time onwards, the reports of the advice offices figured largely in national conferences and the Sash magazine, and often received good press coverage. Whatever misgivings there had been about the appropriateness of this work for the organisation melted away in the face of the overwhelming injustice of the pass laws.

The advice offices in Cape Town and Johannesburg could rely on the support of a dedicated group of voluntary workers, on financial contributions from the general membership, on assistance from lawyers, and on a fairly sympathetic press. They continued to grow, to see large numbers of cases – over 5,000 in 1964 – and to take a number of them through the courts.[16]

The smaller regions of the Sash found this work more difficult to sustain. 'Despite the early successes of the advice offices in Durban, East London and Port Elizabeth, 1965 saw their rapid demise. Harassment by the police intensified after 1964, with Sash workers in East London having to endure frequent Security Police "visits" to the advice office, resulting eventually in its closure. The Eastern Cape advice office in Port Elizabeth also closed temporarily following police warnings in early 1965, and subsequently found it almost impossible to summon up the resources to re-open until 1982.'[17]

Somewhat different circumstances obtained in Durban, where 'Natal Coastal also closed its advice office in early 1965, but through lack of work rather than intimidation. Almost full employment in the Durban area, the fact that women were not being endorsed out of the city, and the relatively sympathetic attitude of many officials, meant that very few people came to the office for help. Although the office managed to open again in May 1966, this situation persisted, and by

1968 the region reported that fewer than five people had come to the office between December 1967 and October 1968.'[18] It was another five years before it became fully active once more.

As in the Eastern Cape, 'The Athlone and Johannesburg advice offices also suffered their share of Security Police harassment, including a much-publicised raid on the Athlone office in July 1965 during which files were seized. However, both Cape Western and Transvaal regions were strong enough to resist intimidation and their advice offices continued to flourish.'[19]

Even in the apple-orchard lands of Elgin, not far from Cape Town, Sash members opened a small office in January 1964. They were responding to the problems of migrant workers, especially those who were employed only during the fruit-picking season, who faced arrests in terms of the pass laws and illegal squatting during the rest of the year. Eventually most of these workers and their families were driven away, but although the office lasted only a year members kept in touch with those who had been sent to the Eastern Cape. In July 1968 Trish Denniston reported that they had been 'equipping the families that have to leave with such necessities as stoves and cupboards to take with them ... the Women's Guild had donated R70 to the fund', and in November she described her visit to the Eastern Cape resettlement camp of Sada and to East London to follow up.[20]

The advice offices differed according to their context and problems brought to them, and changed over time. Jillian Nicholson, advice office coordinator in Durban, described how Natal Coastal region encountered a political and diplomatic challenge after the KwaZulu 'homeland' opted to accept self-government status. Mangosuthu Buthelezi, leader of the homeland, refused the 'independence' imposed on the other Bantustans, trying to straddle the pressure from the National Party government as well as the policy of non-cooperation of the ANC and other resistance movements. The kind of self-government on offer, however, was as much a fiction as 'independence'. The new self-governing KwaZulu inevitably had to accept responsibility for many of the roles the central government had once played, such as dealing with social grants, education, health and labour. The advice office continued to witness the same problems people had experienced previously, now continuing under the KwaZulu government. It soon found itself in major confrontations with Chief Buthelezi and senior officials.[21]

The Grahamstown advice office opened for the first time on 12 May 1973, jointly run by the Black Sash, the Institute of Race Relations and students of Rhodes University. It became concerned immediately with the government's plan 'to deprive black Fingo Villagers of their right to own property in Grahamstown and to send thousands of them to Committees Drift, 22 miles away'.[22]

In East London the advice office was reopened in the offices of the Institute of Race Relations on 8 September 1973. It soon noted concerns over critical levels of unemployment, with '160,000 adults living in Mdantsane [a large resettlement town on the outskirts of the city], 46,000 adults in Duncan Village plus 100,000 people who are living illegally in the East London area. Only about 30,000 people are employed in the city'.[23] In 1975 the advice office was reporting on the depressing nature of its work: 'We do not have endorsement-out problems like Cape Western and Johannesburg. We are the place to which people are endorsed out'.[24] By 1977 it was seeing over 200 cases a year.

In 1975 the Natal Midlands region announced that it was starting an advice office in premises shared with a trade union in Pietermaritzburg. Over the next years the majority of its casework was concerned with work-related matters – pay disputes, low wages, the Unemployment Insurance Fund and workmen's compensation. As Jennifer Scott comments, 'This was part of a resurgence of the Black Sash advice offices nationwide that was prompted primarily by the declining economic situation.' It provided, she says, 'an extremely valuable source of information on the effects on Africans of the workings of the South African economy ... the offices in the '70s sensitised the organisation to economic injustices prevalent in South Africa.'[25]

As the Sash advice offices were situated in cities and towns where there was a membership base, it became increasingly evident that this work was also needed in places outside their reach. The impact of apartheid policies was particularly severe beyond the urban areas. Various strategies were adopted to try to address this. Some offices, first of all in Johannesburg, provided training courses to support the setting up of independent offices in other areas, usually under the auspices of the churches. The objective was to assist people themselves to undertake advice office work. Training courses were designed to prepare individuals and groups to establish structures, with community support and oversight. There was a growing awareness of the potential role of advice offices, and that they did not need an expensive infrastructure. Training became an important part of the advice office work, and a number of churches saw the need for communities to manage their own offices and were willing to make space available to them.

Training workshops and the development of training manuals were undertaken in other centres too. Port Elizabeth began training programmes in the early 1990s.[26] In Cape Town there was also an emphasis on training and making resources available; several workshops were offered jointly with LEAP (the Legal Education Action Project), and training manuals produced.

Volunteer support groups from within the Sash were dedicated to other aspects of the outreach work, particularly in opposing the process of forced removals of entire communities. In Johannesburg the Sash had set up a Resettlement Committee in 1979 to gather information, and in 1981 was asked to visit Mathopestad, 'a prosperous and orderly rural community'[27] which was to be moved to Onverwacht. The committee did its utmost to support them, writing letters to the relevant minister (Dr Piet Koornhof), encouraging members and others to visit the area, and continuing to study and record the entire process of forced removals, as well as the growth of violence and of vigilantism in rural areas. This work grew rapidly and expanded to some other regions, such as the Western Cape's Rural Interest Group. In the Eastern Cape contact was maintained over many years with a number of small towns and villages where people were under threat.

Responding to appeals often meant travelling long distances out of town, and although many links were established in this way, the task became too great to manage on a voluntary basis. In order to ensure this work could continue, it became necessary to employ first one, and then several, full-time workers to undertake and coordinate it. Thus the Transvaal Rural Action Committee (TRAC) was formed.[28] Aninka Claassens was its first fieldworker, followed by several more, and Marj Brown was employed as the national researcher to draw all the threads together.

The Cape Town office appointed a rural fieldworker, Philip van Ryneveld, in response to appeals for help from various country areas, and he was succeeded by Annemarie Hendrikz. By 1990 there were six fieldworkers employed in the different regions, giving the Black Sash a means of extending its work, and a greater awareness of the hardships experienced by people out of the public eye. The fieldworkers had their base in the advice offices, and also worked closely with groups of the volunteer membership.

Members and fieldworkers alike found added strength in working in partnership with other organisations. As the process of forcible removal of settled African communities speeded up in the 1980s, so groups formed to resist it. In the Southern Cape a coalition of organisations, including Sash members, formed SCAR, Southern Cape Against Removals. A Sash advice office was opened in Knysna, and then East Cape Against Removals (ECAR) followed, as did the Association for Rural Advancement (AFRA) in Pietermaritzburg. All of these ventures expanded the network of organisations providing support and services to people outside the main centres, and allowed for the sharing of skills and experience among the participants. The Sash in turn learned more at first hand about the circumstances of people and communities facing the threat of losing their land and homes as well as their citizenship.

This expansion of work and of numbers of employees necessarily led to rapidly increasing costs. It also gradually created a distinction between those who were paid to work full-time and those who volunteered such time as they had available. The most pressing need was for additional funds, and the Black Sash leadership worked hard to find donor partners and to acquire the necessary fundraising and reporting skills to meet the funders' requirements. Although this enabled the Black Sash to meet the ever-increasing demands on its offices, eventually the distinction between workers and volunteers would create difficulties for the management of the organisation.

It was clear that what had started in 1958 as an amateur response to a perceived need was being forced to become more sophisticated and professional. During Sheena Duncan's six-week trip to the United States in 1974, she had many discussions and meetings with organisations engaged in similar work there, and when she returned she brought back to the Sash the term 'paralegal' and compared the advice office work with the 'paralegal clinics' she had visited.

As part of the development in the early 1980s of community-based structures which would eventually lead to the United Democratic Front, local committees began to establish advice offices or similar projects. Black Sash offices were approached for assistance, for example in the Eastern Cape. At the same time, more and more lawyers were being drawn into the legal aspects of this kind of work, and into developing programmes to train paralegal assistants. Since the formation of the Legal Resources Centre in 1979, it had become possible to take up many more legal challenges. Professional paralegal training and some form of accreditation would be a great advantage in developing further opportunities for this work. For the Black Sash, however, the concept of giving the best possible advice, free of charge, to the poorest sectors of society remained the preferred option.

Across the country community organisations, too, were creating structures that would provide for people to come together to discuss their common problems and campaign for their rights, in rural as well as urban areas. Resistance to oppression could come from a variety of ventures, and building community resources and belief in their own capacity was very important. The advice office movement became part of the forces for change. There was a risk that the rise of community-based advice offices, some of them grouped under the banner of the Advice Office Forum, would lead to tensions with the Black Sash, which was sometimes viewed as having greater resources but being less committed to participating in community structures. Questions were asked whether the Black Sash could be seen as having a mandate from the community to carry out its work, and how committed it was to a real transformation of society. The best way to deal with such questions was to hold open discussions, and eventually most of them were resolved.

It was true that the Sash had degrees of protection that many smaller organisations did not. In the 1980s the states of emergency and long trials, as well as detentions and persecution, kept many community leaders out of circulation. The Sash had some security, was able to hold meetings, pickets and demonstrations, and could keep up to date with the laws and their effects, to write fact papers and reports which could be taken up by the media. Similarly, it seemed to have the capacity to obtain increased funding over the years to carry out its work.

It made use of these advantages, while its ultimate goal was always to assist and enable people to seek ways of addressing the problems of the whole community, not simply winning individual cases. A favourable court judgment could mean a victory for thousands of people in similar situations. Training for advice office workers, especially in rural areas, multiplied the skills available. Engaging in solidarity with other organisations strengthened the capacity of all. The Sash sought to use every angle and all the information gathered to oppose unjust laws in every possible way.

The organisation was at pains to ensure it did not convey attitudes that could be seen as patronising or insensitive, and it deliberately fostered ways of working with people which enhanced participation and consultation. Sheena Duncan, for instance, insisted that she and all advice office workers should sit on the same side of the table as advice-seekers, emphasising their goal of seeking jointly the solutions to a problem. Still, when the international press or foreign diplomats came to witness advice office work, they wrote about Sheena Duncan or Judy Chalmers or Noël Robb, and their comprehensive knowledge, while the person seeking advice often remained simply an illustration of the problem.

Briefing the media and international visitors in the 1980s, especially during states of emergency when so much information was unavailable and so many leaders banned or underground, was an important contribution to change. The Sash understood this, and kept its focus on the overall objective: 'We must make absolutely sure that we are not assisting the government by making the wheels run more smoothly. Our aim is to get rid of unjust laws altogether. The information we provide is used to fight them.'[29]

After the momentous political changes of 1990, when it was possible to believe that negotiations would lead to the first-ever democratic elections in South Africa in which every citizen could vote, the Sash advice offices were part of the broad sweep of organisations involved in voter education and preparation. They provided an ideal place for information, for workshops simulating election processes, for strengthening belief in a democratic process, and for sustaining hope during the years of waiting. Gille de Vlieg was appointed to coordinate voter education projects, and all regions participated with enthusiasm.

With the end of apartheid legislation in sight, the advice offices still had much work to do, and found they could return to focus on other aspects of injustice. The organisation's particular interest in the lives of women, and its concern for the rights of domestic workers, led to several surveys and questionnaires. Penny Geerdts, who was by then the coordinator of the Pretoria advice office, produced a book about their rights entitled *Masisebenzisane / Let Us Work Together: A Handbook for Domestic Workers and Their Employers.*[30]

The pass laws were rendered almost obsolete by popular resistance in the early 1980s. When they were then repealed in 1986, the Sash was occasionally asked if there was any work left for the advice offices to do. Many issues persisted well beyond the end of apartheid: social services such as pensions and grants; corruption and disregard on the part of public servants; inequality and poverty. It became more important than ever to find ways of serving the broader community – not only individuals seeking help – to offer skills and training, to demand accountability from those in power.

The advice offices had served the public for 35 years. They had dealt with the huge task of the thousands of cases brought to them, and they had spurred the documentation and exposure of the harshest aspects of apartheid. They had been the support base from which the work had been carried outwards from the cities, and the foundation of the monitoring work that became an integral part of the Sash itself. They had served as the basis of the Sash's mandate and the legitimacy of its advocacy work, which was based on actual knowledge and personal experience rather than theory. The protest campaigns of the Sash were grounded in that knowledge.

When the Black Sash moved from being a membership-based organisation addressing a range of political issues to becoming a professionally run non-profit organisation in 1995, it chose as its focus the work of the advice offices. This transition is described in the final chapter of this book. Still today, the Black Sash Trust continues to fulfil its dual role of assisting people to obtain access to justice and urging the government to offer better systems and services for all.

4

BEARING WITNESS

*'This was one of those countless days when we were
struggling against apartheid, when all you could do was
to witness, be present and stand up to be counted there,
with the people.'*
– Archbishop Desmond Tutu[1]

The practice of personal observation at sites and incidents of injustice
began early in the Black Sash, and it continued in different forms
throughout its history. Members who were alerted to forced removals
of individuals and communities, involving the destruction of homes
and shelters, or to plans to segregate the cities by shunting entire
neighbourhoods to the outlying areas, were prompted to take action.
If they could find ways to protest against or to oppose the actions, they
would do so; at least they could witness and record what took place.
Where events took place far from the major cities, it was particularly
important to document their impact.

Where there were Black Sash members in small country towns from
the late 1950s, they soon witnessed the impact of the pass laws. Two
of them were drawn into the case of a particular family in Wellington,
near Cape Town. Anna Pearce lived in Wellington and Mary Birt in
Cape Town, where she worked in the advice office.

Anna came to know Kleinbooi Sikade and his wife Pauline, who lived in a tin shack in Sakkieskamp in Wellington with their two small children, and who had their lives totally disrupted by the pass laws. He had been working as a street sweeper, but was 'endorsed out' of the area because his pass showed he did not qualify to live there. He had nowhere else to go, but was then arrested because he had not left, and he lost his job. Several months went by, and then Pauline (who had tuberculosis) was arrested, also for being in the area without permission. By this time the family had no money, since Kleinbooi could not obtain work. He had developed asthma, and the children were also ill. They were willing to leave Wellington if they had to, but had no means to do so. After consulting the Advice Office in Cape Town, Anna helped them to apply for a railway warrant so that the family could travel to Lady Frere, where he had been born. He had no home there, nor any relatives except for his stepmother. Months passed: permission had to be obtained from the Native Commissioner or headman in Lady Frere agreeing that they could come. There was no reply. Nor was the application for a rail warrant granted. The Black Sash stepped in again. A telegram was sent to the Native Commissioner, railway tickets were purchased and eventually arrangements made for the transport of the family and its possessions to the railway station.

They boarded the train a little before midnight on a Sunday night, safely seen off by a group of Black Sash members. It had been agreed that Mary Birt would travel with them to Queenstown. It was not Black Sash policy to do 'welfare work', but this case typified that of so many other families, and illustrated the cruelty – and the inefficiency – of the pass laws so clearly, that they felt something had to be done. Mary takes up the story: 'I had their tickets, the correspondence with the various permissions for them to go, medical certificates, and money for their food on the journey.' However, she was obliged to travel in the front part of the train reserved for 'whites' and had to go back and forth through the crowded train to see the Sikade family. 'I had been given instructions not to lose the family ... having seen at De Aar that they had all they needed

for the night I went to bed.' Early next morning she discovered to her
horror that all the third class coaches had been uncoupled along the way.
The conductor stepped in to help, so although the Sikade family did not
have their tickets, they were allowed to continue the journey, and arrived
in Queenstown a few hours after she did.

There they were met by Daphne Curry, East London chairperson of the
Sash, who had driven through the early hours of the morning, and who
had a vehicle large enough for them all and their voluminous luggage.
Mary Birt's account then describes the miserable process of meeting the
Assistant Magistrate of Lady Frere, who was singularly unhelpful, and
then the District Surgeon, who said Pauline Sikade would have to walk
25 km twice a week to obtain the necessary treatment for the tuberculosis.
No-one could offer encouragement as to whether her husband might be
able to find work. At last they were able to deliver the family to the tiny
homestead where his stepmother lived. They were made welcome, more
fortunate than the thousands of other families who had nowhere to go at
all, and no-one to help them. Daphne Curry and another Border region
member from Queenstown went back to visit them some time later, and
found them adjusting bravely to their new and difficult situation.[2]

The story was published in the *Sash* magazine of March 1961 and
reprinted in the *Cape Argus*. The Black Sash was learning at first hand
about the iniquities of the system, and devising ways to make them
known.

Other lessons were also being learned: in the June 1961 issue of the
Sash magazine, a correspondent criticised the article for its use of first
names, rather than the more respectful 'Mr and Mrs Sikade'. The editor
justified it on this occasion on the grounds of the long association
between the family and the Black Sash, but she acknowledged the
correctness of the criticism. Later reports referred to people only as
'Mr B' or 'Mrs Y' in order to protect their identity.

Twenty years later an entirely separate event offered an echo to this
journey.

In August 1981 over 2,000 people living as squatters in Nyanga, Cape Town, faced deportation from the area after many were arrested and all their shelters destroyed. Hundreds were sent by bus and train to Umtata in the Transkei, an action justified by Foreign Minister Pik Botha who said, 'They are not South African citizens. They are like the Mexicans in the United States.'[3] Some of the women were separated from their children in the confusion. The demolition and deportation aroused a public outcry, and organisations rallied to assist. The Anglican and Roman Catholic churches in Umtata and in Cape Town offered shelter and help where they could. Kathy Luckett, wife of the Rev. Sid Luckett and herself a member of the Anglican Board of Social Responsibility, decided to travel to Umtata to locate mothers of missing children and to act as a link between the churches. She expressed her horror at the way in which people were being 'sorted and dispersed in trucks and buses by the Transkei army' to rural areas regarded as their places of origin. Eventually a small number of people were given 14-day passes by the Transkei authorities and a bus was provided to take them back to Cape Town to find and collect children or to retrieve important personal belongings. 54 people begged her to go with them on the bus, and even the Transkei's Deputy Secretary of the Interior and Social Services encouraged her to do so. The journey was a nightmare, encountering seven police roadblocks, driving through freezing and snowy conditions, and facing arrests of the majority of travellers. Officials refused to recognise the travel documents; from the many people who had tried to return (she counted six buses at the first roadblock in Queenstown) only 15 women were allowed to continue, a 'bedraggled and exhausted group'.[4]

Kathy Luckett's account of this particular episode in the long struggle of thousands of people to live and work in their place of choice was reported in detail in the press, and added immensely to national and international concern. Prayers, publicity and practical assistance were the principal means of support in the campaigns to bring an end to these brutal tactics. Soon after her return to Cape Town, Kathy became a member of the Black Sash and joined the team monitoring pass law cases in the Langa court.

On the last day of August 1981 Joan Grover (chair of the Western Cape region) received a late-night phone call from a reporter straight out of Parliament, informing her that the Black Sash had been named by the minister of cooperation and development, Dr Koornhof, as one of the organisations behind an orchestrated campaign to return evicted Nyanga squatters to the Cape Peninsula. Kathy Luckett and the churches were also mentioned in these allegations.[5]

These stories lead me to wonder what it is that draws anyone into political or social action to change an unjust situation. The answer seems to be that something prompts you to put a toe in the water, and you quickly find you are in it up to your knees. You may learn that it is deeper and darker than you had thought, but once you have seen the damage it causes, you cannot draw back.

Most of us who became active in the Black Sash learned about the effects of discrimination and apartheid policies through personal observation and witness. This first-hand experience led us into greater involvement, through direct contact with the victims of the system, or through learning about the laws and their implementation. The growing knowledge and understanding of individual members contributed to the organisation's capacity to speak with confidence about the injustices and brutality inherent in the system.

Over the next decades hundreds of us attended protest meetings and rallies, monitored and opposed forced removals of entire communities, sat in courts during political trials, and joined the throngs at funerals of political activists. We were demonstrating solidarity with those who resisted apartheid, and also keeping a watching brief. For many of us these were new and challenging experiences. Yet bearing witness to injustice had been an early part of the organisation's work, and had contributed to its survival.

As we have seen, it began with the pass laws. The cases that were brought to the advice offices prompted members to attend the courts where the laws were enforced. In Johannesburg members attended the native commissioner's courts even before their region had opened an advice office.[6] In Cape Town, 'Sashers in Action' described a day at the court in 1959: 'When is a wife not a wife? When she is black and separated from her husband by the pass laws. This we observers learnt when we began to attend the sittings at the Langa court … When we arrived we were horrified to see the number of men and women on trial simply because they did not have the correct piece of paper.'[7]

In Cape Town this court (called the Langa Natives Court in 1959) was until the late 1970s situated in the centre of Langa, the township to which thousands of black people had been moved as early as the 1920s. A new court building was later positioned near the entrance to the township, just off the national road. These courts, often located in the townships where black people were obliged to live, were not administered under the Department of Justice, but fell under the administration of what was called variously over the years Native Affairs, Bantu Affairs and Plural Relations. Whatever their name, they were part of the system of apartheid, by which the policy of limiting the presence of black people in white areas was enforced.

Black Sash members attended the court sittings in order to witness the proceedings for themselves. Some went because they had been told about night raids during which African women were picked up and driven around until the police vans were full, and then made to appear in the court still in their night clothes, some clutching babies, some having been made to leave their children unattended. Other Sashers were persuaded to go after hearing a report from an advice office volunteer. Sometimes they were there in order to follow up the case of a particular individual who had approached the advice office, and who was going to be represented by a lawyer briefed by the Black Sash. Sometimes one of the interpreters who worked for the Black Sash would also be present. Visitors to South Africa and journalists would often ask to accompany them.

Their reports demonstrated clearly how the participation of a lawyer, and even the presence of witnesses, improved the way in which the case was run, and also the treatment of the people whose cases were being processed. They observed the arrival of the accused, brought there in police vans, having been picked up during the night. Each person would be called up, told of the charge against them, that of being illegally in the area, and, unless they could produce any evidence that they had not contravened the pass laws, were 'endorsed out' of the area, and sometimes also sentenced to a fine. Being endorsed out meant that those words were stamped into the pass book, and the person was informed that she or he must leave the area within 72 hours. The records showed that cases could be dealt with in as little as two minutes, with scant opportunity for the person to speak. The court interpreter would give the commissioner a brief version of what the person had said, and the commissioner would base his verdict on that.

The monitors (who were referred to as 'observers' at the time, before the term of human rights monitor became widespread) were told by the people they met that when they were there, the commissioner and the interpreter were more careful to listen to the people charged, and to explain the decisions reached. This alone would have strengthened the value of maintaining their presence. In addition, it enabled the Black Sash to report with authenticity about the proceedings. There were times when witnessing seemed too painful and depressing, and attendance fell away.[8] Yet it revived again, and the reports continued.

As the advice office workers became more familiar with the law, they would occasionally identify a case in which it seemed there might be the chance of an acquittal or of having the charges withdrawn. The person might then receive the assistance of a lawyer: this meant that the entire process was slowed down, and arguments were allowed in defence or in mitigation. In such cases the Black Sash monitors reported that there was a different atmosphere in the court, more careful attention given to the case, even if the outcome was the same. Sometimes, even, it was possible to bring to the attention of the commissioner circumstances that led to the case being dismissed. The monitors, too, learned to understand the law, and to think of processes to be followed which might help. Their familiar presence in the courts meant that people in the community began to trust them, so that the work grew over the years. People who were at risk of being arrested, or endorsed out, approached them for advice and assistance, and could be referred to the advice office.

In one of her letters to her mother in the United States, Candy Malherbe described proceedings on 11 July 1975 when she and a friend went to the court: 'We got to hear several other cases before ours came up and one would have thought that the dispensation of justice was a pretty amusing business – much camaraderie among the Commissioner, interpreter, prosecutor and other court functionaries. But when our case came up the atmosphere changed and I was absolutely amazed at the hostility which eventually became fury registered by the Commissioner towards our lawyer, David Dallas … David couldn't have been more polite and mild – it was simply the matter of challenging the procedures of the B.A.D. [Bantu Affairs Department] which caused the Commissioner to lose his cool so badly. I am anxious to know if this was unusual or if David always has such a tough time when he represents Advice Office cases.'

When he read this recently, David Dallas commented, 'It was in reality a kangaroo court the sole purpose of which was to process alleged pass law offenders and thereby demonstrate to the world at large a modicum of justice. The judicial officer in question was unqualified, clueless, and had one aim in the discharge of his judicial responsibilities, which was to please his masters. He and I had a perfectly cordial relationship and I would often have a cup of tea with him and the prosecutor. I cannot recall that he was ever rude to me in court although, inevitably, we would have had disagreements. Frankly most of my legal arguments clearly went over the top of his head and he would have been well aware that a number of his judgments in my cases were later overturned by the Supreme Court. I cannot recall that he ever acquitted any of my clients!'

David added, 'The prosecutor was a retired policeman. He was doing a job that I suspect he found boring and very possibly didn't much enjoy. He was a quiet, gentle man whom I quite liked and he often spoke about his wife and home somewhere in the northern suburbs. No doubt his upbringing and police background led him to support the Pass Laws. Others, possibly less conservative than he, certainly did! The interpreter of course was an African and my relationship with him was restricted to the courtroom. I was never sure how accurately he was portraying my client's testimony. The attitude of court officials generally to all Africans was usually overbearing, aggressive, and so Candy's reaction in that regard does not surprise me.'[9]

Diana Ractliffe, of the Cape Western region, reported in 1979 that 'while court visiting can be monotonous and at times very depressing, we do feel that it is important to know what is happening in the Bantu Commissioners' Courts ... In July 1978 the court moved to a new building situated on the outskirts of Langa. The building is a vast improvement on the very dilapidated old one. A new black prosecutor was appointed, as on busy mornings there are two courts in operation, and as a result more time can be spent on each case, although it is still possible for cases to go through at the rate of one every two minutes ... According to Hansard, 12,006 persons were tried and 10,074 persons were convicted of offences relating to influx control and identity documents in the Langa Commissioner's Court in 1977. This was an average of 46 a day. There is no indication as to how many of these were women.'[10]

She pointed out that 'all observers feel that there are many reasons why it is important for us to visit the courts': 'to represent the public in the courts, which are open; to educate ourselves about the operation of the courts and the laws involved; to inform the accused of assistance they might receive from the Advice Office, after the completion of the case; to give moral support to attorneys when they defend Advice Office cases; to inform the Advice Office of any irregularities which need looking into, such as prosecution of juveniles.' She concluded that 'we remain convinced by our own observations that the overriding concern remains the laws which apply to one section of the population only and which give rise to perpetual insecurity, financial loss, harassment and humiliation'.[11]

People coming to the advice offices brought other problems in addition to the pass laws. Among them were many complaints about the provision of old age pensions and other social grants. Not only did the amounts differ according to racial classification, but the payment system was an enormous burden. All over the country African people were obliged to wait in long queues at pay-out points every month, sometimes every second month, and when they did eventually receive the pension it was not always the correct amount. Those who were illiterate were brusquely fobbed off and made to place their thumbprints on receipts which they could not read. Black Sash monitors were drawn into observing the practices at these points.

Busi Nyide of the Pietermaritzburg advice office said, 'we did start going out to monitor pensions, which really helped because when we got there the pensioners asked us to come every month. When we were there, there was no chance of others taking their money ... having the Black Sash at the pay points made a difference.'[12] Pessa Weinberg of the same office related that she and Pat Merrett 'would go to Vulindlela [a 'reserve' and township west of Maritzburg] and we would see that the people got their pensions'.[13] Assisting people with applications for pensions and in obtaining them continued to be a significant part of the advice office work.

In the 1980s there were many calls from rural areas for Black Sash assistance. In March 1983 Johannesburg members Ethel Walt, Sue Sher, Dawn Ingle and Josie Adler responded to a request from women in Driefontein, a 'black spot' near Wakkerstroom in present-day Mpumalanga, to attend the pension pay-out. They were accompanied by Joanne Collinge of *The Star* newspaper. 'The pension payout point was at a shop ... when we arrived hundreds of people had already gathered to wait. The atmosphere was lively, and vendors were selling pots, apples and brew ... We split up, each with an interpreter co-opted from the crowd ... About 50 or 60 people listened to each question-and-answer session.' Most of the women were awaiting assessment of their qualification to receive a pension, but some had been 'chased away' from the regional office at Wakkerstroom and told rudely that they were not old enough, or that they should find a husband to look after them. The Sash members were helping them to write letters stating their case, when three or four police trucks arrived. The police found no fault with the letter-writing, but turned on the surrounding vendors, confiscating goods and issuing summonses.[14]

In the early 1980s Merle Beetge, who lived in Walkerville outside Johannesburg, began to help local people with pension problems and soon became a one-person advice office. She recounted in precise detail the enormous difficulties experienced, first, in making application for an old age pension or a disability grant, and then in receiving it: inefficient bureaucracy, lengthy delays before the applicant's age or disability was established, long queues at the pay-out points, physical obstacles for disabled people, and unequal policies and systems discriminating against black pensioners.[15]

After 1976, with the establishment of the 'independent' states of Transkei, Venda, Ciskei and Bophuthatswana, and the self-governing status of KwaZulu, the administration of pensions became part of the responsibilities of those governments, which led to escalating tensions between their administrations and the Black Sash.

While office intervention could help in individual cases, it was also vital to address the whole system. The advice office reports provided a massive body of evidence of injustice and discrimination in the sphere of social benefits. Neither protest demonstrations nor approaches to government had any effect at this time, but after the political changes of 1990 the expertise of Sash members was put to good use when new social benefit policies were being developed. The new ministry of social development drew in organisations of civil society and paid attention to their recommendations, and the Black Sash's knowledge about pensions, child care benefits and other social security measures provided a strong contribution.

∽

The goal of keeping political and economic power in South Africa in the hands of its white population required elaborate systems of racially based classification and control over where people could live and own property. Various forms of residential segregation had existed in South Africa long before the National Party came to power. Black South Africans were, for instance, subject to the pass laws and the Land Acts, which dictated where they could live and work. Especially for people classified as 'coloured' or 'Indian', apartheid brought stricter enforcement of residential segregation by law throughout the country, and unleashed a vast process of compulsory uprooting and removal of people. In 1950 the Group Areas Act placed coloured people under provisions for the separation of residential areas on the basis of race, and contributed further to the sorrow and hardship of thousands of African and Indian families all over the country.[16] Over the years this entailed the hounding of individuals and families out of the supposedly white cities and suburbs, and also the forced removal of entire communities away from places where they had lived for generations. Thus arose a new field of monitoring challenges for the Black Sash.

Under the Group Areas Act, villages, neighbourhoods and towns all over the country where people of different cultures and languages had lived together for generations were designated for ownership and occupation by one group only. Africans were moved out of areas now to be occupied only by Indians, losing their homes and access to places of work and recreation; Indians were moved out of places to be sold to whites, losing long-established businesses and homes; coloured people also lost homes and shops; and the compensation was never sufficient to buy anything comparable in the areas in which each group was now supposed to live. The loss was not only financial:

heartbreak accompanied the disruption of neighbourhoods, the impact on access to schooling and health care, and the loss of all that was familiar and loved. By the end of 1976, 349,616 coloured persons had been moved in terms of the Group Areas Act, and 91,427 were still to be moved; the numbers of Indian people moved were 163,770, with 66,655 awaiting removal.[17] Sash members in all regions began to follow the proclamations of Group Areas and then in due course the removals themselves.[18] Protests everywhere by the people most directly affected were simply ignored by the government.

Already by 1958 the leadership of the Black Sash had identified the Group Areas Act as 'one of the ten major blots on our Statute Book', saying that it sought 'to reshuffle our population in accordance with a Master Plan that is as cruel as it is unworkable'.[19] Members in Cape Town were part of a Group Areas Co-ordinating Committee, together with the Civil Rights League and the Institute of Race Relations, that held a two-day Group Areas conference in February 1958. Not long after that, they began the long battles against the implementation of the Act in specific places.

The first step in identifying areas where the law would be enforced was the proclamation of a particular place as being for the use of a specific 'population group'. The procedure for such an area to be 'proclaimed' included a public hearing by the Group Areas Board. Black Sash members (often impeccably hatted and gloved) would attend such a hearing, and would rise to voice the organisation's objection, in principle, to the proclamation of the area in question for reservation for only one group. The presiding officer would invariably rule out such an objection, since the purpose of the hearing was merely to discuss detail, such as exactly where the boundary lines of a 'group area' should be located. For the remainder of the session, there was nothing to do but to listen to the tragic pleas of those who were to lose their homes and often their livelihoods as well.

An account of one such hearing described the chairman's reaction to Mary Birt: 'We all know the stand the Black Sash has made against

Group Areas ... but if you have any factual evidence to bring forward you are at liberty to do so.' She described how people were too frightened to make representations, or cynical about the value of such hearings, and urged the chairman to put forward their plight to the minister. When the members of the board adjourned to go on a tour of inspection of the area, an offer was made to introduce them to people living there. The chairman replied, 'No, thank you. We don't wish to meet anyone or have any discussion with people. We've had quite enough of that ... We shall drive through the area and apprise ourselves of the conditions.'[20]

Group Areas had a particularly drastic effect in the Western Cape, where many areas had been racially integrated for generations. The first protest stand I ever joined was on a warm sunny morning in Kalk Bay, a long-established fishing village along the way from Cape Town to Simonstown. The suburban railway line ran along the shore, between the sea and the road, and the harbour was filled with colourful boats, busy fishermen tossing their catch onto the docks, and loud bargaining from those who had come to buy. The fisher families lived in cottages on the sloping hillside, from where they could gauge the wind, the sea and the weather. Now they were threatened with a Group Areas proclamation, declaring this picturesque place – their home and livelihood – to be for 'whites only'. How could they endure a removal to a dreary inland township, how would they live? We stood along the roadside facing the sea with heavy hearts and angry posters.

In Simonstown, the naval base on the southern peninsula of Cape Town, the first proposal for a Group Areas declaration was advertised in 1959. Barbara Willis (Sash regional treasurer for many years) and her husband lived in Boulders House, overlooking the beach. They immediately became involved in establishing a local committee, made up of representatives of the churches, the local mosque trustees, the ratepayers' associations, the Chamber of Commerce, the Black Sash and a number of other bodies such as sports organisations. This Group Areas Liaison Committee (GALC), which was chaired by Barbara, waged a long campaign opposing the proposal. It resisted the Group

Areas Board for years, drawing in support from the town council itself and a number of politicians. It held public meetings, drew up a petition, and organised individual representations. These last had to be in quintuplicate, so the committee drew up two versions, stating 'I am an owner/occupier' or 'I am a trader/fisherman', and then 'roneoed them and stapled them into fives to be taken from house to house'. This resulted in 733 representations from owners/occupiers and 27 from traders. Other petitions were organised by the local Chamber of Commerce. The Sash arranged for the GALC petitions to be independently counted and they were delivered 'in a huge carton' to the Department of Planning on 31 December 1964. It was a brave and determined effort, and there was consolation in the support received from a wide range of people, even though it had been conducted through the busy period of Christmas, New Year and Ramadan. It succeeded only in delaying matters, and finally it was of no avail: the whole municipal area of Simonstown was declared a Group Area for 'whites only' in 1967.[21]

The False Bay branch of the Black Sash was equally dedicated to the effort to prevent the proclamation of Kalk Bay, as Monica Ritchken described in a vivid article outlining the long and rich history of the fishing community, the beauty of its setting, and the protection of its harbour. Drawing on the experience of Barbara Willis, they too called in the support of local residents, briefed legal counsel (Advocate Robin Marais) to represent them at the public inquiry, and drew up petitions and memoranda. Monica managed to locate a film which had been made in 1955 by the State Information Department called *The Fisherfolk of Kalk Bay* and persuade the chairman of the inquiry to allow it to be shown, 'providing a dramatic ending to the hearing and I trust the Chairman's heart was moved'.[22]

When District Six in the heart of Cape Town was proclaimed a white Group Area, the shock reverberated around the country. This long-established neighbourhood had been home to generations of families, and the more than 28,000 people who lived in it were officially described as coloured, Indian and white. The Cape Town City Council stated in a memorandum that 'The removal of a community of this size ... will cause disruption of the greatest magnitude and will create a wave of disharmony and bitterness.'[23] The Sash joined the thousands who protested against this proclamation. A young English member, relatively new to South Africa, took part in the stand, and wrote a poem:

> *District Six is declared white*
> It's something I can do, this standing
> with Mary, Nel, Beth, the others. We wear
> our black sashes over our frocks, right shoulder
> to left hip. We're still, silent, hold posters
> protesting the latest forced removals:
> *We mourn the loss of livelihoods and homes.*
>
> This placard half-shields me from the swirl
> of traffic, discomfited shoppers' stares, a fist
> shaken from a car. A man with a briefcase
> murmurs *Thank you.* Office girls snigger.
> Sweat trickles. My back aches.
>
> By General Smuts's statue, a long lens glints,
> points at each of us in turn. I wait
> for the relief of *Time's up!*,
> stowing the boards in Mary's car boot
> ready for next time.[24]

District Six in Cape Town, like Sophiatown in Johannesburg, is etched into the memory of South Africa's shameful destruction of settled communities by the Group Areas Act, but there were hundreds more, and thousands of lives were damaged.[25]

While the Group Areas Act provided the legislative framework for the forced removal of people in urban areas, the history of forced removal of black African people from rural areas where they had lived for generations was defined by a series of devastating laws and policies, of which the hated Natives Land Act of 1913 was only one.

'Relocation', 'resettlement' and 'removals' became ominously familiar terms in South African policy during the apartheid era. All in all, the precise total number of people forcibly removed 'will never be known' according to the Surplus People Project, which estimated that between 1960 and mid-1983 the figure stood at 3,500,000.[26]

The National Party government elected into office in 1948 inherited the colonial division of the country into the four provinces and the allocation of portions of land to black South Africans known as the 'African reserves'. These were first legally defined by the Natives Land Act of 1913 and were categorised as 'scheduled areas'. In 1936 the Native Trust and Land Act provided for an additional allocation of portions of land, to be known as the 'released areas'. The land thus allocated made up a total of 13.7 per cent of the country. No black person could buy or own land outside those areas, which were scattered in separate pieces over much of the country (except for the Western Cape).

From the 1950s onwards the National Party government began to formalise its policy of 'separate development', designed eventually to create nine semi-independent states or Bantustans out of the areas occupied by the 'African reserves'. Black people would have rights to land and self-determination only within them, and would only be tolerated in the white-owned parts of the country when needed for their labour. The children and the elderly, as well as women who did not work in the white 'prescribed areas', were regarded as 'surplus people' or 'superfluous appendages' who should be forcibly settled in the Bantustans.

Enforcing this plan was like putting together the scattered pieces of a jigsaw puzzle. Some pieces did not seem to belong together at all, or fit where one would expect. In the Bantustan policy, these were often the 'black spots', the places where black people had managed to acquire land, and from which they had to be moved. In their quest for a measure of security in the anxious years before 1913, some black African people had invested in land ownership. Land could be bought by an individual, often a chief on behalf of his followers, all of whom contributed to the purchase price. It was also not unusual for a group of relatively well-off families to share their resources to buy a farm. This took place, for example, in the area of Rustenburg, near Standerton and Wakkerstroom, as well as in other parts of the Transvaal and Natal. The provision in the bitterly resented 1913 Land Act prohibiting Africans from buying land outside the reserve areas was designed to bring this to an end. The Act also prohibited sharecropping and transformed all labour tenants into servants, covered by the Masters and Servants legislation. 'The immediate effect of the 1913 Act was a massive dispersal of black farm tenant families ... [which] was so widespread and so traumatic as to classify as the first really comprehensive forced removal from the so-called white rural areas in 20th century South Africa.'[27] Increasing mechanisation on farms also led to the eviction of farmworkers and their families.

The impact of the policy of forced removals or 'resettlement' of entire communities of African people whose homes were not 'conveniently situated' in terms of apartheid was even more dramatic. Whether or not they had enjoyed the sense of security which lay in ownership or long-term occupation of their land, if they lived in what was defined as a 'black spot' within an area designated for white people, they were to be moved to an area within a 'homeland' or an independent Bantustan to which they were deemed to belong.

Cosmas Desmond's accounts of some of these resettlements, starting with the story of the people moved to Limehill in northern Natal in 1968, broke into public awareness with his book *The Discarded People* (1970), though it was banned in South Africa. Names of settlements at Dimbaza, Sada and Ilingi in the Eastern Cape contributed to the list of suffering, and began to make national and international news. Starting in 1979, a national research project on forced relocation, the

Surplus People Project (SPP), gathered information from all areas with the assistance of many organisations, including the Black Sash. Its name was taken from the infamous statement by a government spokesperson, referring to the wives, children and other dependants of African workers as 'surplus people'. The SPP authors, Laurine Platzky and Cherryl Walker, published a meticulously detailed five-volume report in 1983, and a shorter version in 1985.[28]

The Black Sash's actions in opposition to the entire policy of forced removals had two main aspects. The first lay in responding to appeals from communities threatened with removal or those actually removed, and drawing public attention to their plight and to the immense suffering and injustice involved. The second was in seeking to document, analyse and understand the political and economic circumstances which led to the policy and legislation, in order to protest. Support and solidarity for the thousands of people affected was vitally important, but even more so was opposition to the policy itself. The artificially created homelands, the loss of South African citizenship, the denial of basic human rights – these were the factors that must be resisted.

Some members of the Black Sash were alert to this even in the earliest days of the organisation. 'In 1959 members of the Addo branch (Cape Eastern) fought against the removal of Africans from settled locations in Kirkwood to Bontrug, a bare hillside far from the town. They were successful in halting the removals ... Later the Municipality again dumped Africans on the bare hillside. This time, however, Kirkwood residents and the Press joined the Sash in battle with the local Native Affairs Department.' These efforts were recorded in several articles in the *Sash* magazine, including an account of a detailed survey undertaken by members of the Port Elizabeth, Addo and Kirkwood branches, in which they described 'upward of 2000 people existing in primitive conditions',[29] struggling for shelter, water, health care and employment. One of the accompanying photographs is a pitiful picture of an elderly couple who 'slept in the veld covered by zinc and sacking'.[30]

Almost ten years later Doreen Patrick, the regional secretary in Natal Coastal, described the events taking place in the Dundee area of northern Natal, with a focus on Limehill.[31] In the removals process, there were two types of settlement: agricultural settlements (where families were allowed to take some of their stock with them and to resume farming); and township settlements, defined in the Acts as 'closer settlements' (where families were given a plot about 50 yards square), as in Limehill. The Black Sash had visited the area, and approached Denis Hurley, the Catholic archbishop of Durban, to ask if he would chair a meeting convened by him and the Black Sash. This took place on 5 December 1967, and was well attended by clergy and 'prominent citizens'. A church committee was formed, and letters of appeal as well as telegrams were sent to the minister of Bantu development, M.C. Botha.

In January and February 1968 three more visits to Limehill (400 miles for the return trip) were undertaken by Archbishop Hurley and Black Sash members, and reports given to the church committee. Sash members in Pietermaritzburg and Durban had by then joined forces, and Bunty Biggs, of Natal Midlands Black Sash, visited the chief Bantu affairs commissioner in Pietermaritzburg. The women went to Limehill again in March, and in April took in a visit to the 'orphan settlement near Weenen – a black spot of a special kind which demands our compassion and our aid'.[32]

All through the following months they wrote to the press and accompanied prominent visitors to the area, including MPs and leading church members and citizens. An important gathering in August led to the establishment of the Natal Citizens Association, and the chair and secretary of the Sash region, Mary Grice and Doreen Patrick, were elected onto its committee.

At the same time, a national campaign was growing, and citizens' action committees were formed in several cities. A memorandum to the state president was drafted and delivered in November 1968, together with a national petition signed by over 21,000 people.[33] The memorandum gave detailed statistics about the removals of whole communities in terms of resettlement and black spot or Group Areas policies and of individuals under the pass laws or slum clearance provisions.[34]

In Grahamstown, Priscilla Hall gathered information about removals into the Ciskei homeland, and identified four distinct waves of resettlement, starting in the 1960s with largely urban removal. By 1976 the people who were being forcibly moved were mainly those fleeing from the Transkei when it became 'independent'. At about the same time evictions of farmworkers and their families from farms began in earnest. The fourth phase was about to begin as consolidation of the Ciskei homeland took place – its 19 scattered areas were meant to be converted into a single block by the end of 1982.[35]

Despite all protests, and in the face of international hostility, the government was unrelenting and the removals continued. Year after year the Black Sash did all it could to expose what was taking place, and to protest against the policy. One of its most successful publications was the 'removals map', drawn up by Barbara Waite and other members in 1972, depicting the astounding number of people and groups who had been moved around the country under apartheid policies over the years. Accompanied by an explanatory text, it was a vivid visual demonstration of what had been done, marked by arrows showing the origin and arrival point of each move. It was widely used, and reissued in an updated version by Ethel Walt in 1982.[36]

The Johannesburg Sash's Resettlement Committee, chaired by Prue Crosoer, went to the homeland of KwaNdebele, which they described as a dumping ground; to Kliptown, near Johannesburg, the site at which the Freedom Charter was first adopted, where squatters were being evicted; to Boons and Mathopestad in the western Transvaal, where a 'black spot' of about 3,000 people, who had owned their land since 1911, were to be moved to the homeland of Bophuthatswana; and the settlement of Rooigrond, near Mafikeng, which was intended to be a temporary site, but where people were still being dumped after 11 years.[37]

Prue had joined the Sash in Durban, and a few years later ('when I was about 28' she said), she and her family moved to Johannesburg, where she was soon drawn into the Black Sash by Jill Wentzel. The small group making up the Resettlement Committee visited communities about to be moved, and documented the events. She remembers how the people 'kept so carefully every single letter and document, always hoping that the Black Sash could help them to resist the removal'. They agonised over the experience of the people of Botshabelo (outside Bloemfontein) when they learned of the babies who died during or after the removal there. To her and the other young women in the group, it 'seemed like a policy of genocide', and she reflects on how they drew strength from one another: 'at least you could be together in it'.[38]

Driefontein was a settled community in the eastern Transvaal that became well known to the Resettlement Committee. Together with its neighbours, KwaNgema and Daggaskraal, it was threatened with removal. This typical 'black spot' – a place where rural life was steady, where many people were relatively prosperous, covering about 3,000 morgen and supporting some 300 landowners and about 7,000 people – was to be destroyed, and the people divided into ethnic groups and settled in different places. The community was determined not to move, and had sought the advice of Geoff Budlender of the Legal Resources Centre. Sash members assisted with collecting affidavits and made several visits to Driefontein, where they noted that 'harassment has stiffened the community spirit' and where they came to know many of the residents, particularly their leader, Saul Mkhize.[39] Not long after, the 17-year-old son of Saul Mkhize was severely beaten, allegedly by members of the police.

Sashers learned the history of Driefontein, which had been in existence since before 1913, when Pixley ka Seme (editor, attorney, and later president of the ANC) was chairman of the local Native Farmers' Association. They witnessed the community's encounters with government officials, and were desolate when in April 1983 Saul Mkhize was shot dead by a policeman during the Easter weekend.

'From now on, here in South Africa, the rich symbolism of Easter will be loaded with the memory of Saul's life and death and the knowledge of the pain of forced removal.'[40]

It is a bitter irony to note that ANC leader Chris Hani was assassinated at Easter exactly ten years later, in completely different circumstances, and after the negotiations towards a new constitution had begun. These were two men among the many who will be remembered for their efforts to create a society built on justice, and whose deaths were a loss to the new democracy.

As the number of forced removals increased, the Black Sash received more and more requests for assistance, so that the work became imposs-ible to sustain with part-time volunteers. In 1983 it established the Transvaal Rural Action Committee (TRAC), with full-time staff members and with Ethel Walt as its chair and a number of Sash members as active supporters. Aninka Claassens was the first fieldworker employed, and soon thereafter others were added, including Marj Brown, Joanne Yawitch and Lydia Kompe, known to all as Mam' Lydia.

The complete story of TRAC would require a book all to itself. For the next nine years it was a vital part of the Black Sash's ability to monitor and record events around proposed or actual removals in the Transvaal and some parts of the northern Cape and the Orange Free State. It produced a remarkable series of newsletters, in clear straightforward language, chronicling the organisation and resistance in the various communities and the supportive work of other groups. It assisted communities in their desperate efforts to resist being forcibly moved, or to return to their land even after this had happened. It also supported the formation of an important Rural Women's Movement, largely thanks to the work of Mam' Lydia. By the time she was elected to Parliament in 1994, she had years of experience and a deep knowledge of that constituency. Other TRAC members also contributed their skills to the new society in various representative bodies.

By 1992 TRAC was firmly established, and became independent of the Sash, with its own structure, which included Sash members on its advisory board. When the policy of forced removals was officially abandoned in 1987, TRAC continued to support the rights of people who had been moved off their land, and to explore environmental and development practices. Its experience and detailed knowledge, and that of the other regional organisations opposing forced removals, were put to good use in developing land policy in the years after the political transition of the 1990s.

One consequence of the policy of separate development and the establishment of the homelands was an acute housing crisis for African families in many cities of South Africa. Previously the larger municipalities, such as those of Cape Town and Johannesburg, had been able to allocate a portion of their general resources to meet at least some of the needs of the townships they administered. But from 1971, with the introduction of the Bantu Affairs Administration Act, Administration Boards were put in charge of the townships, and were designed to be self-financing. There was neither the will nor the money to build housing for a population that was intended to be pushed back into rural homelands.

The struggle for a decent place to live was particularly harsh in Cape Town, where, because of the deliberate 'coloured labour preference policy', almost no family housing had been built in African residential areas for decades and municipal housing was appallingly overcrowded. Despite the government's resolve to repatriate Africans to their rural 'homelands', the urban population increased dramatically as families moved from the impoverished rural areas seeking work opportunities and the possibility of living together as a family. Self-built shacks rose up on the periphery of the city. In the advice office, Noël Robb noted a significant change in the attitudes of people since her work had begun over 25 years earlier: their quest was no longer for the permit to live in the city, but for housing. They were prepared to defy the hated pass laws in their desire to live together as a family, in an area where they could find work and build a future. The people themselves had created a tide that could not be reversed.

Their determination could not create houses, but nor would the authorities tolerate informal settlements. A major confrontation arose in August 1977 when hundreds of shacks on Modderdam Road, followed by those in the nearby settlements of Unibel and Werkgenot, were demolished by government vehicles, leaving their inhabitants abandoned on the side of the road with their belongings. The Black Sash was by no means the only group witnessing these events and recording them: a number of civil society organisations and a large contingent of the press were present, and some individuals bravely challenged the officials enforcing the action. Margaret Nash and the Rev. David Russell placed themselves in front of the bulldozers (which were said by the authorities to be not bulldozers but front-end loaders, as though terminology could make a difference to anyone whose house was being destroyed). Tear gas was used to try to drive the protesters away, although the Cape's strong winds made this a risky tactic, blowing the tear gas back towards the very police who had fired the canisters.

Eventually thousands of people thus evicted moved to a large piece of land that became known as Crossroads, which formed the centre of a historic battle between them and the authorities. Leaders arose within it, who articulated the needs and demands of the people. Lawyers, faith organisations, human rights supporters and urban development experts all contributed to debates about what should be done. The Sash advice office established a temporary presence there in an effort to assist. As the authorities remained adamant, disputes within the Crossroads community arose, and were exploited by the government, which offered an alternative site further from the city, to be named Khayelitsha. A Squatter Support Group made up of various bodies met regularly to try to resolve the tensions within the community. Political dynamics and individual struggles for power came into play and violence broke out, reflecting the wider spread of violence around the country at the time, which was met by the declaration of a national state of emergency in June 1986. Many of the relationships which Black Sash members had established with residents of Crossroads endured beyond that time, and allowed them to understand some of the harsh outcomes of the ensuing years.

Similar demolitions of shacks and evictions of people from the land they were occupying took place everywhere in the country against homeless, landless people defined as 'squatters'. It was at times like these that the advice offices might be filled with large crowds of people seeking help, and the staff would be stretched beyond capacity. They could call on the support of the Sash membership, and many who were not regular advice office workers would come forward to make lists of supplies needed or find places that would offer temporary shelter. We learned to take statements from those who had been injured or had lost property as well as homes. We crowded into the offices, making use of any surface to write what individuals or groups were telling us, or we were sent off with our clipboards to gather information on site, or travelled further to wherever a problem might have occurred. For me, these times were windows into the work of the advice offices, as I saw for myself the roadworkers living for years in a 'temporary' campsite in Swellendam, encountered a delegation of community leaders from Worcester, or spent time in George when the people of Lawaaikamp were threatened with the demolition of their homes.

As the political climate changed after 1990, we could begin to hope that more positive solutions could be found. In Johannesburg, a Sash committee was established to consider problems of urban home-lessness, with Josie Adler as its chair, working with the region's urban fieldworker, Glenda Glover. At its 1992 national conference, the Sash discussed at length the issues of land and rights, of low-cost housing and an enabling infrastructure. It supported the concept of a land claims court and the basic right to shelter and to access to land, arguing that these should be taken into account in the framing of the new national constitution and a bill of rights.[41]

∞

This experience of witnessing, monitoring and recording expanded over the years into other forms. As the inevitable resistance against apartheid grew, so increased levels of repression were used to enforce it. Confrontations between the authorities and communities became more frequent and more violent. After the student revolts in Soweto in 1976, such confrontations spread rapidly. The security legislation was tightened, demonstrations were legally restricted, detention without trial increased, and bannings and banishments were more frequently imposed.

The Sash began to receive reports of police action, and appeals to respond. Members reacted by providing an increasing presence at events, rallies, marches and public protests, offering solidarity and also recording what they witnessed. When hundreds of protesters were arrested, and charges of public violence, illegal demonstrations, supporting the aims of banned organisations and other accusations filled the formal courts of justice, again a roster was drawn up, and Sash members attended the hearings. They kept meticulous records of those accused, their lawyers, of cases remanded time after time, and of people, even minors, held in prison without bail.

The records provide an amazing account of the vast state machinery required to enforce government policies. They demonstrate how unjust laws were given legitimacy by being passed in Parliament, and administered through a system of justice in which judges and magistrates operated under a system of law, instead of a system of 'the rule of law'. All too few of them questioned the justice of the laws they were employed to administer.

The Sash members who attended the courts acquired a great deal of understanding of how this was happening. They also became familiar figures in the courts, and came to know the accused, their families and their lawyers. In Cape Town, Rosalind Bush described one incident in which she met the families of a series of young people who were arrested on charges of public violence, and understood the impact upon them: 'Not only were the parents anxious, and sometimes angry with either their children or the authorities or both, but they were desperately trying to earn their living, and could not afford to be absent from work for the many days of the trials. That burden often fell on grandparents, and we found ourselves worrying almost as much about them as about the youths. The difficulties and expense of public transport often made it hard for them to get to the courts, and we would find ways of fetching them to ensure that they could be there. We came to believe that the frequent remands which sent the youths back to prison numerous times after brief appearances were little more than a mechanism to keep them in custody – sometimes in prison cells with adult criminals, with all the negative results which that entailed – without having to employ the tactic of detention without trial.'

She went on to say that some of the monitors who attended the courts dutifully kept records and passed them on to those who collated all of them. This in itself was valuable, ensuring that they gave as complete a picture as possible. Others became ever more deeply committed to offering as much support as possible to those charged and to their families. Their knowledge grew of the conditions which led to the anger and resistance of communities living under discrimination and repression.

Those who took on the monitoring tasks were a special band of women. They were efficient and dedicated, and brought a particular commitment to justice and dignity to their work. Rosalind Bush remembers the sense of extraordinary separation of the different aspects of her life – partly wife and mother in a comfortable home, partly busy activist attending trials, meeting people under enormous stress, comforting parents whose children had been arrested, or hunting for political leaders who had disappeared. Nearly 30 years later she brings out the books in which the meticulous records were kept – who would be at which court, what cases were heard, what the outcomes were. Muriel Crewe was the chief organiser and set up the system for recording the roster and the reports. Rosalind mourns the fact she is no longer alive. The records are her legacy.

Rosalind, like many other second-generation Sash members, grew up in a family who could be described as traditional 'white liberals'. Her mother was a member, her father a businessman who was involved in a variety of projects to improve the lives of young black people. Her husband shares her values of justice, equality and freedom. She had been active in church projects to work for change. Above all, it was her work as a court monitor that gave her a true insight into the lives of other South Africans and that continues to drive her to greater efforts to bring about a new and democratic society.

As the monitors became a familiar presence in the courts, they were sought after and often told about other people who were missing during the waves of police arrests and detentions in the late 1970s and 1980s. They hunted for them in police stations or hospitals. They attended funerals, and witnessed the way in which these turned into political rallies. They started to understand some of the complexities of the struggles that were being waged, and of the contestations between political groupings already becoming evident. They were asked for help, for transport, for a supportive presence. 'We were seeing children of 13 or 14, bail was not given unless we pushed for it, they dropped out of the school system, and were at risk of falling under the influence of criminals.'

The reports speak of people being accused of public violence, of the possession of banned books, of contravening the provisions of the state of emergency, of professional people losing their livelihoods and having their lives ruined because of long court cases. The monitors relate that, however painful it was to witness, they are grateful to have had that insight, to understand how the destruction of lives through such mechanised repression had effects on people which still can be seen 20 or 30 years later.

Anne Greenwell came to live in South Africa in the 1980s, and found a place in the Black Sash where she could use her skills and her desire to help end apartheid. She became active in the monitoring work, and like others found that it brought her a strong link with the lives of people in the squatter settlements and also with activists building the mass democratic movement. She speaks of the way in which they 'got into the heart of the devastating machinery on a very personal level'.

They were often told that they did make a difference, either by their supportive presence, or by being able to achieve exposure through the press of what was happening, or even by offering a degree of protection when they attended potentially explosive events. Sometimes they felt that, even if they did no more than show that people cared about the situation, it was worth doing. From the Black Sash point of view, they performed an essential service in bringing to the organisation their first-hand accounts of what they had seen.

Yet they sometimes felt that even in the Sash they were not heard as strongly as they wished. They were closely connected with entire communities in a way that other members were not. They witnessed the conditions which led to the anger and resistance of communities living under discrimination and repression. They felt that their reports were 'just a part of the agenda' at Sash meetings held in safe neighbourhood homes, or in the regional offices where so many other urgent issues took up time. Committee members acknowledged their importance, but did not always respond with the urgency and desperation that the monitors felt appropriate. 'Not everybody supported what we were doing,' and indeed there were some members who worried that their work was taking the organisation into an uncertain area, where it was not always possible to discern the whole picture, where it might appear for instance that the Sash supported the use of violence by the resistance movements, or might take sides in a dispute.

Such misgivings did not prevent the Sash from responding to the evident need to continue to watch, listen and learn, and to react when there were clear signs that help was required. For example, Rosalind Bush recounts the experience of rushing to Hermanus, a hundred kilometres from Cape Town, in response to reports that young people

Based on a design by Sheila Nowers, the Black Sash tree banner, symbolising optimism and growth, was first used at the national conference in Cape Town in 1987. (© Iziko Museums of South Africa Social History Collections. Photo by Thom Pierce)

(Above) Carrying petitions, Black Sash women stride up the hill to the Union Buildings, 28 June 1955. In the front row, behind the drummer, are (left to right) Bessie Brummer, Jean Sinclair, Ruth Foley, Marjorie Juta. (Independent Newspapers, courtesy of UCT Libraries)

(Above) In November 1955, Black Sash members held protest marches in many cities, including this one in Cape Town, carrying the constitution book. (Independent Newspapers, courtesy of UCT Libraries)

(Opposite) Jessie Power, in her green Morris Minor carrying the sash-draped book of the constitution, leads the convoy of cars to Parliament, 13 February 1956. (Independent Newspapers, courtesy of UCT Libraries)

Black Sash advice to pensioners, Driefontein, Mpumalanga, 10 May 1983.
(Photo by Gille de Vlieg)

Glenda Glover speaking to residents of Varkfontein, Ekurhuleni, 3 November 1987. (Photo by Gille de Vlieg)

Audrey Coleman taking statements from young men about events in Thabong, Free State, 7 June 1985. (Photo by Gille de Vlieg)

Tinkie Mathope and Jill Pointer discussing the threat of forced removal, Mathopestad, North West Province, 9 March 1984. (Photo by Gille de Vlieg)

Margaret Nash (above) and Mary Livingstone (below). (Photos by Eric Miller)

(Right) Sheena Duncan and Beyers Naudé at a meeting after the shootings at Langa, Uitenhage, on 21 March 1985. (Photo by Eric Miller)

(Below left) Anne Greenwell. (Photo by Mary Burton)

(Below right) Di Oliver and Di Davis. (Photo by Mary Burton)

(Above) Protest against the Senate Act, held in the Mayor's Garden, Port Elizabeth, while one member beats a muffled drum, 25 November 1955. (From Mirabel Rogers, 'The Black Sash')

(Below) Port Elizabeth group, 2 March 2010. Seated: Baa Thompson, Mary Burton, Bobby Melunsky, Judy Chalmers. Standing: Debbie Mattheus, June Crichton, Cathy Binnell, Val Hunt, Leslie Greensmith, Zoë Tookey, Lindsay Woods, Vicky Proudlock (partly obscured). (Photo by Debbie Mattheus, courtesy of UCT Libraries)

(Above) The Western Cape delegation to a national conference (with Sheena Duncan of Johannesburg on the right). (Courtesy of UCT Libraries)

(Below) Two of the smaller regions, Cape Eastern and Albany, at the same national conference. (Courtesy of UCT Libraries)

(Above) End Conscription Campaign meeting. (Photo by Eric Miller)

(Opposite) Albertina Sisulu, at the Children's Festival, part of the Free the Children campaign, Johannesburg, 1 June 1987. (Photos by Gille de Vlieg)

(Below) Funeral in Lingelihle of the 'Cradock Four', 19 July 1985. (Photo by Gille de Vlieg)

(Above) Black Sash members who were part of a Five Freedoms Forum meeting with the ANC in Lusaka, June 1989. (From left): Fidela Fouché, Sandy Stewart, Judy Chalmers, Glenda Glover, Jenny de Tolly, Beva Runciman, Sarah Burns, Judith Hawarden, Joyce Harris (missing from the photo is Kerry Harris). (Photo by Gille de Vlieg)

(Below) Helen Suzman, with a portion of the Peace Ribbon, Johannesburg, 30 November 1985. (Photo by Gille de Vlieg)

(Above) Protest in Greenmarket Square, Cape Town, as part of the defiance campaign against apartheid, 24 August 1989. (Photo by Eric Miller)

(Below) At the same protest, police arrest Anne Schuster and Frances Whitehead (with Rosalind Bush in the background, wearing a sash). (Photo by Eric Miller)

After 29 years, during which all demonstrations were banned there, the Johannesburg City Hall steps are reclaimed by the Black Sash, 28 June 1991. (Photo by Gille de Vlieg)

(Above) Black Sash members form a guard of honour at the funeral of Helen Joseph. Johannesburg, 7 January 1993. (Photo by Gille de Vlieg)

(Below) Black Sash members, together with Ellen Kuzwayo and Joyce Serote, at the funeral of Chris Hani, held at Soccer City, Soweto, 18 April 1993. (Photo by Gille de Vlieg)

A voter education event, Johannesburg, 10 December 1993. (Photo by Gille de Vlieg)

(Right) A Black Sash vigil on St George's Cathedral steps, Cape Town, December 2013, in memory of Nelson Mandela. (Photo by Eric Miller)

(Overleaf) The Black Sash commemorative cloth, created in 1993, displayed by Jenny de Tolly, Patricia Davison, Sue Townsend and Sue Clark. (Photo by Thom Pierce)

(Above) Trustees of the Black Sash at the Cape Town offices, 2009: Mary
Kleinenberg, Sibongile Mkhabela, Yasmin Sooka, Dolly Khumalo, Mary
Burton, Nyami Mbhele, Rosemary van Wyk Smith, Jenny de Tolly, Hilary
Southall (missing were Di Oliver, Jessie Turton and Mary-Jane Morifi).
(Photo by Elroy Paulus)

(Left) Karin Chubb with Womandla T-shirt. (Photo by Thom Pierce)

(Right) Sue Townsend, with commemorative cloth shirt. (Photo by Thom Pierce)

(Below) Sue van der Merwe, at a training workshop, 'Working for Justice', July 1990. (Courtesy of UCT Libraries)

Amanda Louw herself, in a blue version of the Womandla badge, created by Gus Ferguson. (Photo by Gille de Vlieg)

(Previous page) Collage of Black Sash posters, cards, publications, pamphlets, cartoons. (Photo by Thom Pierce)

had been detained in the police cells there and were being severely assaulted.

As conflict grew all around the country in the late 1980s, Black Sash members became more and more involved in responding to calls from communities that were experiencing brutal repression. They would attend political rallies, which were sometimes disrupted and broken up, either by opposing groups or by security forces. They became accustomed to meeting groups of people who had been beaten, teargassed or shot, and to taking accurate statements from individuals which would form the basis for wider investigations, and publicising the actions of those responsible.

When people were killed, Black Sash members would be among the thousands at the funerals, once again providing a witnessing presence. All too often the funeral itself would become a scene of conflict: the police would impose restrictions (on numbers attending or on duration), and attempt to enforce them; the mourners would attempt to place the banned ANC flag on the coffin as it was lowered into the grave, and the police would attack; further injuries and even deaths could result.

The monitoring of the courts was matched by the monitoring of increasing repression and violence, as Sash members joined others in recording events and trying to keep track of people who were missing. In each region Repression Monitoring Groups (RMGs) were established, and information was recorded. The national conferences of the Sash in 1987 and 1988 received lengthy reports from the RMGs of the numbers of those who were presumed to be detained, exiled, in hiding or killed, especially from the Johannesburg area and from KwaZulu-Natal, where the conflict was at its most brutal.

As the country slid into civil war, the tally of deaths grew. The numbers of people who died while in police custody were added to the Sash's list and read at the start of all its meetings, engraving their names in the memories of those who regularly read the list.

When at last in 1990 government recognised the need to resolve the conflict by negotiation rather than repression, a National Peace Accord was established, and the monitoring skills and experience of Sash members could be drawn upon for peace monitoring. In the anxious years before the eventual elections in 1994, when what continued to be described as 'unrest' often reached heights of violence even worse than earlier, this was a time of see-sawing hope and despair.

Monitoring the preparations for the democratic elections in April 1994 was widely recognised as vitally important, and arrangements were made for national as well as international monitors and observers. Sashers were active all over the country during the pre-election period and for the election itself. Their knowledge of local conditions and their extensive contacts were of considerable value, and their efforts rewarded by the final peaceful outcome, although violence continued in many parts of the country.

There were other forms of monitoring that did not require a physical presence in courts or at public events. These made good use of special skills and dedication on the part of members: they spent hours reading the *Government Gazette* and the Hansard records of parliamentary debates. They alerted the Sash to new issues, or impending changes to laws or regulations. Questions were formulated which could be put to cabinet ministers by supportive MPs. These raised issues that would otherwise not elicit attention, and obliged ministers to make at least some effort to find explanations. The processing of bills through Parliament was closely watched and, if necessary, plans to demonstrate against them were timed to coincide with the debates. Very few members had specialised legal knowledge, but they acquired experience and astuteness. Sash members in Cape Town set up a Legislation Watch group known as Legiwatch and produced a useful document called *Tracking a Bill*, which explained the process of how laws became part of the statute book. They attended parliamentary debates and kept records of information gathered. In the 1990s Alison Tilley, a qualified lawyer, was employed to assist and take forward this work. Under the new government after 1994, this work was taken on by a new structure, the Parliamentary Monitoring Group (PMG), made up of Black Sash members and others.

The advice and the monitoring were areas of solidarity with those who suffered and those who resisted. They needed skills of empathy, of caring deeply for people, of being prepared to sacrifice time and skills and resources to help them overcome their suffering. Rewards came in many forms – gratitude, friendship, knowledge, understanding and self-awareness. The goal was not merely to relieve the suffering, the impact, the effects of injustice, but to tackle the cause. Hence the quest for knowledge of the law and of political systems, of strategy and mechanisms to bring change. This dual task formed the core of the organisation.

5

REPRESSION AND
THE EASTERN CAPE

*'When you are on the periphery, the
periphery is the centre.'*
– Mary Robinson[1]

*From Grahamstown a number of spindly roads fan out in an arc across
the grey-green ridges and flatlands of the Eastern Cape, connecting the
town to a number of small and widely scattered communities: moving
clockwise from the south, Port Alfred and Kenton on the coast; Alexandria
a little inland; Alicedale and Riebeeck East to the west; then Somerset
East, Cookhouse, Bedford and Adelaide in a sweep to the north, and
finally Fort Beaufort on the Ciskei border. They are tiny towns, their
populations ranging from 1,500 to 12,000, largely unknown in other
parts of the country ... Despite their smallness, their isolation and the
endemic poverty, the level of politicisation among the black population
of these towns is remarkably high ... it is important that a record of the
terrible things that people are enduring in the townships and in the jails
should be preserved ... Can spring really be so exuberant during a State
of Emergency – can jacaranda blooms be so blue?[2]*

The Eastern Cape has a special place in the story of South Africa.
For over a hundred years it was a frontier between white settlers and

local Xhosa-speaking people, who confronted each other in what has become known as the Hundred Years War. In popular memory the history of the Eastern Cape is a story of resistance, led by a series of remarkable chiefly warriors such as Makhanda, Hintsa and Sarhili. But in addition to conflict, the Eastern Cape was also a zone of interaction and cooperation. It saw the earliest development in South Africa of a new class of educated, Christianised African men and women who sought to forge a place for themselves in the common society that was taking shape. The Eastern Cape boasted some of the oldest and finest schools and colleges for Africans, including Lovedale, Healdtown, St Matthew's Keiskammahoek and St John's Umtata. Fort Hare University College, established in the early 20th century, drew students not only from the whole country, but also from beyond its borders, and many of them were to become significant leaders – among them Nelson Mandela, Robert Sobukwe and Robert Mugabe. The first members of the ANC Youth League, founded in 1943, included graduates of Fort Hare.

The Eastern Cape was also a leading agricultural centre, famed for its sheep farms established by enterprising British settlers and also for a prosperous African peasantry that turned the province into a granary. But gradually, as the economic centre of gravity in the country shifted to the Witwatersrand, the Eastern Cape began to decline and its large 'native reserves' became reservoirs of cheap labour for the mines on the Rand, exporting men and importing remittances. Over the course of the 20th century, desperate poverty combined with a tradition of resistance made for a turbulent history, which in turn evoked intense government repression from the 1950s onwards.

Even after I joined the Black Sash and began to learn about South Africa's history, I took some time to begin to appreciate the complexity of this part of the country. Almost everything I have learned has been mediated through the experience of the Black Sash members in this harshly beautiful area. Their own knowledge was garnered over 40 years of activism, and as their awareness grew, even while their numbers dwindled, they were propelled into stronger opposition to injustice. They established contacts throughout the whole area with communities struggling under great hardship, and their reports provided a rich store of confirmation of the battles those communities waged, continuing the legacy of their ancestors. I was fascinated by the inspiring early stories of the establishment of the Black Sash in this area. It was not until 1976, when the national conference was held in Grahamstown, that I encountered the region for the first time. By then, the combined forces of climate, urbanisation, overcrowding, unemployment and apartheid policies had turned it into an area of extreme poverty and state repression.

Twenty years earlier, the formation of the Women's Defence of the Constitution League had evoked immediate strong support in the Eastern Cape, not only in its cities, but also in the smaller towns. The women who first joined were caught up in the excitement of the moment, and their reports reflect this. The first Black Sash 'regions' established were known as Border, based in East London, and Cape Eastern, with its centre in Port Elizabeth. Members in Grahamstown were part of Cape Eastern until they established the Albany region in 1972. In April 1956 Middelburg (Cape) was also listed as a region, known as Cape Midlands,[3] but it suffered the general decline in membership in country areas, and soon disbanded.

It is not difficult to see why these women became so enthusiastic about the Black Sash. They were intelligent and energetic, often frustrated and disappointed by politicians, eager to work for change but far from the centres of power and decision-making. Here at last were opportunities for them to demonstrate their commitment and channel their activities into a common cause. Di Davis recalled the first meeting in Port Elizabeth, 'with a lot of people in my sitting-room. I said at the beginning, "I am not the slightest bit interested in politics, and we're only having the meeting here because Ruth Foley is Bill's aunt and she is staying with us." But Ruth was very inspiring, and by the end of the meeting we had a committee, with Alison Pirie as chair, and I was the secretary.' Convinced that the pending Senate Act was unfair and immoral, they immediately rushed into collecting signatures for the petition. 'Everyone was mad keen ... It was something we were looking for ... None of the political parties had offered us anything where we could express ourselves in that way.'[4]

These women had the support of the local press, and a good deal of sympathy from the public in those early days. The newspapers helped by sending the petitions out with their delivery lorries, so that they were quickly and widely distributed throughout the area. Gathering signatures for the petitions was less daunting for these new activists than taking part in protest stands. 'I was frightened every time we stood – we were terribly few.' On one occasion, 'down at North End, and it was terribly dark,' Di suggested her husband might come with her, and keep watch from behind a nearby tree, but he said, 'Certainly not! You got into this.' On another occasion, 'We had a whole lot of terrible Nats [National Party supporters] pushing us from behind – I don't think I've ever been so scared, and though we weren't supposed to talk when protesting, I murmured to the person next to me, "Are we all mad?" but it was Mrs Ritchie and she said, "Nonsense, my dear, I was a suffragette," and I felt better straight away.'[5] She and many others, including Alison Pirie and Peggy Levey, continued as active office-bearers for many years, and their names appear and reappear in the records.

Di Davis may not have been politically active before joining the Black Sash, but there were others among those women who did have more political experience. Peggy Levey and Alison Pirie were re-membered by Hilda Tshaka as having participated with ANC women in the Defiance Campaign of 1952. 'Mrs Levey was a strong woman in Port Elizabeth. She was our good friend and we made her "Nokhaya" ... So many were arrested ... We used to collect the names of those taken and take them to Mrs Levey; she would find lawyers for us.'[6] In the Black Sash they found a structure where they could contribute their skills and experience. New members in the smaller towns, even while some of them worried about their lack of experience and bemoaned the conservatism of their neighbours, took part eagerly wherever opportunity presented itself, and they grew in confidence.

The anti-pass campaigns, which led to the proclamation of a state of emergency in 1960 and the banning of the ANC and the PAC, resulted in a mass of arrests over the next few months and years. 'Repression was enforced with particular ruthlessness in the Eastern Cape, the worst affected area being Port Elizabeth ... [where] over 1,000 people were detained by security police between October 1964 and June 1965.'[7] During the state of emergency, Black Sash members in all regions became involved in relief committees, helping the families of prisoners. In the Eastern Cape, too, they were active in supporting the dependants of detainees and in the work of the organisation Defence and Aid, which provided support for people arrested and tried. Money, food and clothing were distributed, and funds raised for legal representation. Outside the Port Elizabeth jail they did 'jail duty' on two days every week, helping those inside as well as outside the prison, and earning considerable respect from the public and the press.[8]

Optimism and commitment became quite difficult to sustain. Public opinion among the white population grew more critical as the Black Sash voice became louder. In small towns and rural communities the price for being outspoken was rejection by neighbours and friends. Police harassment increased, as it did in other parts of the country. Membership declined sharply, despite help and encouragement from the national leadership. Eulalie Stott, as national president, visited the Eastern Cape in July 1961, and addressed meetings in the smaller towns.[9] At the national conference hosted by Border in October 1961, a delegate was heard to say that a sure way of dealing with difficult husbands was to have Eulalie Stott to stay.[10]

In this hostile climate, there were often discussions about whether the Black Sash should embark on welfare projects, since these might be more favourably viewed by the public and also provide fulfilling work for the members; but this was firmly rejected by national decisions.

Members were encouraged to participate in charitable work in other established organisations: the Black Sash was to remain a politically motivated one. In spite of this, it is notable that in the Eastern Cape there was a consistent thread of support work of two main kinds: in educational projects such as pre-school crèches and libraries for African schools; and in remembering the people who were banished by the government to remote areas far from their homes. Funds were raised (kept carefully separate from the Black Sash funds) to assist scholars to meet their school fees, and also to send parcels of food and clothing, as well as money, to banished people.

Banishment was a particularly cruel and unjust punishment for resistance. Its justification in law dated back to the Natal Code of Native Law of 1891, according to which the governor could remove an African subject from any part of the colony to any other part without any trial. The Native Administration Act of 1927 generalised this to the whole of the country. This punishment usually meant being banished with no income or support system, to a place where even the local language might be unfamiliar. Saleem Badat's book *The Forgotten People* is a devastating record of banishment, written as a result of a promise made to Helen Joseph, who in 1962 undertook a trip around South Africa with Amina Cachalia to visit all the banned people known to be hidden away from public scrutiny.[11] It was through their vigilance that organisations like the Black Sash, the Civil Rights League and the Christian Institute were able to document the extent of the banishments, and try to provide some support.[12] The Eastern Cape regions of the Black Sash regularly reported on their efforts.[13]

Inevitably the Sash attracted the attention of the security forces, and from the mid-1960s it became almost impossible in the Eastern Cape to sustain the organisation's work. In Port Elizabeth in 1966, 'three members of Regional Council were warned by Special Branch' and two were 'forced by circumstances' to resign.[14] In 1964 Peggy Levey was 'warned' in terms of the Suppression of Communism Act, her house was raided and her passport removed.[15] The Port Elizabeth advice office started in 1964 but closed in 1965, and the Cape Eastern region itself eventually closed in 1978 'due to Security Police harassment'.[16] Yet members there retained their commitment, and even if there was not an official Sash regional presence, there were individuals who continued to do what they could. About 30 years later, when Judy Chalmers gathered together a group of long-standing members so that they could tell me of their memories, Bobby Melunsky was firmly convinced that the Black Sash in Port Elizabeth had never closed.[17] Indeed, it probably seemed so to her, since she and Peggy Levey had continued to help people with pension problems. Many others had also supported the people forcibly moved to the notorious settlement camp of Dimbaza between 1967 and 1969. Dimbaza was established as an 'elementary closer settlement' in the Ciskei homeland near to Kingwilliamstown. People were taken there by truck after being evicted from 'white' areas.[18] Following the revelations of their plight by Cosmas Desmond, there was national and international condemnation. In response, Sash members found ways to assist, to record and to protest. The region may have been formally inactive, but its members could be roused to action by particular events or causes, as the example of Dimbaza shows.

When we met at Judy Chalmers's house in 2009, the members spoke of the difficulties they had with organising protest stands in the early years, which were usually held in front of the mayor's office in Port Elizabeth, around a circular garden, until they were denied permission. Lionel Melunsky, who was an attorney (and after 1994 became a judge), took up the matter, and permission was reinstated – Bobby said this put her in good standing with the Sash. In June 1981 a first-time participant was removed from the steps of a church in Main Street, Port Elizabeth, and told she was constituting a riotous assembly. The Sash women battled with the authorities over their right to stand, and by August were once again protesting against bannings and detentions, and insisting 'Scrap apartheid'. In a protest on the beachfront against beach apartheid 'our revered and loved founding member Joy Alder was manhandled and sworn at … Her dignified and gentle bearing …

received front page treatment' in the local newspapers.

It was not unusual for there to be a web of connectedness between Black Sash members and their families, stretching across all the regions, as well as the generations. The daughters of a number of the founding generation became active members, or joined other organisations working for change. Di Davis, for example, remembered that she was friendly with the mother of Molly Blackburn and Judy Chalmers ('she was a chum') and also knew Bobby Melunsky's mother. Di and her family moved from Port Elizabeth in about 1976, but before then she had sought to persuade Molly and Judy to join the Black Sash. At that time they were too busy raising their young families, but when they did so in 1981 they had an incalculable impact on the entire region, and not only on the Black Sash.

Di Bishop Oliver recalls that 'Judy was active in Sash before Molly was. Molly was impressed with our Cape Town advice office and its outreach during the Crossroads "squatter crisis". She familiarised herself with how we worked when she came to Cape Town for her orientation as an MPC [member of the Cape Provincial Council]. Then when she started to get a profile through the media as a result of her activism, Molly had a long queue of people coming to see her at the PFP [Progressive Federal Party] offices ... She told Sash members she would join if they reopened the advice office, which is what happened.'[19] The Cape Eastern region was formally revived again in 1980, and the Port Elizabeth advice office reopened in May 1982.[20]

That 2009 conversation with the Port Elizabeth group was lively and informative, as members spoke of the sense of excitement and risk they had felt, and the urgency of the 1980s. Zoë Tookey (Riordan) said afterwards, 'What a great bunch of ladies, delightfully eccentric some of them, but all worth their weight in gold. In the midst of terrible trauma, we were fortunate to have uniquely rewarding experiences.'[21] June Crichton described being taken to a pension pay-out point by Cathy Binell: 'It was at Centenary Hall. There was a closed-off area where people had to wait for hours, with huge gates holding them back.

It was very hot and the people were getting angry, and we could see there could be trouble. Cathy climbed up onto the gates and started to sing "Nkosi Sikelel' iAfrika", and people joined in.'[22]

The Border region, centred on East London, also had a history of early enthusiasm followed by a decline. The chairperson was Daphne Curry, who for ten years led the organisation in East London with great energy and commitment. It was she who went to Queenstown in response to an appeal for help from Mary Birt when accompanying the Sikade family after they had been endorsed out of Wellington, as we have seen earlier.[23] As she had promised, she returned in 1961 to visit the family in the Lady Grey reserve, accompanied by Mrs Grainger from Queenstown. They found that Mr Sikade had obtained work with a road gang, earning R12 per month, and that his wife, although finding their new life of poverty very hard, appeared in better health, and was delighted to see the visitors.[24]

Members of the Eastern Cape regions participated actively in the national discussions about Black Sash policies. Border was particularly influential in several major decisions regarding the opening of membership and support for a universal franchise. Yet many of their members lived far from the cities and found it difficult to participate in any activities, even if they valued the contact through newsletters and contributed their subscriptions. When the national conference was held in November 1961 in East London, members came together from the whole region to provide the necessary hospitality and practical arrangements. These occasions provided opportunities for them to maintain their links to the Sash.

Daphne Curry was re-elected once more in 1965, but this time she shared the chair with five others since she was returning to full-time employment. The pressure from the police made any work very difficult, and the region might not have survived had it not been for the next chairperson, Deena Streek, who remained at the helm until 1975. Deena was a staunch liberal, and could rely on the support of her husband, Frank, who was general manager of the regional newspaper, the *Daily Dispatch*. In 1975 the new chair was Liz Kaye-Eddie, whose husband was also connected with the *Daily Dispatch*. Wendy Woods was a member, and wife of Donald Woods, its editor from 1965 until he was banned on 19 October 1977. The family was the target of vicious attacks by state agents and was forced to leave South Africa.

Border region had also opened an advice office in East London on 8 April 1964. However, it too was forced to close again by 1965 because of security police harassment. Public protests attracted considerable hostility, and were greatly curtailed, but its members continued to meet and kept up a variety of activities. They looked for new ventures that might have a more positive impact. They visited the African location, accompanied by two municipal officials, and reported on the housing conditions. They held monthly meetings with discussions on a variety of topics, and opposed the segregation of the public library; originally they had some success.[25]

The ability to manage the administrative work of a region fluctuated according to the number of members and the time they had available. Larger centres such as Johannesburg and Cape Town could depend on an active core of members, but in the smaller areas it was much more difficult. Although the Eastern Cape Sash went through lean years in the 1960s, it never died away entirely, and the next decade brought new growth.

Ever since 1955 Sash members in Grahamstown had constituted a 'branch' of the Cape Eastern region. Betty Davenport was one of the dedicated group who revived the branch and built it into a new 'Albany region'. She had moved from Cape Town to Grahamstown in 1965 and recalls how 'like-minded people' had helped her to settle. Their main focus at first was on vigorous opposition to forced removals. Later, in the 1980s, they played a large role in responding to the detention of great numbers of people. At one stage in the mid-1980s, when 'frightful tensions' escalated, 'we had a meeting every night'.[26]

During Port Elizabeth's dormant period, its members 'fell under Albany's wing' and were in their turn regarded as 'country members'.[27]

Gradually the three regions – Albany, Border and Cape Eastern – grew closer together, with Grahamstown often the meeting point. In 1972 Jill Joubert was the Albany delegate to the national conference and reported a membership of 57, including those at Port Alfred. In May 1973 an advice office opened in Grahamstown under joint responsibility with the Institute of Race Relations, at the same premises as the Legal Aid office and with the assistance of students from Rhodes University. Betty Davenport was one of the 20 or so members who worked to establish it, and staff it every Saturday.[28]

In East London, too, the Black Sash had a new spurt of energy in the early 1970s. Deena Streek reported that 'the whole outlook has changed': the average age had dropped, their protest stands were carried out by 'attractive young women', and in 1973 they had 45 members (ten more than the previous year). The advice office reopened from 8 September 1972, on Saturday mornings, in the Institute of Race Relations office.[29] The Black Sash's national executive welcomed this revival of activity in the area.[30] Rosemary van Wyk Smith was particularly dedicated to making this cooperation work well and to keeping the regions close. The national conferences for 1976 and 1981 were held in Grahamstown, and each time the Sash was reminded of the invaluable work being carried out locally. The year 1976 marked the first anniversary of Sheena Duncan's presidency, in a time of considerable anxiety about the future of the country. Her opening address was titled 'We must go on', and it was evident that in Grahamstown and the surrounding areas the work was indeed continuing.

These regions of the Eastern Cape managed to survive public hostility, very small membership and continued security police surveillance and pressure, and to make a substantial contribution to the whole organisation's understanding of the impact of apartheid policies. Their annual reports give membership figures that varied from 35 to about 60, and yet they sustained advice offices for much of the time, gathered information about forced removals, political resistance, poverty and repression, and made it available not only to the Black

Sash, but to journalists and diplomats, who knew they could rely on its accuracy.

Val Viljoen (previously Sullivan), who came to East London in the early 1970s with a background in Britain of support for the anti-apartheid movement and the Liberal Party, sought out the Black Sash and soon became a vital part of its work. She described with some amusement how she was so keen to join that Deena Streek thought she must be a spy. The small number of people in East London who were working for change constituted quite a close community, who knew one another well. Most belonged to the Institute of Race Relations, the Dependants' Conference and the Border Council of Churches, as well as non-racial sports organisations, and they tended to view outsiders with mistrust. Indeed, they were probably wise to do so, as was shown when an eager member took over the advice office in 1976 and 1977 and was then discovered to be handing information to the security police. Despite this, Val said she never felt threatened, and for quite a long time this was the experience of many Black Sash members, probably because their white skins and their positions in apartheid society did give them a measure of protection. 'Although I knew our phones were tapped I was quite naive,' she said, 'and only later did I discover that they had a special branch policeman just for me.' Pondering the interest of the security forces, she said, 'If they were so worried about us, we must have been doing something right.' It must surely have been the continued ability of the Black Sash to portray the ugly reality of apartheid to the outside world, even if much of white South Africa did not wish to see it.[31]

By 1973 Val Viljoen had become the regional secretary. She had formed a strong friendship with Dr Trudy Thomas, whose work in local state hospitals for black people remains legendary. Together they worked with Steve Biko and the Black Community Programmes, the developmental wing of the black consciousness (BC) movement, in Kingwilliamstown. Val acknowledged the importance of BC, and the role played by the *Daily Dispatch* under Donald Woods in giving space to and providing understanding of the movement in its pages.[32] The East London advice office had a particular emphasis on socio-economic issues, since acute poverty was the greatest problem in the area. As the 'grand apartheid' plan developed, and black people were increasingly and forcibly moved out of white areas into the 'homelands' of Transkei and Ciskei, poverty, unemployment and the removals became the focus of Black Sash concerns.

Val remembers the older members with affection and respect – 'they were so strong!' She speaks of the years of leadership of Daphne Curry and Deena Streek as vibrant, but then came a downturn after the shocks of the Soweto student uprising in 1976 and the killing of Steve Biko in detention and the subsequent clampdown on major black organisations in 1977. The next years were very difficult. In 1982 East London's Norah Squires gave a verbal report to the national conference in which she said that Border region had only five active members, who shared the leadership, but they had managed to hold several protest stands and had close contact with the people of Duncan Village, scheduled for removal to Mdantsane. They were now ready to resume management of their region, they had plans for the future, and the advice office still survived. 'Later, Susie Power arrived and it all took off again!'[33]

During the late 1970s and the 1980s wave after wave of popular resistance and violent retaliation by the state pounded South Africa. In large cities and small towns people came together in angry desperation to end the poverty and injustice of their lives. Young people, workers and women's groups all made sacrifices and ran risks to exert pressure on the state and its allies. School boycotts and work stoppages spread, and while the government tried to stabilise the situation by banning public gatherings and holding people in preventive detention, rioting and protests continued. In those dark years the ability of the Black Sash to respond to crises and to calls for support from threatened communities, as well as to sustain its monitoring and reporting work, was tested to the utmost.

Many of the conflicts and much of the violence occurred in the cities, but they were even more acute in the small towns, further from the public eye. Gathering accurate information therefore became an important way of opposing state repression. Molly Blackburn of Port Elizabeth and Di Bishop of Cape Town, who had both been elected as Progressive Federal Party members of the Cape Provincial Council in 1981, were called with increasing frequency to go and see what was happening. (The Council was responsible for the whole of the Cape Province, which then included the Eastern Cape.) They responded to calls for help from many groups and individuals, travelling throughout the entire province, taking statements and affidavits, and exposing the brutal repression which was the government's response to the widespread resistance. They regarded this as an essential part of their public service, and were able to draw on the support and help of the Black Sash in several areas. The full story of their remarkable contribution is still to be told, but there is plenty of evidence of the trust and respect they received.

When the Sash national conference in March 1985 was held in Port Elizabeth, it was natural that some of the events they had witnessed and the people they had met should form a major part of the agenda. A trio of guest speakers gave delegates a deeper understanding of the turbulence in the area: Matthew Goniwe, a teacher and the chairman of the Cradock Residents' Association; Mkhuseli Jack, a leader of the Port Elizabeth Youth Congress; and the Rev. Michael Mjekula of the Port Elizabeth Ministers Fraternal. All three made a powerful impact on us, and there were murmured hopes that some wonderful day in the future Matthew Goniwe might be a fine minister of education. The cold reality was that before his words could be printed in the *Sash* magazine, he had been listed in terms of the Suppression of Communism Act,[34] which meant that he could not be quoted, and by June he had been killed by security police.

That conference was a turning point for many of us, and for the Black Sash itself. Reports from all regions described townships in turmoil throughout the country. Now we were also drawn in to witness at first hand the impact this was having on the region. Audrey Coleman recounts the calls for help that interrupted the conference proceedings. She tells how on the Friday night Molly Blackburn had been visited by someone who had just been released from Port Elizabeth's 'Rooi Hel' prison, and who was extremely upset by the number of children he had seen being held there, as many as a hundred, who had told him they were being abused. The next morning the conference decided to send three delegates to see the magistrate, and at the same time to contact various other organisations, seek an interdict to get the children released, and draw up a national memorandum. The three Sashers were accompanied by lawyers (Lionel Melunsky was one of them) and met Port Elizabeth's chief magistrate, the chief magistrate of Uitenhage and the commander of the prison. They conceded that there were children in the prison, but not that they were being abused, and the only positive outcome was the permission granted for parents to visit their children.

On Sunday, 17 March there was a further desperate call for help, asking for someone to come to nearby Uitenhage immediately, as parents feared for the safety of their children being detained there. Nine delegates were appointed to accompany Molly Blackburn. They told the horrifying story of how in the police station they had discovered a young man, manacled to a table and bleeding from his injuries, while three others nearby said they had also been assaulted. It was all too clear from the attitudes of the police that they felt able to act with absolute impunity, although as a result of the Sash intervention these four young men were subsequently released. Audrey said, 'For us the whole episode was breathtaking. There was not even a pretence of bringing wrong-doers to book. There was a latent sense of violence.' Sashers gathered affidavits for a memorandum on police conduct. It condemned the 'mindless brutality indulged in by members of the police force in the Eastern Cape [which] can only destroy their own moral fibre, in addition to fostering feelings of anger, frustration and hatred in the black community'.[35]

Four days later, on 21 March, ironically the anniversary of the 1960 massacre in Sharpeville, there was a funeral procession in Langa, the township adjacent to Uitenhage, to which the police responded with particular force, resulting in the deaths of 20 people and injuries to 27.[36] On and on, throughout that year, it seemed that elements in the security forces were able to act with impunity to detain, torture and kill. The resistance became more violent, too, and clashes occurred between community organisations and other bodies suspected of collaborating with the authorities. On 8 May the 'PEBCO Three', leaders of the Port Elizabeth Black Civic Organisation, were abducted and killed. On 27 June the 'Cradock Four', Matthew Goniwe and his colleagues, were assassinated on a lonely stretch of road between Port Elizabeth and Cradock. The Eastern Cape would never be the same again.

The funeral of Goniwe, Sparrow Mkhonto, Fort Calata and Sicelo Mhlauli was held in Lingelihle, the township of Cradock, on 20 July 1985. Thousands of people, mostly supporters of the United Democratic Front (UDF), made their way from all over the country. Many Black Sash members were among them, particularly those who had been so impressed by Matthew Goniwe and felt the impact of the brutal killing most deeply. Some came by car, some rode in the buses hired to carry people from various cities. All of us joined in the huge throngs which filled the dry and dusty sports stadium, and all of us experienced warm welcomes and the sense of strength, solidarity and anger of the people. Flags, banners, songs and hymns, prayers and speeches contributed to the emotional force of the occasion. On the hills that surrounded the stadium – Karoo koppies that typified the area – were massed police forces and vehicles. They took no action against this remarkable demonstration of enormous sorrow and of a determination to sustain every possible effort to end apartheid.

Returning to Cape Town that night on the buses, we heard the news that a state of emergency had been put into effect in 36 magisterial districts, including Cradock. Altogether 7,996 people were detained during the seven months of that state of emergency, of whom 3,681 were under 21 years old. There were restrictions on funerals and memorial services, curfews, banning of gatherings, restrictions on the media and on a number of organisations, and there were many deaths – 545 according to the Institute of Race Relations, which included people killed by security forces.[37]

Many of those affected were known to Black Sash members. They received word, for example, of the death in Steytlerville of Mzwandile Miggels (aged 20) on 3 July 1985 and of his nephew Johannes Spogter (age given as 13) on 5 July after they were arrested 'in connection with public violence'.[38] Post-mortem examinations revealed extensive injuries. It was the death of Johannes Spogter that prompted two Black Sash members in Cape Town to chain themselves to the railings of Parliament in protest.[39] Di and Brian Bishop attended the funerals, and in a moving account Di described the experience. 'At first we were regarded with some mistrust by some of the young comrades there, but they warmed to us when they noticed that we joined in the singing of "Nkosi Sikelel' iAfrika" – the unofficial national anthem – which few white people knew. Afterwards, when they heard I was a Black Sash member, they clustered around me, asking, "Is it really true that those white women chained themselves to the railings because of *our* Johannes?" And then one added, "That is really what I call non-racialism."'[40]

The final devastating blow to the Black Sash came at the end of that year, when on 28 December, in a suspicious car accident that has never been fully explained, Brian Bishop and Molly Blackburn were killed, Di was seriously injured and Judy Chalmers less seriously so. The mass funerals of Molly and Brian, in Port Elizabeth and Cape Town, were testimony to the selfless dedication of all four of them.[41] The impact on the Sash itself was immeasurable. Every one of us who had worked closely with them experienced anger and despair, and all had to search for ways to support Di and Judy, and to increase our activity and commitment.

Through all this time, the advice offices continued to deal with the many problems facing local communities, while members became increasingly aware of the impact of state repression and continued to document it. They collected statements and affidavits, and directed people who needed help to various agencies, such as lawyers, doctors and detainees' support groups. They ensured that the number of detentions was recorded as well as possible, and made widely known. In 1984, for example, they recorded that 'there were an estimated 1,149 detentions'.[42] They helped to conduct counselling and debriefing programmes for those affected. Sash members also organised food parcels and reading materials for detainees being held in prisons near them. The Sashers themselves became targets of repression, and by 1986 a number of them were detained.

Although the Black Sash did not suffer anything like the brutal repression vented on the majority of those who participated in the struggle against apartheid, its members and staff were not immune to the actions of the security forces, or to acts of violence by bigoted apartheid supporters. They endured surveillance and intimidation, and some were arrested, or detained without charge, in various parts of the country. It is no surprise that some of the worst of this harassment took place in the Eastern Cape. During 1984 the Port Elizabeth advice office suffered a series of damages, including a burning tyre pushed against its door causing a fire, and was obliged to leave its premises. The Grahamstown advice office was completely gutted in one of several arson attacks on a number of institutions. On 21 October 1988 the whole (new) Port Elizabeth advice office was destroyed by a fire-bomb.

Even when they were not violent, the instances of hostility and intimidation could be infuriating. Shirley Smith of East London laid charges against two men who threw ink at her while she was taking part in a protest stand against detention without trial. In spite of her detailed evidence about the event, she was made to feel that the case was 'the joke of the year' and the men were acquitted.[43] On 5, 6 and 7 May 1986 the Black Sash held a stand outside East London's City Hall to protest about the detention of Duncan Village leaders. Three members went each day: one stood, while the other two sat on a bus-stop bench about 12 metres away (in order to abide by the regulations that only one person could stage a protest stand). There was contact between members only when the poster changed hands. The police watched and took photographs (as they usually did during such stands). On 7 May a photo was taken of four women at the bus-stop before the stand itself began. A fourth member had come along to tell the others of the threatening calls she had received, namely that if the Sash kept up the protest, somebody would be severely injured. The four were not wearing sashes at the time but the wording on the poster, 'Talk to the leaders – don't jail them', was clearly visible. The four were charged with contravening a section of the Internal Security Act prohibiting gatherings. On 19 December they were found guilty and received suspended sentences.[44] The following year their appeal against conviction was upheld in the Grahamstown Supreme Court, but not before one of them had lost a job opportunity as a result of the episode.

Susie Power told of other actions against the Border members, whom the security police 'delighted in tormenting … They would slash members' tyres (preferably two at a time, to make it difficult to get home) … They sent us flowers, party orders of alcohol, coffins (all to be charged to our own accounts) and phoned us at all hours of the day and night … They finally dreamed up a scheme that they felt sure would discredit us in the eyes of the black community.' In April 1989 the police distributed thousands of pamphlets throughout the townships advertising a 'Black Sash Winter Care' programme which would give food, clothing, jobs and shelter to people presenting themselves at the local chairperson's home. Hundreds of people turned up at the Powers' house. Border members leapt into action, explaining the hoax, but also producing a mass of sandwiches and soup. Best of all, 'the resultant publicity produced an unexpected response from the East London community who donated so much food, clothing and housing materials that they were almost able to meet the promises made by the police!'[45]

In all parts of the country, 'the Black Sash also bore the brunt of many violent attacks'.[46] A journalist reported that Sheena Duncan was accustomed to finding 'a brace of dead cats swinging from her doorpost', or having 250 sandwiches that she hadn't ordered delivered to her house.[47] Esther Levitan, an active and 'staunch' member in Johannesburg, was detained by the security police on 5 January 1982 and subsequently redetained under section 6 of the Terrorism Act, which provided for indefinite detention without charge or trial.[48]

Other, less visible means of harassment and intimidation were used. Sandy Stewart (now Hoffman) was one of several Port Elizabeth members detained, after which she lost her job, and so did her father (who was an engineer based in Cradock). Both Sandy and Mkhuseli Jack, of the Port Elizabeth Youth Congress, who had also been detained, were then employed by Des Chalmers, Judy's husband, in his business as a supplier of building materials. A security policeman (who later confessed to Des and asked forgiveness) distributed leaflets discouraging support of his business 'because he employed terrorists'. The business was forced into bankruptcy, and the Chalmerses were obliged to sell their home.

Although some new members joined the Black Sash during the 1980s, it remained a small organisation, and its smallest regions definitely punched above their weight. Membership reports at the 1985 conference recorded a total paid-up membership of 1,353. 'Of these Transvaal had the most, with 658, Cape Western 400, Natal Coastal 117, Natal Midlands 78 and the other regions each under 40.'[49]

Clearly the smaller regions needed help as the demands of the work grew. It was only with the advent of substantial financial support from outside its own membership that the organisation was able to employ additional staff members as fieldworkers and researchers to take on some of this work so as to underpin the volunteer component. In the Eastern Cape this was to add a particularly valuable strength. Judy Chalmers herself became the Port Elizabeth fieldworker in 1986, and travelled extensively through the area to the north-west: Cookhouse,

Somerset East, Pearston, Graaff-Reinet, Jansenville, Klipplaat, Steytlerville, Cradock, Kirkwood and Addo. This outreach built on the work already done by the Port Elizabeth advice office, which had, for example, helped to set up an advice office in Uitenhage after the Langa massacre of 1985. Many of those towns had been visited by Molly Blackburn and Di Bishop, together with Brian Bishop and Judy Chalmers, so there were already good relationships of trust. Now Judy could rely on Sash members and advice office workers for support.

In Jansenville, 'which was beleaguered because it had an active group of youth, Shelagh Hurley and I used to hold an advice office day regularly in the home of a marvellous old lady, Nellie McGee Grootboom. The police used to surround the house and make notes of all who came in and out. Then Nellie's grandson Temba was killed by the *kitskonstabels* [auxiliary policemen] and Shelagh and I attended the funeral. Nellie was undaunted and we continued to run our regular sessions in her house.'[50]

'The youth in Cookhouse wanted an advice office, so Cate Turner (who was then working in the PE office) and I went up and helped them form a committee, found a venue and a bit of start-up funding. Cate then went up and stayed in the township for a week to do training and get them going. The first night she was there the police arrived at 3 am and took her off for questioning. Cate was undaunted and most irate and refused to answer any questions "until you give me a cigarette". That advice office ran for some years and really made a difference in the community.'[51]

Judy described Klipplaat as 'the most back-of-beyond place. Shelagh and I used to stay with a marvellous old lady, "old soldier" she called herself, Ma Lilian Blaauw, and ran an advice office from a local church hall. We also ran workshops on committee management and the like. Lilian's son Mannetjie and I used to distribute *Saamstaan* [a community newssheet] to the surrounding towns; he was always in hiding so it was risky. He is now mayor of Ikwezi Municipality there.'[52]

Judy, together with Shelagh, Cate and also Cathy Binell, helped many other Eastern Cape towns to establish advice offices, providing training and support, and visited them often, taking statements from people who had suffered at the hands of the police. Her reports provide an impressive account of the extent of the repression in the area – reports which went not only to the Black Sash itself, but to the Sash's funding partners abroad, spreading awareness of conditions that were generally out of the public eye.

In Grahamstown, Rosemary Smith takes pride in having been instrumental in employing Cherryl Walker as the first fieldworker and researcher for the Albany region in 1986. Now a highly respected professor of sociology at the University of Stellenbosch, Cherryl was an excellent appointment. Her meticulous research, detailed reports and an ability to communicate with many different people laid a firm foundation for the work. She started in August 1986, when three key members of the volunteer group were in detention. It was nearly two months into the state of emergency. Her task was to coordinate and develop the work of the volunteers, to ensure ongoing monitoring of events, to maintain systems of documentation and analysis, as well as dissemination of information, and to keep in touch with other groups with similar objectives. Cherryl laid the foundations for this work in Grahamstown, and when in 1987 she moved to Durban, her successor, Janet Small, was able to take over where she had left off.

In her report for July 1987, Janet listed the detention in Port Elizabeth of Murphy Morobe and Mohammed Valli Moosa, 'two of the last remaining UDF national executive committee members' who had been in hiding for over a year, and noted the murder near Kingwilliamstown of Eric Mntonga of the Institute for a Democratic South Africa (IDASA). In Grahamstown itself, threatening graffiti messages had been directed towards Black Sash members and a muti-lated doll hung on the door of one woman's house. While there was good news that Sash member Janet Cherry had been released in Port Elizabeth after almost a year in detention, Sue Lund of Grahamstown would be 'alone in a cell in North End prison as the only white woman in detention in the Eastern Cape (and in the country as far as we know)'. Janet estimated that 472 people were still being held from the Albany area, and that the total number detained there since the proclamation of the nationwide state of emergency on 12 June 1986 was 1,069. A woman who had been held in North End prison for nearly a year had died, reportedly after a stroke. Organisations were working together to sustain the flow of information as well as support for detainees and for those released.[53]

Janet speaks in glowing terms of Cherryl Walker's work and her 'wonderful reports, full of information and in lyrical language'.[54] The Black Sash was greatly enriched by these full-time appointments in several regions to strengthen and coordinate the work of the volunteer monitoring groups, and to enhance links with the advice offices as well as with other organisations. Janet's own reports eloquently portray the tensions of the time, and the importance of maintaining contact with the small towns around Grahamstown where people suffered extreme repression, and often felt forgotten. The personal contacts built up were valuable and provided the main source of information when people did not trust the telephone. Not everyone would have been brave enough to undertake those long dusty drives through conflict-ridden countryside, but Janet says she felt almost as if she was in a safe bubble, protected by her white skin and by the status of the Black Sash.

That protection did not save her from being detained in May 1988 and held for over three months. When she was released, she was restricted to Cape Town, not allowed to leave her parents' house at night, not allowed to continue her work or take part in any Black Sash activity, write for publication, or speak to the press or to any group of more than five people. This was not the end of Janet Small's commitment to the Black Sash, as a few years later she became one of the fieldworkers in its Transvaal Rural Action Committee (TRAC).[55]

Janet's detention prompted the Sash to develop formal policies for the continued support of its employees in such an event – continuing to pay salaries and benefits until their release. Some of the Sash members and staff in all parts of the country who were detained in 1986 were Sandy Stewart, Louise Vale, Bridget Hilton-Barber, Ann Burroughs, Priscilla Hall, Peter Kerchoff and Victoria Vena. Those released included Annica van Gylswyk (she was forced to leave South Africa), Liz Kistner, Joy Harnden and Gille de Vlieg.[56] By the following year, some had been released and restricted: Ann Burroughs, Priscilla Hall, Joy Harnden, Bridget Hilton-Barber and Louise Vale (Albany); Sandy Stewart (Cape Eastern); and Jill Pointer and Dawn Ingle (Transvaal). Janet Cherry (Cape Eastern) was redetained, and Victoria Vena (Cape Eastern) was released.[57] The Sash protested vigorously against all these detentions.

The fieldworkers in every region had the effect of multiplying the Sash's capacity to monitor and record events, and to respond to appeals for help from far-flung areas. Their reports provided a composite picture of conflict, resistance and violent repression. They established networks with other organisations, they travelled long distances to meet communities in small towns, and they ran many risks in order to tell the reality of what they encountered. As Janet Small said in her report for July 1987, 'The Eastern Cape certainly managed to live up to its reputation as one of the most harshly repressive regions in the country during the past two weeks.'[58] In such conditions, the fieldworkers, several of whom were dedicated young men, were the highly visible presence of the Black Sash.

Support groups were important for them, and in each centre there were committees of Black Sash people who did their best to provide help and encouragement. In the event of detention support was available for staff and members alike, and the Sash tried to offer this too for other detainees, and to support the work of the Detainees' Parents Support Committee. In Grahamstown a particularly strong and well-documented programme was set up, led by Priscilla Hall. Janet Small remembers that when the police arrived to detain her, she knew exactly what she should pack and take with her to jail, thanks to Priscilla and the group.

A poem for two Janets[59]
janet, the small
beginnings are hard
hard as a rock, as a seed
hard as a prison wall

janet, the small
consolation might be
that the cell, the lock,
the cold, hard wall
acquaint you with the rock:
  against silence and fear
  you turn inward like a stone
  hug your knees, feel your bone:

    you are bone
    you are rock
    at the core
    taste the iron in your blood.

janet, the small
seed of hope in it all
is that now they are striking the rock!

Priscilla Hall and Marianne Roux wrote an account of their work, together with a small team of women, interviewing and offering support to more than 200 people as they came out of detention in the Eastern Cape. The Black Sash in the Albany region had been monitoring such detentions in ten Eastern Cape towns. In June 1987 the debriefing project began, enabling them to systematise detention data and identify trends. They suggested that the underlying purpose of detention was destabilisation or disorganisation, intended to suppress community mobilisation. Community leaders and trade union officials had been detained, redetained and warned. They were usually the ones to be interrogated, while others were never questioned or given any reason for their arrest and continued detention. 'Randomness is also strategic, as it is used to unnerve communities and break down people.'[60]

They recorded in detail the conditions in prison – the two mats and few dirty blankets as bedding, the terrible food, and the detainees' anxiety and uncertainty about their future and that of their families. They recorded, too, the support provided by the Legal Resources Centre and certain law firms, the Dependants' Conference, SACHED (the South African Committee on Higher Education), and the psychology clinic at Rhodes University and the outpatients staff at Fort England psychiatric hospital, as well as the Black Sash and individuals and families.

Equally important was the support for ex-detainees and for their families. For released detainees, the first immediate needs were medical and psychological examination and treatment. Lack of jobs and other opportunities contributed to depression and a sense of isolation. A study programme was initiated by SACHED and the Dependants' Conference, known as EWE (Each Working in Education – *ewe* also means 'yes' in Xhosa), and set up in all the towns that were part of the debriefing project.[61]

In a later report, Albany members revealed the impact of the detention of male activists on the women left behind.[62] Drawing on interviews with women in Grahamstown, Bedford, Adelaide and Fort Beaufort, they looked at the burden of coping strategies which fell on the shoulders of women, who had to face financial hardship, emotional suffering, anxiety for themselves and their families as well as for the detainee, and the need to hide their feelings and present a cheerful face. The financial support from the Dependants' Conference, together with solidarity among the relatives, helped to ease some of this load.

Priscilla Hall and Marianne Roux concluded that, although long periods of detention had a damaging effect (they mention that on average the detainees they interviewed had been held for ten months and over half were under 26), their impact had not been entirely negative. Detention had brought together hundreds of people from all over the region 'at a time when not even ten people could meet together in one township'. Activists from different organisations were thrown together and were able to engage in political discussions, which had become almost impossible anywhere else. Furthermore, the experience of their families and communities working together to provide support could sometimes contribute to a process of reorganisation.[63]

Through its projects, its advice offices and its teams of monitors, researchers and fieldworkers, the Black Sash in the Eastern Cape continued to resist the oppressive forces of apartheid. As its voice refused to be silenced, and in fact became still more effective in drawing national and international attention to the real nature of government actions, the surveillance and the threats increased.

Yet even in circumstances of arrest and detention, there was often the uncomfortable awareness that the treatment of white women was different from the conditions for black ones, and that their voices were heard in different ways and with different attention. For the Sash, this meant that in addition to speaking out, we had to be constantly aware of our task as offering skills and resources while trying not to usurp the space of those voices that were often silenced.

Located geographically on the periphery, the people of the Eastern Cape sometimes felt themselves to be marginalised in terms of national decision-making. The area was frequently described as a microcosm of the whole apartheid system, or the crucible where the suffering was greatest. In spite of this, when policies were being drafted or budgets allocated by national organisations of civil society, or in opposition political structures, the needs of the region tended to receive scant attention. For the Black Sash in that area, it was no different.

Sashers in the Eastern Cape sometimes expressed their frustration at being seen as marginal. National conferences of the Black Sash were an annual reflection of the organisation, its work, its members, its concerns. Year after year reports were prepared and decisions taken, and delegates grew to know one another and to understand the differences as well as the commonalities between their regions. The smaller regions were very conscious of the fact that they could not control the decision-making at national conferences because of the numerical superiority of Cape Town and Johannesburg. Their representatives were remarkable women, with strong views, and leaders in their own areas, but always in the minority in the Black Sash. In an effort to recognise this, the representation system provided for a minimum of three delegates from each region, even if the membership did not reach a hundred. Where there was a larger membership further delegates were added accordingly, so this situation persisted. This is reflected visually in photographs of national conferences, where two long tables each held anything from eight to twelve delegates from the large regions, and the other regions were represented by their three.

The two Natal regions, Coastal and Midlands, experienced the same inability to set the agenda of the organisation. 'We felt your power,' said Jillian Nicholson.[64] There were impressive fact papers presented and statements made about the smaller regions, but there was not enough time allocated at the conferences for discussion of some of their most pressing concerns. They felt themselves to be on the periphery, and viewed the two large regions as being always in competition for control. As part of one of the large regions, I was insufficiently sensitive to the depth of this feeling until we in Cape Western became national headquarters and had responsibility for the whole organisation – and perhaps not even then.

It has been in speaking to people all over the country that I have heard with some chagrin of their sense of having been disregarded. I believe firmly that everyone in the Black Sash acknowledged the vital importance of the work of the small regions in particular, because it was so greatly needed there. Many of us would insist that without understanding the conditions under apartheid in the Eastern Cape, one could not understand the impact of apartheid itself. Yet that was not the perception of many in those regions. This has taught me the importance not only of recognition, but of creating structures that allow for all participants to feel equally able to influence outcomes. When Mary Robinson accepted nomination for election as president of Ireland, the election campaign provided an opportunity for her to travel around the country, 'beginning a journey that changed and enriched me. I saw the beauty of the landscape and the calibre of the people in places such as Allihies [in County Cork], where I attended a conference about communities on the periphery coming together in mutual support. Their conviction that when you are on the periphery the periphery is the centre was an early lesson in the importance of small places.'[65]

Smaller communities can develop particular strengths in working together, as illustrated by the Black Sash and other organisations in the Eastern Cape. Building successful organisations and sustaining them depends on making opportunities for all their constituent parts to share responsibility and receive equal acknowledgement.

6

CREATIVITY AND INNOVATION

The seriousness of the Black Sash's work was enlivened by many of its artistic and talented members, whose creative imaginations and varied skills introduced original ideas, entertaining events and beautiful artworks. They also produced plays, wrote songs and poems, made items for fundraising and were renowned for their delicious food.

Imaginative ideas had always helped the Sash to capture public interest. The symbol of the black sash draped across a book representing the constitution and mourning its desecration, coupled with the wearing of the black sashes, became imprinted in the public mind as the image of the organisation. When it was not possible to wear the sashes, ingenious ways were found around the problem. Told they could not wear them in the public gallery of Parliament, the women bought long black gloves, and wore them at the appropriate angle. Another member sewed a black band across the front of her dress. Failing all else, a black satin rose was a good substitute.

The creation of these visual images at times resulted in profoundly moving and effective occasions. One such was the public meeting of the Black Sash's annual national conference in 1988, held in the Claremont Civic Centre in Cape Town. It was opened with a silent procession that moved slowly from the back of the hall up to the stage, where each member laid a white carnation on the platform while Di Bishop read the names of those who had died while held in detention by the security police. This act of memory and mourning held the audience in spellbound silence. Many years later I was told of a young German researcher working in the archives at the University of Cape Town who broke into tears as he read the account.

Another imaginative idea from the early days was the 'haunting' of cabinet ministers. This certainly had the effect of humiliating them, and they did their best to avoid such encounters at airports, train stations, public meetings, even restaurants. The planning of these 'haunts' required considerable ingenuity. A system was devised whereby each minister was allocated a flower as a code name. Joan Pare, a leading member of the Cape Western region, was a professional florist, and her office was used to transmit messages and arrange assignations such as 'Roses need to be met at Cape Town central station at 11.00 am on Wednesday' or 'Orchids will be delivered to Johannesburg airport at noon on Friday'. Interviewed decades later, Joan said triumphantly, 'They never cracked our code.'

In 1993 a small team worked together to design and print a Black Sash cloth to celebrate the long-negotiated Interim Constitution, which was to pave the way for the national elections of 1994. Inspired by the tradition of celebratory African fabrics, they chose symbols of the Sash's own story – the black sash itself, the black roses that were sometimes a substitute for the sash, the map of Africa, the dove of peace, and a golden border representing sheaves of corn. For the central medallion they selected 'Amanda Louw', the sturdy Black Sasher invented by the poet and illustrator Gus Ferguson, her name almost an anagram for Womandla, her sash draped from the 'wrong' shoulder, her arm raised and her fist clenched in perennial protest. Patricia Davison, with her expert knowledge of commemorative cloths in Africa, sparked early ideas. Such cloths had been used for over a hundred years to celebrate events and people in many countries on the continent, and were a distinctively African method of communication as well as an adornment.[1]

This Black Sash commemorative cloth was an appropriate way to welcome the political changes taking place and to recall that nearly 40 years earlier the organisation had arisen out of a constitutional issue. Members received its creation with delight, and it had great success at the annual morning market, sold as cloth but also made up into shirts, waistcoats, a noticeboard, shopping bags and backpacks. The design was reproduced on the covers of a leaflet and several annual reports. 'The Black Sash will be sold by the metre' advertised the *Cape Times*, and both it and the *Southern Suburbs Tatler* published photographs of the cloth being worn in various forms.

Many Black Sash women grew up in situations in which they were encouraged to acquire domestic and artistic skills, with a focus on managing their own homes. Seen in the context of a society where they were part of a privileged minority, these skills might be thought frivolous, but the women found ways to put their abilities into a wider challenge to change the nature of the society itself. A major vehicle for fundraising through creative work in several regions was the annual morning market or Black Sash fete. Held in church or municipal halls, or in the large gardens of some members, these sales not only provided a major contribution to the regional budgets but created strong bonds of friendship and solidarity as the women – and often their supportive male friends and families – worked together in preparation.

The first of these fundraising ventures, in December 1957, was described in the *Sash* magazine: 'The members of the Johannesburg Region showed themselves to be women of many parts when they held a Morning Market at Mrs D. Hill's home early in December. An almost bewildering variety of Christmas fare was on sale and one wondered where members had found time to make the many beautiful articles for sale on the needle-work, novelty and children's stalls. The total amount raised by this venture was over 730 pounds!'[2]

For all the years that followed, similar events took place around the country. For months beforehand members would knit, sew, make preserves and jams, gather second-hand books and other articles, or create decorations for Christmas and other special occasions. Many of us found ourselves acquiring new skills in a variety of crafts. I remember spending many hilarious days learning how to do batik work and manage melting wax on cloths or shirts. At branch meetings, while listening to reports or an invited speaker, we kept our hands busy producing massive artificial flowers at a time when these were a passing fashion. Long-time national president Jean Sinclair was renowned for her Black Rose floor polishing wax, which could be bought at Thrupps, a well-known Johannesburg supermarket, as well as at our annual markets.

In the final days before the market, expert cooks and willing sous-chefs filled various kitchens to produce wonderful pies, salads and other gourmet items. Every member, skilled baker or not, was exhorted to provide a number of cakes, and the cake stall was always sold out before the morning was halfway through. A four-part series of recipe books, titled *Cordon Noir*, is now a coveted collector's item. Christmas puddings and Christmas cakes were made in large quantities, often mixed in a bathtub at Sarah-Anne Raynham's house. She also made her kitchen available for a series of lessons in vegetarian cooking.

One of Cape Western region's members, Ann van der Riet, recalls that 'the annual Black Sash fete, as well as being one of the main fundraisers, was also an opportunity for some fun. Our Media Group came up with some great ideas for screenprinted slogans such as "For this I went to university", "A woman's place is in the struggle" and "Equal opportunity apron", which were printed onto aprons and other fabrics. We produced mugs too, one saying "War is not healthy for children and other living things", and another "Overconsumption, racism, sexism, pollution, dogmatism are *also* unhealthy for children and other living things". We made greetings cards from three of Marguerite Bolland's etchings, and of course Amanda Louw's picture as well as pictures of the "Creatures" which were the inventions of the irrepressible Gus Ferguson. The Womandla lady was not only used for cards – she was also used for the design of wrapping paper, on T-shirts and of course the wonderful little leather badges. We all found the designing of the cards and wrapping paper, the layout and getting the printing done a very rewarding exercise.'[3]

Gus Ferguson donated his original creation of Womandla and her alter ego, Amanda Louw, to the Sash, where she took on a life of her own. Among her many appearances were the T-shirts and tablecloths printed by the Gardens branch on fabrics provided by Cassandra Parker, who remembers them being hung out to dry on the branches of trees in her garden. Other writers, artists and cartoonists were generous supporters, too. In Johannesburg in the 1950s and 1960s, Bob Connolly was prolific in his cartoons depicting the Black Sash in full haunting mode, and he gave several of his originals to individual members and to the organisation. In Cape Town the Media Group organised three annual calendars of cartoons for sale, and were particularly grateful to the cartoonist Tony Grogan of the *Cape Times* for donating his work and being involved in the selection for these calendars. The 1987 and 1991 calendars consisted entirely of his cartoons; while the one for 1989 had four each of Grogan's, Zapiro's and Stent's work.

The Cape Town potter Hyme Rabinowitz and other artists also willingly donated work. Black Sash members were diligent in their search for desirable items, and some were known for their ability to garner treasures for the markets. Lily Herbstein used to say that her friends hid their favourite treasures when she visited them, for fear of being obliged to donate them to her 'white elephant' stall. These morning market occasions brought friends and supporters of the Black Sash, as well as members of the curious public, to spend their time and money and see a different side of the organisation. They provided an opportunity for earnest conversation about the state of the nation at the tea and coffee tables, but also evidence that Black Sash members and their families had a variety of interests and talents, in addition to their deep concern for justice and equality.

Fundraising was necessary all year round. Some Black Sash members had beautiful gardens, and were willing to make them available for shows and afternoon teas, and to sell plants and flowers to swell the coffers. Flowers were available for pleasure too – seldom would the Sash hold a monthly membership meeting, or a public meeting in a large hall, without a magnificent display of flowers provided and arranged by one or more of its enthusiastic members.

Jenny de Tolly came up with the idea of auctions with a difference: 'dream auctions', where the item offered might be a dinner for eight catered in one's own home by one of the Sash's excellent cooks, or a weekend in someone's beautiful beachside cottage. Sue van der Merwe (later a deputy minister in the new Parliament) was a vibrant and outrageous auctioneer at events that included dinner (provided by members, of course) and even a fashion show of 'boutique' clothing donated for sale. At one particularly hilarious evening, some unlisted items were auctioned: the company for dinner of Sue's husband, the MP Tiaan van der Merwe, and of Charles Grover, much-loved volunteer bookkeeper and husband of the regional secretary, Joan Grover. The hilarity of the evening was enhanced by the wine provided by Jenny, whose family produced the Thelema wines. In those years, when the vineyard was new, some of the first wines, not considered ready to be launched onto the open market and suitably named La Rejection, were greatly enjoyed at Sash functions.

The Black Sash was fortunate to have several highly competent amateur photographers among its members, and their work forms a valuable part of the organisation's records. It was also the beneficiary of the professional skill and ongoing commitment of Gille de Vlieg, who was involved in many of the important projects of the Black Sash, whether it was the resistance against forced removals, the opposition to growing militarisation, the strengthening of women's groups and, eventually, voter education and preparation for the 1994 elections. She was a member of the AFRAPIX collective of photographers and over the years she has exhibited widely in South Africa and internationally. In September 2012 Gille participated in an exhibition on 'The rise and fall of apartheid' in New York, at the International Center of Photography, where her work attracted considerable attention. A review pointed out: 'as this show suggests, theater became an important element in both apartheid-era politics and photography, as in pictures of the Women's Defense of the Constitution League, known as the Black Sash, in the mid-1950s. A coalition of white women opposed to apartheid, its members staged choreographed protests, standing, impeccably dressed, in silent formation, all wearing identical black sashes over one shoulder. This is how they appear, holding placards on the steps of Johannesburg City Hall, in an enlarged 1956 photo dominating the first floor. They make an unforgettable sight. And while their performance – that's what it is – may have been directed toward a street audience, it was also calculatedly photogenic.'[4]

A year after the New York exhibition, a performing arts programme in Mississippi state created and produced a play inspired by Gille's photographs. Tonya Hays explained how it came about: 'I saw an exhibit on apartheid in the Museum of Photography in NYC last year. I was intrigued by the many pictures of the women with the Black Sashes and asked in the gift shop who they were. I was told very little but that the organization started out with a few women who decided to make a difference.

'I work with the WINGS Performing Arts Program at the Lynn Meadows Discovery Center, a not-for-profit children's museum in Gulfport, Mississippi. Our program is dedicated to nurturing talent, spirit and leadership in children and youth, through quality performing arts programs, community service and leadership opportunities. Three of my high school girls became fascinated with the Black Sash and wanted to collaborate on a play about your incredible work. We all read everything we could get our hands on, including books we ordered. We also were able to meet with a couple of South Africans who grew up during apartheid.

'The cast and crew of the show have learned so much through their research on this play, apartheid and what a difference a small group of people can make.'[5]

The Black Sash itself found some unsuspected dramatic talents among members. There were various plays devised and performed in different regions, some for educational purposes such as voter education, some for entertainment. Two plays put together and performed by members of the Cape Western region caused much amusement. The first was largely devised by Annemarie Hendrikz, for performance at an all-day First Cape Women's Festival, organised by FSAW and held in the Samaj Centre in Rylands, Cape Town, in April 1988.[6] It portrayed the way the Black Sash originated, with members frantically making dozens of phone calls to rally support, and with founding Cape Town member Noël Robb in a leading role, and then went on to show the protest demonstrations. Annemarie provided an outrageous commentary, first as a tennis-playing housewife and then as a street-seller of newspapers; her representation of the security police's Special Branch was the waving aloft of a tree's branch. Coming amid a day of serious speeches and angry struggle songs, this light-hearted take-off by the Black Sash brought the release of laughter. Several comments expressed astonishment at the ability of the organisation to laugh at itself, and the play probably brought about some revised opinions about those middle-class white women.

The second play was presented as entertainment at a Black Sash national conference, and took the form of an allegorical life story of 'Samantha Sash'. I was apparently a natural choice to take the role of Samantha's 'Mother Mary' and Samantha herself was played by Thisbe Clegg, first seen in a baby's basket, then growing up in a middle-class family taking ballet and riding lessons and being groomed for marriage to a suitable young man, portrayed by an all-in-one piece of underwear stuffed with cushions. Alas, Samantha was led astray by a progressive friend, with Sue Philcox in this role, who introduced her to the occasional use of marijuana and to left-wing politics.

Samantha was transformed into a typically over-extended activist and inevitably attracted the attention of the security police. All this was counterpointed by a subversive group of singing women acting as a Greek chorus in a closet.

Singing had been a central element of resistance throughout South African history, and Black Sash women learned to sing in mass meetings and in smaller groups. We learned to sing hymns, to worry about the violence expressed in some of the struggle songs but to sing them anyway, and to give voice to what was to become the South African national anthem long before most white South Africans had even heard of it. We also learned international songs of resistance, like 'Bread and roses' and 'We shall overcome'. Still more avant-garde was the creation of brilliantly topical rap songs by Marj Brown, sometimes learned and performed by groups of delegates at conferences.

Many forms of music are integral to the South African story, and the organising committee for one of the Black Sash national conferences decided to arrange for some local musicians to play during the dinner party held as part of the conference entertainment. A new band named Amampondo was starting to make its name in Cape Town, and was invited to perform. The dinner was held at my house and, rather to the astonishment of my family, the musicians appeared early in the afternoon to prepare for the event. They requested electric heaters to warm the skins of their drums, and generally took over the verandah for their instruments. The guests arrived, the musicians played and, as the evening wore on, the decibels rose. Fascinated neighbours hung over the hedge, and I heard next day that one young spectator ran home and breathlessly announced to his parents, 'Listen, listen, the revolution has started in the Burtons' garden.'

Among the members and supporters of the Black Sash were museum and gallery curators and highly talented and successful artists, including women like Marguerite Bolland and Sheila Nowers, who willingly contributed their skills in various ways, including donating some of their works. In Durban, Coral Vinsen, a member of the Black

Sash and the Detainees Parents' Support Committee, and Lorna Ferguson, also a Black Sash member, were instrumental in putting together a project to celebrate International Human Rights Day on 10 December 1988. They formed the Artists for Human Rights committee which organised two major events – a workshop for teenagers, and an exhibition of entries for a national art and photographic competition. In 1990 an exhibition was held showing selected works by the young people at the workshop, and in subsequent years Coral organised AIDS awareness and human rights art exhibitions. In 1996 she convened a committee which produced a limited-edition print portfolio of 'Images of human rights'. She has continued to work in this field and to be actively involved in the Artists for Human Rights Trust.[7]

In the 1950s, when the Group Areas Act was dividing South Africa's cities into racially segregated zones, Eulalie Stott was instrumental in producing a film, *Notice to Quit*, which told the tragic stories of the people who were being forced to move. The film was made by Esdon Frost, who was the brother of Joan Grover, later to become a very active member of the Sash in Cape Town. Decades later a project was initiated by Cassandra Parker and Denise Ackermann to record some of the early history of the Sash by filming interviews with founding members. This developed into the film *The Black Sash: The Early Years*, which was produced and directed by Cassandra, Denise and the Cape Town filmmaker Nodi Murphy, and was made with almost entirely voluntary work.[8] A number of the original 1955 members were interviewed, and then a group was brought together to exchange memories. The film is a marvellous portrayal of those intrepid women, whom Jenny de Tolly described as 'those funky women who are our ancestors'.[9]

During the 1980s, when many organisations banded together in the United Democratic Front, large joint meetings were held in halls in a variety of centres and towns. It became common practice for each organisation to put up a banner to signify its presence and support, while also providing a strong and clear image for television coverage. Delighted in particular by the End Conscription Campaign's creative use of words and images, a group of members wanted to see the Black Sash also producing its own banners and projecting a more modern approach. Some of the new banners were beautiful works in themselves. Sheila Nowers, a noted artist and miniaturist, was an inspiring creator of some, but did not wish to be acknowledged at the time. When the banners were displayed at Sash meetings, or used in publications, they sometimes stimulated debate about the motifs, with more traditional members asking, 'Since when did the Black Sash symbol become a tree, instead of the sash itself?' Nevertheless, the banners made a strong impact and were proudly displayed.[10]

Many members were engaged in producing publicity material that was intended to make a public statement or get a public message across. Cape Western's Media Group participated in the production of leaflets, which would be distributed by one Sash member during a protest stand while the others stood silently with the posters. Ann van der Riet recalls 'the pamphlet explaining the truth about the massacre by the South African Defence Force in May 1978 at SWAPO's Angolan camp of Kassinga[11] – an awful message. I am not sure how or where we distributed these, but I do remember very clearly getting a phone call from Beva Runciman telling me that the pamphlet had been banned – she was very proud of the fact that this was the first product of the Sash to be banned. I am sure whoever did the banning could hardly have realised that their action had made us proud.'

The same Media Group also produced various stickers: 'Apartheid free zone', 'All God's beaches for all God's children', 'No constitution based on colour'. 'The layout, design and organisation of many of these items gave the group a great deal of pleasure,' Ann van der Riet remembers, 'and the creativity involved was somehow a release from the tensions of their messages. The meetings to discuss them were also fun – lots of laughter in spite of the seriousness of projects.'

The production of ideas was equally important. Finding the right words for posters held in protest stands was a constant challenge. A team would get together and brainstorm ideas, inspiring one another to choose the best, most concise phrase to make the necessary point, often with very little time to bring it all together. Others would opt for the painting of the words onto the posters – carefully, precisely, clearly legible even from a distance. Some of the wording was truly memorable. One of the earliest referred to the passing of the Senate Act: its words 'Legal now, immoral forever' were to be used several times over the years as unjust laws were successively enacted. To mark the opening of Parliament in 1958, Cape Western members managed to commandeer a large lorry on which they created a float displaying the words 'Justice, freedom, democracy'.

During the 1980s, as young people of South Africa became more and more active in the struggle to bring about change, many of them were taken into detention for lengthy periods without any charge or trial. The Black Sash took up the issue, and produced documents, organised protests, and participated in campaigns to bring an end to this practice. Joyce Harris wrote a 'Memorandum on the sufferings of children in South Africa' in April 1986. Then, too, Black Sash's creative members put their skills to use in joint action with others in the Free the Children campaign. They arranged for a day when hundreds gathered to release yellow balloons into the sky. Ann Finsen had the ingenious idea of yellow T-shirt-shaped stickers printed with 'Free the children' and 'Children need peace'. These were soon to be seen everywhere. Mary Livingstone found them reminiscent of a similar venture in the very early days of the Sash, when small buttons – paper circles – were printed with the words 'Defend our constitution', and were worn as lapel buttons, or dropped into sugar bowls in restaurants and tea rooms, or slipped into library books and the magazines in doctors' waiting rooms.

Working in support of the End Conscription Campaign, the Cape Town Media Group also printed posters: 'Our children need peace not bullets, 'Their right to share a future without war'. Brightly coloured sweatshirts printed with 'Another mother for peace' were popular, and T-shirts carried a variety of witty slogans with a tough punch.

In 1985, at the height of official repression and popular resistance, a meeting of the Southern Transvaal regional council of Black Sash discussed the question of violence again. Sheena Duncan shared the news of women in the United States who had made a peace ribbon that year, to mark the 40th anniversary of the bombing of Hiroshima.[12] Pieces of cloth had been made into banners, each representing a symbol of peace or a statement against violence, and the banners were then attached to each other. When completed, the ribbon was ten miles long, more than enough to tie around the intended target – the Pentagon. The regional council decided that this would be a way for women in South Africa to express a similar abhorrence of the spreading violence in the country. Other NGOs were contacted and meetings of women's organisations were held in October 1985. The outcome was a new umbrella body, the Committee of Concerned Women (CCW), which was given the task of coordinating the making of a peace ribbon in South Africa. The chair was Ethel Walt, of the Southern Transvaal Black Sash.

CCW issued a pamphlet titled *Join Up and Make the Peace Ribbon*. The pamphlet and letters of invitation, to make a positive contribution for 'a just peace and a new South Africa', were distributed through NGOs and other institutions opposed to apartheid. They hoped 'in the making of our South African Peace Ribbon to bring South Africans closer together' and explained the necessary requirements: pieces had to be 60 cm from top to bottom and of any length; they could be made from any cloth and the concept of peace could be shown using paint, embroidery or appliqué; and because the ribbon could not be used to promote any organisation, the names or logos of organisations should not appear.

Women responded in exceedingly creative ways. One woman, herself in detention for organising a protest against children in detention, took her T-shirt off in prison, unravelled her prison blanket and sewed her square with these materials. She smuggled the piece out of prison for it to become a part of this rich tapestry and testament to the courage and determination of women. Women from outside South Africa heard of the peace ribbon and also began sending squares as well, in solidarity.

At meetings organised by CCW, broader aspects of the anti-apartheid struggle were discussed and women's role within this. For example, on 13 February 1986 the committee issued letters of invitation to a panel discussion on 'Women in crisis', held at the Temple Emanuel, in Johannesburg. A report sent out with this invitation summarised a talk given by Albertina Sisulu, one of the patrons of the UDF, quoting her as saying that the peace ribbon offered South African women an opportunity to reach out to the many whites 'who are horrified by the present violence in our country'. In a later newsletter, three speakers were reported as addressing a meeting of the CCW – an ex-detainee, a member of the Soweto Parents' Crisis Committee and a white mother. The committee was indeed bringing women of all walks of life together in South Africa.[13] Suggestions for action followed and a telegram was sent protesting against the detention of children.

Under the state of emergency then in force, many meetings were prohibited, and even the peace ribbon was seen as a threat: permission was refused to show the ribbon on 3 and 13 April 1986 at the City Hall and Zoo Lake, respectively. Despite this, the ribbon was displayed wherever women who supported it were gathered in defiance of state policies. Often, because of its size, only sections of the ribbon were used. According to Ethel Walt, before a display of the peace ribbon was allowed, a member of the City Council perused each piece carefully and decided which pieces could be used. This sparked off a debate among the women: some wanted to use only the pieces that were allowed by the state, while others said there should be no self-censorship on the part of the women.

Most of this activity took place in the Johannesburg region, where the Black Sash kept the peace ribbon, but the pieces came from all over the country and some from abroad. Harriet Gavshon was inspired to make a film called *The Ribbon*, monitoring the first eight months of the making of the ribbon, which eventually grew in length to more than 500 metres. The film showed how the women of the Black Sash, as well as from other traditionally white organisations, united with women from Soweto and others to form a new identity as women from all classes opposed to the victimisation of their sons by apartheid and to the brutality of apartheid. Conscription, policing, repression and military aggression were focal points in galvanising the women portrayed in the film,[14] which went on to be a finalist in the 1988 American Film and Video Film Festival.

The ECC organised a march with the peace ribbon for 28 October 1986, and for months before the march about 50 women planned and held workshops in anticipation of the event. The main aim of the march was to protest against 'the increased militarisation of our society'.[15] Six prominent anti-apartheid activists were due to head the march: Sheena Duncan, Leah Tutu, Winnie Mandela, Molly Sklaar, Emma Mashinini and Albertina Sisulu. Just shortly before the march, Mozambican President Samora Machel's plane crashed under mysterious circumstances, causing the VIPs to withdraw from the march in the ensuing chaos of the days that followed. The marchers decided to carry sections of the peace ribbon, as they would converge on the Wits Command military headquarters from different directions. A spy alerted the police to the intended march, with the result that streets leading to Wits Command were cordoned off and armoured cars and police with dogs were waiting as small groups of women approached the building, with pieces of the ribbon. Only 15 women got through the roadblocks and were sitting down outside Wits Command when ordered to disperse. They refused and were arrested. Of these, six elected to plead not guilty when arrested, and were sentenced to five days' imprisonment. The police confiscated the sections of the peace ribbons carried by the women who managed to get through the cordons. When Ethel Walt wrote to the police to request the return of the sections of peace ribbon, she was told they had been burnt.

Women who were involved in making pieces of the ribbon have reflected on their involvement in this project. 'In the 1980s everything was banned ... the ribbon was something we could do ... it made one feel part of a broader women's movement and no-one could come into your house and tell you that you could not sew your views onto this piece of cloth; they could not take your creative spirit away' – Ethel Walt. 'The peace ribbon had such a wide range of contributors, it was a melting pot. There was a strong gender component to it. Women needed to do something creative during this militaristic time, in the deep darkness of apartheid. The peace ribbon brought in many people who felt powerless. Some of our leaders now have no understanding of the '80s, and reject this time. If so, they do not understand the deep pain' – Gille de Vlieg. 'The peace ribbon was a symbolic expression of a vision of a different society. Different groups of women used it in different ways. It had adaptability, but spoke to many in our society. Currently much of the heritage stuff is big stuff, yet this ribbon reminds us of ordinary people who in a group made little responses, little actions, to contribute to fighting apartheid' – Adele Kirsten (chair of the ECC and leader of the march to Wits Command).

Of all the creative and dedicated tasks of the Black Sash, its magazine, *Sash*, produced over nearly 40 years by members on an entirely voluntary basis, was the most sustained and important. Started as a weekly newsletter, it underwent many changes over the years and served as a vital part of the organisation's communication with its members and the public. It was a vehicle for the ideas and knowledge of the leadership and of the many members who wrote articles for it or engaged with some of its debates. It informed members about a variety of political issues, building unity and confidence. It offered a platform for the expression of different political opinions, and invited many distinguished academics and activists to write articles. It had a series of highly dedicated editors, only some of whom had professional experience.

By 1985 the magazine had become a quarterly, and Glenda Webster was recruited for the task of editor. She continued to produce the *Sash* editions for a year or so after the national headquarters moved to Cape Town in 1986, including the only issue against which the government took action, that of May 1986, volume 29, number 1.[16] It was seized from the premises of the printer, Pacific Press, before most of the copies had been distributed (with the exception of those destined for Cape Western members, who thereby acquired a piece of memorabilia). Despite letters from the Black Sash's legal adviser, Raymond Tucker, the magazines were never returned.

The Cape Town team, which was to produce the magazine for its last seven years, took over from Glenda, and its first issue was published in February 1987. Its editor was Candy Malherbe, with the assistance of an editorial committee whose names and special areas of expertise are listed in it. This was to be the practice for the following years, with various editors alternating the responsibility for the specific issues.[17]

The magazine illustrates yet again how Black Sash members worked together to bring to the organisation their professional and artistic abilities. Even though most of the editorial committee members had full-time or part-time occupations, by sharing the tasks they were able to produce an excellent and factually reliable journal that not only served the needs of the Black Sash, but was also of great interest to a wider national and international readership. The final issue appeared in May 1995 under the guest editorship of Moira Levy, and included on its first page an overview by Sue Philcox of the magazine's 40-year history. She ended her survey by saying, 'The 37 volumes of *Sash* provide a running commentary on a dark period in our country and an organisation comprising a small group of middle-class, white women who soldiered on and are at last living in a country of which they can be proud.'

Some of the most creative women were also those at the forefront of the political work of the Black Sash. The work was stressful and demanding, confronting a cruel and unjust system, and many Black Sash activists found solace in working with their hands as well as their brains. Sheena Duncan's exquisite embroidery of altar cloths used the finest gold thread to create beautiful designs. Admirers of Jean Sinclair were at pains to stress that not only was she a sound political thinker and a brilliant strategist, but also a skilled seamstress who made all her own and her daughters' clothes. A set of beautiful table mats she had made was offered as a prize in a fundraising competition. In all regions, members ensured that the platforms at public meetings were decorated with magnificent flower arrangements. Skilled gardeners held garden parties as a regular means of boosting the organisation's income. Fetes and morning markets were famous for wonderful food and beautiful needlework. Bunty Aitchison is remembered for her fine garden and her magnificent baskets of flowers, and her charming manner. She was also courageous and forthright when voicing her firm opinions, and her life was one of commitment to the cause of equality and human rights. She chaired the Claremont branch for many years, from its first meeting on 2 February 1956.[18] Ingenious and quirky, others found the perfect gift for Annemarie Hendrikz when she moved back into the rural development sector in 1995: a wheelbarrow painted with the colours and design of South Africa's new flag.

The eventual demise of apartheid in South Africa was brought about by a multiplicity of efforts, mainly the upsurge of resistance within the country and the international pressure exerted on the National Party government. A part – possibly a small part – of that pressure was built up by the participation of many organisations, including the Black Sash, in exposing the injustices of the regime. Every member of the Black Sash found a way to contribute in whatever way was possible and appropriate for her, and was able to replenish herself at the wellspring of creativity and solidarity when her energy or optimism flagged.

7

RIPPLES OF CHANGE

The decade between 1965 and 1975 spelt isolation and frustration for the Black Sash. The ruling party seemed impervious to all appeals and protest, the opposition inside Parliament and outside powerless, the white population uncaring. In fact the government portrayed all opposition outside the official apartheid structures as part of a revolutionary mobilisation. Its response was to proscribe black organisations, imprison or persecute their leaders, limit the rights of Africans to the 'white' cities and shunt off the rightless and the unemployed to the 'reserves' where they were to enjoy citizenship in newly created, ostensibly independent 'homelands'. While people defined as 'coloured' or 'Indian' were offered a limited measure of control over their lives, African people were to be denied their South African citizenship and participation in the single, common economy. Migrant labour, resettlement policies, widespread poverty and unemployment continued to create misery for millions of black South Africans.

From the government the Black Sash met with hostility and rejection. From the majority of the white community it faced anger and ostracism. At the same time, most black leaders viewed white people with good intentions as doing no more than soften the edges of the apartheid system. They could not expect that any real change would come from the work of such a small organisation of women, even if some recognised that the Black Sash was at least demonstrating its commitment to a society not built on racism. Indeed, with the growth of black consciousness in the late 1960s a growing number of black leaders argued that change would only come when black people developed their own organisations and built up their power and capacity. Multiracial initiatives such as discussion groups, women's activities, children's parties and social events became more and more difficult to organise, and were often experienced as artificial, even if some valued friendships were created. One black participant said, 'I can't keep coming to these parties. They make me feel soft towards you white people, but these times need me to be hard.' As Jennifer Scott commented, 'By 1962 the Sash was increasingly both politically isolated and impotent. These were to be the defining characteristics of the organisation in the coming decade.'[1]

The Sash was realistic in its assessment that it would not by itself achieve any of the changes it knew to be necessary. It might have been tempted to give up the lonely struggle. Other organisations with similar goals were finding it difficult to sustain membership. Protest activity was curtailed by stringent legislation and fundraising was not easy, particularly after the government restricted funding from abroad in the early 1970s. Yet day after day, the Black Sash advice offices were filled with African people seeking help. If ever the organisation might have thought of giving up, that fact alone would have deterred it. So it simply kept on doing what it believed to be right, trying to help where possible and keep pressing for change.

In 1974 it was difficult to imagine that apartheid could be overcome. Seeing little prospect of major change, the Sash had recommended at least some immediate steps which could be taken. These included building houses for families in the centres where employment opportunities lay; providing freehold tenure for people in the common area where they actually lived, not only in the 'reserves'; removing the curbs on industrial growth and expansion in the existing urban areas; stopping the mass removals of settled communities; giving all

South Africans freedom of movement; and abolishing the pass laws. It concluded, 'These things are *not* impossible. We say we cannot do them because we do not want to do them. Nothing whatever can justify the maintenance of the South African migrant labour system. We have already destroyed everything of value for millions of people. We must build, not bulldoze.'[2]

Yet they had little hope that these things would ever be done. In August 1974, together with the Programme for Social Change,[3] the Black Sash organised a consultation in Johannesburg on migrant labour. Professor Francis Wilson outlined the existing situation, concluding that efforts to change it would best be directed at the micro-level, drawing in churches and universities, bringing pressure to bear on employers, working towards the recognition of trade unions, and disseminating information.[4] That conclusion illustrated why Sash members had little optimism. These micro-level strategies were similar to those they had been undertaking for years, with no visible result.

In March 1975 the Black Sash's national conference marked the twenty years of its existence, and in a major address (which was her last as national president) Jean Sinclair reviewed its history in the context of ever tighter restrictions on human rights and liberties. She said, 'in the early years we may have been euphoric; we certainly were hopeful that with constant pressure we would be able to rouse the White public to take action of some kind … there was excitement, even fun at times … As the years passed so did the light-heartedness we once had. Life became grim and we were absorbed in helping Africans through the maze of the pass laws and trying to make White South Africans realise what it would be like to be Black … there has been a steady erosion of our civil liberties and our basic human rights.'[5] She cited examples of the legislation which had curtailed the right to freedom of assembly, which prevented any organisation declared 'affected' from receiving funds from abroad, which restricted the freedom of universities, which allowed for censorship and limitations on the media, and which forbade non-racial political parties.

In spite of its strong sense of being confronted with an intractable situation, the Black Sash took 'change and action' as its theme for this 1975 national conference. The Cape Western region, as hosts, and the headquarters committee in Johannesburg devised a comprehensive programme, drawing in guest speakers to attract the public and provide the background for the discussions. The opening night audience heard Jean Sinclair and also Helen Suzman, the Progressive Party MP. She paid tribute to Jean, and to the Black Sash, noting its 'transformation from the large and fashionable body of women who haunted Ministers in the Fifties to the small and remarkable band of women who comprise it today; who unfailingly have protested against the repugnant discriminatory legislation, who had stood in rain and cold and burning sun, enduring the taunts, insults and eggs hurled at them, who drove into Langa with lorry loads of food during the dark days after Sharpeville, and most of all who have year in and year out manned the Advice Offices into which thousands of desperate Africans have streamed, seeking a helping hand to guide them through the morass of the pass laws ... The quiet persistence of the Sash ... has had its effects over the years ... I never hesitate to send overseas visitors to Advice Offices – I think that a couple of hours spent in one of them is far more instructive than any amount of talking to politicians.'[6]

In a session (led by Mangosuthu Buthelezi) considering the future role and direction of the Black Sash, Margaret Nash, Sash member and important voice in church structures, said, 'There will come a time when all parties will sit together at the bargaining table and we will have to know what we and the other peoples want.' Other members had referred to the need to consider the country's economic organisation and the production and distribution of wealth, observing that real power lies where the money is and that a vote alone does not constitute active democracy. The Sash was looking towards the future and preparing itself for what lay ahead.

Regional reports to the 1975 conference showed that in spite of the overarching gloom about government repression and public apathy,

Sash members everywhere had created ways to record events, to protest and to ease suffering. Delegates who had come to the conference feeling exhausted and hopeless found ideas for work which would be possible for them, and which would contribute to an overall plan to sustain pressure on the government. A public statement from the conference affirmed its demand: 'The Black Sash calls for direct representation of all South African people in the South African government. Democracy can function only with the consent of the governed. The National Party itself recognises the need for participation of all races in the governing process through the establishment of ethnic councils, but denies them real power which is at present in the hands of the central government. Therefore, direct representation therein is an immediate essential for all South Africa's people.'

Letters of thanks to Cape Western region after the conference convey some of the sense of renewed energy it had generated. Sheena Duncan, newly elected national president, wrote: 'We all came back feeling stimulated, justified, and full of new ideas for action. It really was a great achievement on your part because I think all Regions were having ... doubts about our future ... and I think they now all see quite clearly that we still have a very definite role to play and they also have ideas as to how to play it.' She added thanks for 'the injection of enthusiasm you have managed to give at a time when we were all uncertain as to where to go next'.

The apartheid government may have appeared immovable to the Black Sash at that time. Yet when we look back 40 years later, we can see that simultaneously there were many harbingers of change. We may not always have recognised them, but events were taking place that were often beyond the influence of the government. The citizens of other southern African countries were also increasing the levels of their resistance to apartheid and oppression. Within South Africa clandestine mobilisation was ongoing, even though many paid heavy penalties of imprisonment, detention without trial, and even death. The years ahead would show the strength of that resistance despite the brutality of the government response to popular developments.

After the long 'Indian summer' of the 1960s, when the white regime managed to check the winds of change sweeping across Africa by a combination of economic growth and draconian repression, the 1970s saw South Africa enter a state of permanent crisis that was both economic and political in origin and expression. With the oil-price hike of 1973 the country slipped into a major recession. In the same year dramatic strikes of workers in Durban heralded the arrival of a new era of labour unrest and moves to unionise black workers, who had hitherto been denied the right of collective organisation. At the same time the strikes were indicative of poor pay and poor working conditions, to which the Sash had begun to pay serious attention. The dramatic collapse of Portuguese colonial rule in Mozambique and Angola in the mid-1970s was a major cause for celebration among black people in South Africa, and a serious concern for the government.

The defining moment of the crisis was undoubtedly the revolt of young students in Soweto in June 1976, which soon spread to other parts of the country and became more or less permanent. The original motivation for the protests was an educational one, but the brutal response of the police, and the smouldering anger of young people about apartheid policies in general, ignited a fire that would not be extinguished. It was clear that a new generation had arisen to oppose the injustices of apartheid. When leaders of the schools protest were arrested and charged with sedition, with terrorism as an alternative, Janet Sahli, editor of the *Sash* magazine, attended the trial of the 'Soweto Eleven' together with Jill Wentzel, leading member in the Sash Transvaal region, whose husband, Ernie Wentzel, was the senior advocate for the defence. Janet described her impression of the young accused as mature, highly disciplined, brave and intelligent. She concluded, 'Whatever the ultimate verdict ... it is a tragedy that our country does not use people like these to their full potential. To make them second-class citizens, to destine them for citizenship of a homeland or drive them to militancy is our scandal and our sorrow.'

All these developments had an effect on discussions within the Black Sash. Articles in the *Sash* magazine reflect an ongoing interest in the history and development of black organisations. The number of younger black leaders who were speaking out against apartheid was welcomed as an important signal of change. The concept of black consciousness gave impetus to debates within the Sash, with some members expressing concerns about the risk of a rise of black nationalism in opposition to the white nationalism then ruling the country. Others welcomed the growth of a coherent argument for the involvement of black people in determining their future. Steve Biko himself, as well as the Black People's Convention (BPC) – founded in 1971 with the aim of fostering black consciousness and black solidarity – and its developmental wing, the Black Community Programmes (BCP), made a strong impact on many, inspiring not only black people to recommit themselves to ending apartheid. The BCP sought to strengthen black leadership and enable the black community to mobilise its own resources. After Steve Biko's colleague Dr Mamphela Ramphele started a community health clinic named Zanempilo in the Eastern Cape as part of the BCP, it was visited by Lily Herbstein of the Black Sash's False Bay branch, who described it in glowing terms. She found herself 'completely overwhelmed to see what had been achieved by dedicated communal workers who believe in self-help'.

The ideals of the black consciousness movement had an impact on the student movement and the churches; and members of the Sash, particularly in the Eastern Cape, also established good working relationships with the BPC. Its projects and programmes developing both the theory and practice of initiatives driven by black people, and the power of the arguments articulated by its leaders, all brought about significant growth of the prospects for change.

The years from 1975 onwards, the start of its third decade, brought new developments within the Black Sash as well. Partly in response to the growing sense of crisis and the need for change, the Sash was joined by a new generation of younger white women keen to find a role for themselves and make a difference to their society. In the various regions there were new faces and greater involvement, although the number of members did not change significantly. They were confronted by new challenges and issues that had arisen as a result of the economic and political developments already described, and they pioneered new ways of responding to the needs of the broader population in these different and difficult times. With the advent of a growing national spirit of resistance, the Black Sash also encountered new energy and new ideas in public discourse, which in turn re-energised and transformed the organisation. This change in the Sash, which inaugurated the second period in its history, was marked in many ways by the election of Sheena Duncan as president in 1975. Under her wise and vigorous leadership, the Sash adapted to the new state of the nation and adopted a range of strategies that would allow it to remain relevant to the needs of the poorest and most disadvantaged in society and find a role for itself in the rapidly shifting world of late-apartheid South Africa.

In Sheena's first presidential address in 1976 she recognised the difficulties the organisation faced. She acknowledged that many black people believed that white liberals would leave the country rather than face fundamental changes. 'We must ask ourselves whether we are truly committed to the shared society of which we speak so often. We must ask ourselves if we really believe in the necessity for change and what we are prepared to sacrifice to bring it about.' But, she went on, 'We are in the Black Sash and have worked as we have done for 21 years precisely because we are South Africans. We are committed to this country and to her people.' In sombre terms, she outlined the problems and risks which threatened all organisations working for an end to apartheid: 'One by one over the years we have seen organisations, political parties and people put out of action by the succession of security laws ... If we do not survive as the Black Sash, we will have laid the groundwork for our members to continue that work in other ways.' She rejected the option of succumbing 'to the temptation to say we have done all we can and can now opt out of the fight with a clear conscience', and concluded that while the grand ideals of justice and freedom should always be upheld, what was needed was the 'small words' of 'hard work, truth and reason, a quiet will, to keep faith; love and joy and peace'.[7]

A year later Sheena's presidential address took as a focus 'majority rule' – a topic seen as close to treason by many whites.[8] And in 1978 the Black Sash national conference embraced the concept of universal suffrage, which the organisation had tacitly accepted when it adopted the principles of the Universal Declaration of Human Rights in 1963, but had not actively promoted since then.[9]

This growing understanding in the Sash of the issues at stake gave an added depth to its shock at the force of the government's stony rejection of processes of change. Growing resistance was met with greater repression. There were many arrests and the numbers grew of those detained without trial. On 12 September 1977 the brutal killing of Steve Biko by police deprived the country of a potential future leader and provoked mass protests and serious concern for the prospects of peace. Black Sash members, especially those in the Eastern Cape, had held him in high esteem, and Dr Trudy Thomas wrote an inspired tribute for the *Sash* magazine.[10] In various centres the Black Sash made hundreds of wreaths and distributed them widely. There were student protest meetings, and pressure on the South African Medical Association to discipline the state doctors who had taken no action to save Biko and whose forensic reports had allowed the government to evade responsibility for his murder.

Just over a month after Steve Biko's death, on 19 October 1977, the state struck again. On what came to be known as 'Black Wednesday', three newspapers[11] and 18 organisations[12] were banned and 42 people detained, including Percy Qoboza, editor of *The World*, Aggrey Klaaste, news editor of *Weekend World*, and Thenjiwe Mtintso, formerly of the *Daily Dispatch*. Editors Donald Woods (*Daily Dispatch*) and Cedric Mayson (*Pro Veritate*) were also banned. One of the organisations outlawed was the Christian Institute (CI), with which a number of Sash members had close links. In Cape Town the CI office was in a building just two doors away from the Cape Western region of the Institute of Race Relations, where the Black Sash had moved its regional office in 1976. The advice office had previously moved into the CI building, after it had been forced to vacate its premises closer to Athlone, when a petrol bomb was thrown through its barred windows. These close relationships, including the fact that Helen Kotze, wife of the CI's director, the Rev. Theo Kotze, was a member of the Black Sash, brought the effects of the bannings very close. In Johannesburg, Black Sash members cherished their warm friendships with the Rev. Beyers Naudé and other leaders of the CI, who were also issued with banning orders.[13] In the Eastern Cape regions and in Natal too, these bannings, together with those of dozens of others during that year, silenced many important voices and severely curtailed the work of many organisations.

In an atmosphere where many people were prevented from speaking out, or were afraid to do so, the Black Sash sought to inform the public of the enormous power of the security system. In demonstrations, publications and meetings, the Sash drew attention to those who had disappeared, or had died in detention. In 1974, for example it listed in its magazine the names of 37 people known to be missing, presumably in detention, and asked, 'Where are Lindelwa Mabandla, Brigitte Mabandla, Saths Cooper, Revabalan Cooper, Ahmed Bawa, Harry Singh, Muntu Myeza, Haroon Aziz, Yugen Naidoo, Mosiuoa Lekota, Rev. M. Mayatule, Strini Moodley, Dr Aubrey Mokoape, Ben Langa, Mapetla Mohapi, Pumzile Majeke, Pandelani Nefolovhodwe, Menziwe Mbeo, Nkwenkwe Nkomo, Jerry Modisane, Nyameko Pityana, Danile Landingwe, Mahlomola Skosana, Buna Bukwe, Paul Tsotetsi, Kaunda Sedibe, Cyril Ramaphosa, Zithulele Cindi, Madikwe Manthata, Drake Koka, Aubrey Mokoena, Rubin Hare, Steve Carolus, Harold Dixon, Johnny Issel, Nicky Titus and Albert Beukes?'[14] The Sash kept up to date its list of those known to have died in detention, and read it aloud at all meetings, internal as well as public events. This list became embedded in our memories.

The annual reports from all the regions and the advice offices provided a dismal picture of the damage done to the whole society by apartheid policies. Many reports were prefaced by 'this has been the worst year to date'; 'the office has never seen so much hardship'; 'a year of crises on every level'. In 1978 Sheena Duncan's speech to the national conference began, 'This has been a bad year, a tragic year, for all South Africans who care about justice, about honesty and democracy in government, and about people,' and in 1980 she said, 'We have never experienced a worse year than this one.' The Natal Coastal region noted at the 1981 national conference, 'We meet ... in an atmosphere created by an ever worsening situation of heightened tensions, further polarization, tighter control and the threat of sterner measures still to come.'

These multiple pressures brought about an awareness in many circles that major policy changes were necessary. Even the National Party recognised that some change was inevitable, it made promises and protestations of goodwill to homeland leaders, allowed some token changes to segregation rules (for example, opening the Nico Malan Theatre in Cape Town to all races), and entered into dialogue with Kenneth Kaunda of Zambia. Political scientists, opposition parties, journalists and a number of organisations had begun to talk about alternatives. The *Sash* magazine published some of these debates, while the organisation continued to insist that a workable solution could only be achieved by a truly representative national consultation that would involve the trusted leaders of all South Africans.

By 1979 the Sash was moving well beyond the period of isolation and impotence. It had set out on a road towards a destination that was still uncertain, a road filled with potholes and dangerous twists and turns. Although it could sense many changes ahead, it was likely that there were bitter struggles still to come. The pressure of popular resistance was growing, and the government's response was to give way on some fronts while continuing to maintain rigid control overall.

While the Black Sash's understanding of these developments

deepened, it still had not found a place for itself and a role within the broader movement of opposition to apartheid. Its rejection of the token reform strategies of the government, its outspoken protests, and its detailed and principled examination of legislation, made it a logical ally of the forces ranged against apartheid. Sash monitors and activists had become a visible presence in many situations, and their assistance was often requested in moments of crisis. Yet the organisation's white membership and privileged class base kept it at some distance from internal and external organisations representing the majority. It was not until the early 1980s that this changed significantly.

In 1983 it was clear that an important oppositional coalition was being built in the country, and the Sash was aware of some of the debates surrounding its formation. It had been strongly opposed to the government's recent proposals for a tricameral parliament representing white, coloured and Indian people while denying African people representation except in black local authorities and homelands. If such opposition was also to be the policy of the new coalition, this would be a basis for cooperation. If, too, its principles included the ANC's goals of a non-racist, non-sexist, democratic society, there would be common ground. In some regions of the Black Sash there were members who were enthusiastically in favour of supporting such a coalition, which was starting to be talked about as a 'united front'.

At the March 1983 national conference of the Sash, a discussion about the Freedom Charter (which was adopted by the ANC in 1955) was on the agenda, motivated partly by the possibility that support for the Charter might be a precondition for affiliation to such a united organisation or campaign. It was agreed that the regions would undertake a study of the Charter among their members, with a view to discussing at the next national conference whether the Black Sash should endorse it.

The individuals and organisations involved in building the united front were moving quickly, and the United Democratic Front (UDF) was launched in Mitchell's Plain, Cape Town, in August 1983. Thousands of people were present, including a number of Sash members. The story is told by Noël Robb that Eulalie Stott, an alderman of the Cape Town City Council and one of the founder members of the Black Sash (though no longer very active within it), made it possible for the event to take place when at the last moment there was an insistence that the premises be insured, and the UDF did not have sufficient funds to do this. She found guarantors to allow it to proceed.[15] (This is a story which causes some wry amusement in the Black Sash, since Eulalie was, or became, more critical of the UDF than many others of its members. Perhaps it is precisely an illustration of the ambivalences within the Sash.)

The UDF was supported by trade unions, youth organisations and a wide variety of political and social bodies. It embarked on a 'million signatures' campaign against the new constitution and the tricameral parliament, which the government of P.W. Botha had introduced in a bid to reform apartheid. The UDF was committed to non-racialism and to building unity, although it failed to win over the organisations led by AZAPO (the Azanian People's Organisation), which supported the black consciousness perspective. The Black Sash would have to decide whether it should seek affiliation, and the regions began to discuss the question. The Natal Coastal region of the Black Sash, led by Ann Colvin, who was totally committed to the UDF, had already affiliated to it.

In the Cape Western region, we embarked on a process of consultation, within our own membership as well as with other people. I remember going to see the respected and independent intellectual Neville Alexander, fully aware that he would not himself be likely to support this new venture, based as it was on the demands of the ANC's Freedom Charter. He was somewhat astonished (and, I think, perhaps mildly amused) to hear that some of our members, especially those most closely connected to trade union movements, were opposed to our affiliation on the grounds that the UDF would be a 'bourgeois body', unlikely to address the real economic issues facing the country.

Neville's ideas were always worth learning from and, as I recall, he did not condemn the prospect of a united front as part of a process to force the speed of change, although for himself he would prefer to focus on the ultimate transformation of the society, which was his goal.

By the time of the next Sash national conference, in Johannesburg in March 1984, the UDF was a major force in the country, bringing together hundreds of organisations, many of them small community-based groupings, and many of which had never worked together before. Delegates to the Sash conference came with mandates from their regions, and after an emotionally fraught debate the proposal for affiliation failed to win the two-thirds majority required. The long history of the independence of the Black Sash, which had over the years resisted affiliation to any other organisation, was a powerful influence.

Even those who were opposed to formal affiliation were anxious that this decision should not result in a return to the isolated position of the organisation, nor create a rift with the UDF. A further decision, to seek 'cooperation' and 'observer status', was easily adopted, and rapidly referred to the UDF. The fact that this was generously accepted bears testimony to the claim by its secretary-general, Popo Molefe, that the leadership of the UDF was characterised by a 'high and almost incredible degree of mutual tolerance' and that the 'unique skills and organisational ability' of many of its activists were what had ensured its success.[16] It was a relief for Sash members to receive the message that 'the UDF has officially conceded to our request to be granted observer status on its Councils … I suggest that each of you approach your local UDF committees.'[17]

From then on, it seemed that the Black Sash had achieved the best of both worlds. It had retained its valued independence to act according to its traditional methods and established principles, while being part of the broad movement for change, which brought hope to so many. The fact that its headquarters and the Johannesburg advice office were located in Khotso House, the premises of the South African Council of Churches, and that the UDF's offices were in the same building, made for good communication. In other regions, too, links were built with the member organisations of the UDF – the residents' associations, civic associations, student bodies and workers' forums.

If the years of isolation were over, the years of repression and conflict were not. In August 1984 elections took place in terms of the new constitution, and coloured and Indian MPs were installed in the new tricameral parliament. For Africans political representation would be offered only through the 'homeland' system and at local level through black municipal councils. These provisions were bitterly rejected by extra-parliamentary groups, who did not believe these racially defined structures would ever lead to full and equal participation. The Black Community Councils suffered from the start from a lack of legitimacy and, when they attempted to increase rents, as a way of raising finances, they triggered widespread protests. Rent boycotts were followed by mass stayaways from work, and school boycotts led to marches and rallies. Violent clashes between local civic associations or youth groups and police followed. The government responded by detaining dozens of leaders, arousing even more anger, and by October 1984 it resorted to sending the army into the townships.

Many leaders of organisations were detained without charge for long periods, or were arrested and held through long trials. This deprived their organisations of strong and disciplined guidance. In a number of areas Sash members found themselves called out to meet some of these organisations to discuss what steps might be open to them, or at least to record the events in the area. Foremost among them were Molly Blackburn and Di Bishop, who were able to raise issues in the Cape Provincial Council, and draw the other members of the Progressive Federal Party into first-hand experience of the many problems. They were an inspiration to other Sash members, who made themselves available to answer calls for assistance outside the main centres.

The Sash members were conscious that their position as women, and as white women, gave them a degree of privilege and protection that was not available to others, and that this carried with it a duty to use this privilege for service to others. This was further emphasised by leaders of the black community, who said explicitly, 'You have space and a voice which has been taken from many of us who are in hiding or in detention. You must use it to tell the world what is being done.'

It was not new for the Black Sash to write reports, and to brief the media, the opposition parties and international visitors. The knowledge gained through its advice office work had always been reliably based on fact. Now the experiences of its members involved in so many other ways were being gathered and analysed in order to expose the injustice of the entire system of apartheid and the brutality with which it was being enforced.

One of the exemplary ways in which the Sash worked in these troubled years can be seen in the expert witness that Sheena Duncan provided in a major trial held in Delmas, outside Johannesburg. Nineteen members of the UDF and the Vaal Civic Association stood trial for treason, with three alternative charges of terrorism, subversion and murder. The defence team was made up of the widely respected advocates Arthur Chaskalson, George Bizos, Karel Tip, Zak Yacoob and Gilbert Marcus.

On 2 May 1988 George Bizos called Sheena Duncan, past national president of the Black Sash, as a witness. He asked her about her various roles in the Anglican Church, and in other organisations besides the Black Sash. He quoted from Black Sash documents and the reports of the advice offices, and asked whether she would describe the work as 'mobilisation, conscientisation and politicisation of people'. She responded, 'I think that mobilising and organising citizens of a country against unjust laws is an obligation,' and that the advice offices certainly mobilised members of the Black Sash into understanding the horrors of the apartheid laws.

Central to the case against the accused was the allegation that the UDF, as an organisation, formed part of a conspiracy with the ANC to overthrow the state by violence. Part of the indictment concerned events that took place in the Vaal Triangle in 1984, which resulted in large-scale disturbances and the murder of several community councillors. Although none of the men on trial was accused of having perpetrated any of these murders, they were alleged to have been part of a conspiracy resulting in the deaths. The defence took pains to demonstrate by its questions to Sheena that the issues taken up by the UDF were matters that had been raised by many opponents of apartheid, long before the formation of the UDF. Bizos explained that his reason for tabling so many Black Sash documents was to refute the argument that the language used by the UDF was the language of the ANC. 'Your lordship received those ANC documents ... We are planning to show that the ANC has not got a monopoly of this language.'[18]

Bizos went on to ask Sheena about a range of Black Sash campaigns, particularly the organisation's opposition to the Constitution Act of 1983, which had provided for the tricameral parliament. Referring to the Black Sash's formal resolution (at its national conference in March 1983) to cooperate with groups opposing the constitutional proposals by non-violent means and noting that this was taken before the formation of the UDF, he asked whether the decision had been influenced by the guidance of any other organisation. Sheena replied, 'Taken independently, but we were aware of other groups also opposing the constitution.' In a portion of his examination he asked about the Black Sash's attitude to the Freedom Charter and the UDF, including the phrase 'The people shall govern'. Sheena answered, 'We think that the phrase is one of the basic principles of democracy ... We do not regard it as a statement indicating adherence to violent revolution at all.'[19]

Bizos continued to press her on the question of violence: 'Did you at any stage at any of the meetings that you attended, called by the UDF or any of its affiliates, hear anybody calling for the use of violence in order to achieve any of the objects of the UDF?' To which she replied, 'Never. Never have I heard any person at a UDF meeting call for violence, and that includes not only the public meetings that I have attended but the many meetings that were of a more private nature, workshops with affiliates of the UDF; I have never heard any suggestion that violence be used, quite the opposite. In fact there has always been a stress on the need for non-violent and disciplined, restrained action.'[20]

Under cross-examination by Advocate Jacobs for the state, Sheena took the opportunity presented by his questions to deliver a succinct account of how the Black Sash worked to bring about change. First, he asked about the campaign against the constitutional proposals.

Jacobs: 'What else did you do in this campaign?

Sheena Duncan: 'We produced that document saying: "Vote no", which is amongst the exhibits. We distributed that as widely as possible. We made ourselves available to other organisations who wanted to know the details, we offered speakers to other organisations; for this campaign we did not need to lobby opposition members of Parliament because the Progressive Federal Party at that stage was opposing the proposals themselves.'

Jacobs: 'And after the proposals became law, did you still continue with this campaign?'

Sheena Duncan: 'The proposals became law before the referendum [on the new constitution]. The bill had been passed and the Constitution Act had been passed by Parliament before the referendum was held and we continued right through that period of the referendum campaign, and we have continued since the new constitution came into effect and the tricameral parliament was set up. We continue to oppose the constitutional structure. Because we believe that the present constitution of the Republic of South Africa cannot bring us to any acceptable democratic, non-racial and just constitutional dispensation because it is fundamentally based on race classification.'

Jacobs went on to ask about the campaign against forced removals, and Sheena outlined a classic explanation of how the work was done: 'The purpose of the campaign against removals was to try to prevent that happening, to bring a stop to the removal of people in South Africa from one place to another. We would in the course of our work, in the advice offices or perhaps just as Black Sash people, be approached by people from a community which had been told that it was going to be removed, and we would then first make ourselves knowledgeable with all the necessary information about that community, such as did they own the land, for how long, how many generations had they been in that same place; did they have title deeds, that kind of necessary information. We would then put that community – many of them being rural communities with no access to resources – we put them in touch with legal advice. We would try to raise public interest in the threat that was hanging over them, by taking people out to meet members of the community to learn the story at first hand; to look at the place where they were to be removed to. We sought to raise public concern again through writing articles for the press, publishing pamphlets, publishing books or booklets about a particular place or about removals in general. We held Black Sash pickets to protest against the removals, and in general tried to raise sufficient public concern and public outcry that would make the government desist from its plan to remove a large portion of South Africa's population around.'

Jacobs: 'Was it also to mobilise and politicise people?'

Sheena Duncan: 'Certainly, because you cannot run any successful campaign unless you mobilise and politicise people to support your point of view.'

Jacobs: 'So when you politicise them, surely you would have presented an alternative political view to the people?' (He had to explain that he meant the people who were threatened with removal).

Sheena Duncan: 'There was no need for us to mobilise and politicise people who were going to be removed. The fact that they had been told that they were going to be removed, immediately politicised and mobilised them, which led in turn to them coming to us. We were trying to politicise and mobilise the public into support of the community's resistance to the removal.'

Jacobs: 'And what was the alternative political view that you expressed to the public?'

Sheena Duncan: 'Okay, the alternative political view is that people should not be removed from where they are in the pursuit of an ideology based on race. That people must be left where they are and that if that did not fit in with the constitutional grand plans, particularly in relation to the homelands, that was too bad. That the evil done by the uprooting and removal of communities was so great that it could not be justified for any political purpose whatsoever.'

Jacobs sought to push the questions further, asking whether the Black Sash's work on matters of housing and the situation of homeless people included efforts to 'politicise' them.

Sheena Duncan: 'We find that there is a deep level of politicisation in the black community, particularly in homeless communities whose daily suffering is such that they may not understand how the administrative structures work, but they blame government and the authorities for their position of homelessness. So there is no need for us to politicise black people.'

Earlier in her testimony she had illustrated her understanding of 'politicisation' by citing a group of elderly women who were experiencing problems in receiving their pensions. She had met with them and explained the existing legal and administrative processes, and the women concluded that their problems stemmed from corruption. They themselves had decided what steps to take, and they had been successful. 'Politicisation is as important as mobilisation – there is no issue from the price of bread to worship in church that is not political.'

Jacobs shifted to the Black Sash's focus on education: 'Is it not so that this campaign on education emanated from the ANC in the 1950s?'

'Goodness me,' said Sheena, 'I think education is one of those day-to-day issues when people are always concerned about the education of their children. And if the ANC started a campaign on education in the 1950s, one would have been very surprised if it had not, because the ANC at that time was a legal organisation addressing itself to expressing the political and other grievances of the people, and education as a day-to-day issue is of the utmost importance to people.'

Jacobs: 'Would you agree then that the UDF was bringing together all the people in order to achieve people's power?'

Sheena Duncan: 'If people's power is another way of saying democracy, which I believe it is, yes, I would agree with that statement.'

Jacobs: 'And not just a question of getting civil rights, but it is to take over power?'

Sheena Duncan: 'But if people enjoy civil rights, they also have power; because if they have civil rights they have the power to vote and to choose which government of the people they wish to elect, so I do not see a distinction between civil rights and people's power.'

Jacobs: 'Do you know whether the UDF – you said you knew they were also calling for a national convention. Do you know whether they had any preconditions?'

Sheena Duncan: 'I have not heard of any preconditions other than the three that I mentioned. [Earlier in her testimony she had said that the Black Sash agreed with the UDF that political prisoners must be released, the exiles should be allowed freely to return, and banned organisations should be unbanned, before it would be possible to enter into any process such as a national convention.] I am not aware of any other preconditions.'

Jacobs: 'And if I put it to you that they have other preconditions, what would you say?'

Sheena Duncan: 'Well, I would not contradict Mr Jacobs in the court, m'lord.'

Court: 'Although you would like to?'

Sheena Duncan: 'Well, it depends, I do not know what he is going to put to me.' (*Laughter*)

Jacobs: 'I put to you that one of the preconditions of the UDF is the scrapping or suspension of the constitution in South Africa.'

Sheena Duncan: 'I have not heard that. Not as a precondition to a national convention.'

Jacobs: 'Or that the army and the South African Police are to be unarmed?'

Sheena Duncan: 'I have not heard that.'

Jacobs: 'They must be scrapped.'

Sheena Duncan: 'I have not heard that.'

Jacobs: 'Abolished, dismantled.'

Jacobs: 'Now do you know what is the policy of the UDF to achieve its ultimate aim of a government for the people?'

Sheena Duncan: 'Yes, I believe that the UDF policy or strategy is to use exclusively non-violent means to bring about change in South Africa and I have found them consistently adhere to that principle; whatever strategies are undertaken are non-violent strategies, and where violence has broken out on the fringes during the course of such a campaign, I have found the leadership both at national, regional and local levels concerned to restrain that violence, to stop it; to maintain the discipline in the action, whatever it may be.'

Jacobs reacted strongly, 'How can you say that? Were you present with them, did you attend any of their meetings? How can you say that you found them to restrain violence where it broke out?'

Sheena Duncan: 'They have consistently said so at the public meetings that I have attended. I have consistently found it at the affiliates at a local level, where for example the civic association at Duncan Village in East London, who had invited me to go down to help to do a workshop with various problems that the community had, and one of the problems they raised with me – this was the committee of the civic association – was did I have any idea how they could stop the young elements in Duncan Village, coming from the poorer section, who were using violence and who would come to meetings with the leadership and agree that they would not do it anymore, but the next day would throw bricks or seek to burn down a house or something again. I have at that level seen consistently a great concern to discuss how does leadership in such a position manage to continue to exert that influence for discipline and non-violence, and particularly in cases where, as it so often happens, the respected leadership figures have been taken into detention and are not on the scene.'

Judgment began on 15 November 1988 in the Delmas Trial, the longest treason trial in the history of South Africa. Mr Justice Van Dijkhorst found that the state had proved that a dominant part of the UDF leadership had acted as an internal wing of the banned ANC. He said that it was symptomatic of all speeches given by UDF members and supporters that one did not hear an outright condemnation of violence. Those who were UDF members he found guilty of treason and sentenced to terms of imprisonment: Popo Molefe, Moses Chikane, Mosiuoa Lekota and Tom Manthata. Gcinumuzi Malinda was found guilty of terrorism and sentenced to imprisonment. The other six members of the Vaal Civic Association were given suspended sentences, and were restricted.[21] In December 1989 the five jailed Delmas trialists were freed after the Appellate Division of the Supreme Court overturned their convictions and sentences.[22]

These extracts from Sheena's evidence at the trial are a remarkable testimony to her ability to think clearly and speak convincingly under pressure, and to her own unshakeable principles. They also reveal much about the crises of that period – the long-term detention of a significant part of the leadership of the UDF, which removed an important layer of responsible figures; and the inability of the state to deal with the spreading violence. Sheena's answers also illustrate the way the Black Sash responded to these situations, and how far it had moved in its understanding of the real conditions experienced by the majority of the people, and in its quest for a total change in government.

The comment Sheena made in evidence about how 'mobilisation and politicisation' arose directly out of people's experience was also applicable to some sections of the white population at the time. Women in particular were prompted by escalating violence and government intransigence to join organisations seeking solutions. These included the End Conscription Campaign and the Women's Movement for Peace, as well as a number of other women's organisations which arose at this time. As individuals, Sash members worked within some of those structures. The Black Sash itself participated in meetings and joint programmes that brought women together in discussion and action.

At the same time there was growing contact and cooperation between a wider range of women's organisations. Janet Cherry describes some of these: the formation in the Western Cape of the United Women's Organisation (UWO) in 1980–1, which in 1986 merged with the Women's Front to form the United Women's Congress (UWCO); the Natal Organisation of Women (NOW) in 1983; the Federation of Transvaal Women (FEDTRAW) in 1984; and the Port Elizabeth Women's Organisation (PEWO) in 1983. She provides a detailed account of the work of the women within the mass movement seeking to build a non-racial women's organisation.[23]

In 1986, even under the state of emergency, new organisations came into existence and fostered wider consultation, particularly with the exiled representatives of the ANC. The Institute for a Democratic South Africa (IDASA) and the Five Freedoms Forum, both established in 1986, provided opportunities for white South Africans to demonstrate their willingness to be part of a non-racial society and to start laying down the foundations for a transition to full democracy. In mid-1989 the Five Freedoms Forum held a conference in Lusaka, headquarters of the exiled ANC, at which 114 South Africans, including eight Sash members led by Jenny de Tolly, met a senior ANC delegation. Later that year, a meeting was held in Harare with the theme 'Women and the challenge for peace', led by Jenny Boraine, in which a number of Sashers participated.

Links were strengthened with women's groups in the extra-parliamentary movement, and in 1987 Sashers were included in a national meeting aimed at reviving FEDSAW.[24] Several Sash members were privately invited to travel outside the country to meet exiled ANC women representatives. Even under the restrictions imposed by the state of emergency, opportunities were made to continue contact.

In January 1990 the Malibongwe conference in Amsterdam brought together more than 150 South African women, some from within the country, some from exile in Africa and Europe and beyond. Public meetings, closed sessions, private discussions, and cultural evenings all contributed to the topic of the role of women in the liberation movement and in a future free and democratic South Africa. Preceding as it did the announcement only weeks later of the unbanning of the ANC, the conference did not focus directly on future policy, but it did provide the opportunity to explore some issues where further work would be necessary, such as the role of traditional customs in a democracy and the position of women in all spheres of society. The Sash delegates to the conference, Karin Chubb and Rosemary van Wyk Smith, reported on their experience of the wide-ranging debates and the warmth of the contacts, while noting the need for a 'consistent feminist perspective'.[25]

All these meetings were signs of hope, and were opportunities eagerly grasped by those who longed for a peaceful path to a democratic society. Yet the daily reality was one of violence, not only by agents of the state, but also directed against state institutions and people seen as collaborators. Just as the Black Sash was opposed to military conscription, and to the deployment of the Defence Force within the country as well as on its borders and beyond, it also deplored the use of force, violence and conflict in the fight against apartheid. Its constitution committed it to working by peaceful means. All of its years of work for justice and equality amounted to a plea for an end to apartheid, an end brought about by negotiation rather than by war.

In the 1980s pressures were building up and events were moving too fast for this to seem a possible outcome. How then, if opposed to violence, could an organisation align itself with the forces for change? What effective pressure could be exerted on the government? We began tentatively to consider civil disobedience. Speaking and acting in non-violent ways might nevertheless contravene the law, and have serious consequences. Members became involved in learning techniques of non-violent direct action, and workshops were conducted by the International Fellowship for Reconciliation (IFOR). Members considered how they would react and what support they could offer if one or more of their number decided in good conscience to disobey a law in order to protest; and they debated what forms of civil disobedience might be open to them.

Although the Black Sash did not adopt a strategy of disobedience, a number of its members decided to take such action. Among the first was Barbara Waite's brave choice to serve a prison sentence for employing an African woman without a permit, and in 1977 for refusing to testify about her visit to Winnie Mandela, then banned and banished to Brandfort, which again resulted in months in jail. Another was the action taken by Beva Runciman and Cornelia Bullen-Smith, who chained themselves to the railings around Parliament in 1985, in protest against yet one more death of a youth in detention, that of Johannes Spogter of Steytlerville. By the late 1980s many members were participating in events that formed part of the Standing for the Truth campaign, joining in banned marches and demonstrations.

In the 1980s the growing national and international movement to impose economic and other sanctions on South Africa (such as the sporting and cultural boycotts) challenged the Black Sash to take a position; yet supporting or encouraging economic sanctions was an illegal action. Sheena Duncan took a firm stand as an individual, supporting the disinvestment campaign, but the Black Sash itself did not formally adopt such a decision.

Several peaceful but illegal protest stands took place. These included one outside Parliament about the Sharpeville Six, and another on Greenmarket Square in Cape Town on 29 November 1984. Sheena Duncan described in a national circular the arrests of the theologian Dr Wolfram Kistner and his wife, the legal scholar John Dugard, Max Coleman, six Sash members, students and others.[26] In August 1985 a mass march was planned under the banner of the UDF, with the goal of delivering a message of support to Nelson Mandela, then being held in Pollsmoor Prison in Cape Town. Together with a few other Sash members, I took part in the march, and in my personal capacity participated in its organisation. In the Sash itself we planned a variety of support activities such as monitoring the event and maintaining communication networks which would allow information or calls for assistance to be disseminated. Permission for the march was refused, so it became an illegal action, and when the police broke up the various streams seeking to reach Pollsmoor, there were hundreds of arrests, outbreaks of violence and many injuries. A small group of seven of us were arrested not far from the prison, and held in the Wynberg police station for a couple of nights, during which time we could hear truckloads of other people being brought in. Realising the extent of the damage, and imbued with a sense of responsibility for this outcome, especially as I was the regional chair of the Sash, I wrote a letter to all members after I was released, explaining the background and motivation.[27]

Throughout the next four years of the state of emergency, many Sash members in all parts of the country continued to explore ways of protesting and speaking out that would have an impact, even if this sometimes meant that laws would be broken.

A decision to break the law was one thing, but differing attitudes towards violent resistance provoked some of the most agonised discussions ever held within the Sash. They arose in the early 1980s, initially over differences about whether apartheid could be overcome by gradual, incremental and reformist means or only by radical rejection, non-participation in any government structures, and economic and political sanctions, boycotts and even violent resistance and armed struggle.

At first the debates examined the call from many quarters for boycotts of South Africa. From the liberation movements came pressure for an economic boycott and economic sanctions: many countries and multinational corporations did withdraw or decrease their involvements. The cultural boycott led to artists and academics declining to perform or teach in the country. Sports boycotts isolated South Africa from international competition. There were also boycotts within South Africa directed against commercial enterprises, and a very strong opposition to any participation in new government structures such as black municipal councils and the tricameral parliament.

Arguments about incremental change versus radical transformation gathered momentum in the Sash. On the one hand, there were members who stressed the organisation's long-held principles of human rights and liberties for all, including respect for life and property, and the right to dissent (from whichever ideology or action). They believed that cultural and academic boycotts had the negative effect of cutting off all South Africans from contacts that might have influenced their attitudes. They deplored the lawlessness they perceived in the actions of groups which used violent means to enforce boycotts and non-participation. They defended the rights of those who opted instead for a strategy of participation in transitional structures proposed by the government under the new constitution, and for using such platforms to argue for change.

In an article in *Sash* magazine in November 1984 on 'Strategies of opposition', Joyce Harris described the different choices made by those who decided (or were obliged) to work within the constraints of the existing government system, and those who were totally opposed to participation. She pointed out that in the tricameral parliament, 'The mere fact that people of different skin colour are occasionally meeting together in joint sittings, or are sharing discussions on the standing committees or even in the Cabinet, may gradually alter attitudes as a precursor to encouraging real reform. When there is change of any description there is no knowing where or when or how it will end. Neither is there any real control over the course of events. So that even though this constitution is undemocratic, rigid, exclusive, and a step in the wrong direction, no-one can foretell with any certainty its eventual outcome.'[28]

On the other hand, she conceded, 'Non-participants have a valid argument in not wanting to have anything whatsoever to do with so flawed a constitution, and retain their integrity with their constituents with greater ease than do the participants, who have a need to explain their actions. The campaigns they have been organising have politicised their constituents and given them an understanding of what is at stake. They are not hamstrung by the rigidity of operating within the constitution, though they are obviously at risk from the government, as the spate of detentions has clearly indicated. If extra-parliamentary political activity can remain non-violent, then it remains possible that sufficient pressure can be built up to bring about reform peacefully.'

Joyce was a respected political leader in the Black Sash, and her opinions carried weight. She was deeply committed to the fundamental liberal principle of providing space for all views to be heard, and she agonised over the escalation of violence. 'It is heartbreaking to see so much dissension within the opposition. This holds out scant hope for the future stability of our country. Recent violence in the townships is tragic evidence of this. We are faced with a constitution we all reject. We choose to fight it in different ways. Let us respect each other's strategies and try to accept that they are complementary and not antagonistic. A failure to do so can only result in the emasculation of the opposition.'[29]

Taking a different view were other members who were involved in monitoring situations where violence occurred which demonstrated the over-reaction of members of the police force. Some had taken statements from people who had witnessed events in which community violence had seemed to be deliberately provoked. They were deeply concerned at the spate of detentions and the allegations of police torture which were being received. They argued that angry reactions were inevitable, that there were historical and ongoing reasons for reactive violence. While they did not condone actions such as intimidation and brutality towards people who contravened the boycotts or participated in government structures, they argued that these needed to be understood in the context of structural violence committed by the state. They had no trust that any real change would come about through the tricameral and 'homeland' structures being offered.

At first these views were contained at the level of different opinions and attitudes, which were given space in newsletters and the *Sash* magazine, but they became particularly antagonistic among the members in Johannesburg. Jill Wentzel, as editor of the magazine and a long-time member, wrote several articles defending the policies of participation and negotiation. In response, Sheena Duncan remarked: 'If ever an oppressed people has been prepared to negotiate it has been in this country. The whole history of black resistance has been a history of endless trust in negotiation and endless violations of that trust ... I think there are times when to enter into negotiation is just another trap. Negotiation is not negotiation at all when one of the parties has nothing at all to bargain with ... Should people agree to try yet again? They have tried so often before in Representative Councils, Advisory Committees etc. and they have always been defeated because they entered into conversations with trust and belief in law and honour while the other side had no intention of moving forward but only of emasculating the black leaders while consolidating their own power.

'If you study Gandhian strategies of non-violent coercion there was always love and concern for the opponent, but negotiations came only when there was some kind of balance of strength ... I think the real cause of all our troubles in white liberal circles at the moment is that we are not victims. We stand on the outside and can maintain high moral positions because we are not watching our children die, our mothers being evicted from their houses because someone has bribed someone else, our husbands denied UIF benefits, our daughters and sons refused permission to work or to make the most of their abilities ... I personally find it difficult to come out with high-sounding righteous statements about good and evil, right and wrong.'[30]

She pointed to the importance of action instead, 'the solid, sacrificial hard work done by active members of the Black Sash to further non-violent and effective strategies of opposition ... In all Regions you find us engaged in encouraging, exploring, teaching the law and structures to enable people to find effective ways of insisting on those rights they have and to find strategies for gaining rights they do not have. I do think we expend almost all our resources of time, talent and energy on "finding non-violent ways of compelling change".[31]

The arguments were strong in the regions of the Sash too, but they did not have the same damaging effect as in Johannesburg. There the arguments became more and more painful, despite attempts through workshops and discussions to find a degree of consensus. Divisions took on personal dimensions and individuals found themselves in opposing camps. Jill Wentzel eventually felt so strongly that she moved out of active involvement in the Sash, and wrote a book, *The Liberal Slideaway*, documenting in detail her sense of living with the 'slur' of having become right-wing.[32]

The division reached its deepest point in 1985.[33] It was a time when repression and resistance clashed in confrontational sites of violence around the country, resulting in the proclamation of a partial state of emergency in July, immediately after the funeral of the Cradock Four, and its extension to the nationwide state of emergency in 1986. It was a bleak time in South Africa and in the Black Sash. For me it was a time of deep sorrow, as I witnessed the rifts between women for whom I had great respect. There was no escape from the choices each one of us had to make, and as Cape Western became headquarters in March 1986 and I took on the presidency, we felt a great sense of responsibility. We had to accept that the divisions existed, while sustaining our strong sense of purpose in driving forward to common goals. We had to find ways to respond to the desperate state of conflict in the country, refusing to be paralysed by internal disagreements.

For the Sash this meant continued commitment to the work in the advice offices, and support for similar community-based initiatives. It meant increased efforts to monitor and expose the tactics of the apartheid machinery by first-hand knowledge. Under the four-year state of emergency it meant being willing to take more risks, to participate wherever possible in joint actions with other structures and organisations, to maintain a visible presence at protests and marches, rallies and church services, and to sustain the growing national and international pressure against the government being built by the extra-parliamentary organisations.

As the 1980s drew to a close, this pressure mounted, protest marches continued to take place, and almost all of them, including those led by members of religious faiths, were broken up by the police. The toll of arrests, injuries and deaths grew. Finally in September 1989 a march in Cape Town, led by Archbishop Tutu and many other faith leaders and civic representatives, was allowed to proceed. It was clear that the political cost of trying to maintain apartheid by force was becoming too great, and the march became a landmark on the road to the longed-for peaceful negotiations. Peace marches followed in many other cities.

There were other indicators of coming changes, one of which was the release of some of the leaders among the political prisoners from Robben Island or Pollsmoor. This was cause for great celebrations, particularly at Cowley House in Woodstock, which was usually the first place to which they went. This had become the base of the Cape Town office of the Dependants' Conference, which provided support for the families of political prisoners. Moira Henderson, a founding member of the Sash, had been instrumental in establishing it after the banning of the organisation Defence and Aid.[34] For many years she continued to dedicate herself to this work, and Sash members were drawn into it, giving time to meeting the wives and families who came to Cape Town from all over the country to take up their few opportunities to visit Robben Island or other prisons. The hours before and after visits were long and sad, so invitations to private homes or to visit other parts of town were always welcome.

June Mlangeni visited her husband Andrew, a senior ANC member who had been sentenced in the Rivonia Trial, throughout the 26 years of his imprisonment, and she became friends with Tish Haynes, who wrote, 'I have come to know and love June by driving her and her family to Pollsmoor and offering hospitality. She is a woman of great integrity and has shown wonderful strength of character over the years working and bringing up four children. It was a happy privilege to be their guest in their home in Dube, Soweto, over the weekend of the Welcome Home rally at Soccer City on 29 October 1989. Andrew paid tribute during his speech to the work of the Black Sash.'[35] His invitation to Tish to be present at the celebrations was a tribute to her own dedication.

The released prisoners would arrive by ferry, usually before dawn, at the Cape Town docks, to rapturous welcomes, and the celebrations would continue at Cowley House, which had become a haven for their families. The Trauma Centre for Victims of Violence subsequently made its base there, and the house across the road, where many of the first returning exiles were sheltered, still bears Moira's name.

These indications of change we could see. We did not know much then about initiatives that were being taken to draw the ANC into secret discussions with the government, but we did know that some kind of change must come. It was President F.W. de Klerk's speech to Parliament on 2 February 1990, announcing the unbanning of the ANC and other organisations, and the imminent release of Nelson Mandela, that finally heralded the start of South Africa's transition to democracy.

8

TRANSITION

When Nelson Mandela was installed as president in the seat of government, the Union Buildings in Pretoria, on 10 May 1994, the ceremony was one that many South Africans could scarcely have imagined. The solemn rituals, the enormous and jubilant crowd, the presence of the leaders of the previous government as well as those newly elected, the new flag flying, all emphasised the significance of the changes that had taken place in four years of negotiations and agreements. Special guests represented all sectors of society, and included Sheena Duncan.[1] The fly-past of the aeroplanes of the South African Defence Force provided a dramatic demonstration of the transfer of power from the old to the new.

No doubt all the people of South Africa wondered that day what the future held for them. Certainly, we in the Black Sash were deeply moved by those special moments, and rejoiced that so many of the values for which we had worked for so long were now being honoured in the Interim Constitution. We thought deeply about what we had to offer to the new society. Already a number of our members had been appointed to positions in government, at local or national level, and some had been elected to the new Parliament. We felt sure that there were other ways we could use our skills and knowledge to serve our fellow citizens, and that our organisation was still needed.

Nine years earlier, in very different circumstances, Nelson Mandela had sent a letter to Sheena Duncan in anticipation of the thirtieth anniversary of the Black Sash. From Pollsmoor Prison, he wrote on 1 April 1985:

Dear Mrs Duncan,

In my current position it is by no means easy to keep abreast of the course of events outside prison. It may well be that the membership of the B-Sash has not grown significantly over the last 30 years and that, in this respect, this pattern of development is not likely to be different in the immediate future at least.

But few people will deny that, in spite of its relatively small numbers, the impact of the Sash is quite formidable, and that it has emerged as one of the forces which help to focus attention on those social issues which are shattering the lives of so many people. It is giving a bold lead on how these problems can be concretely tackled and, in this way, it helps to bring a measure of relief and hope to many victims of a degrading social order.

The ideals we cherish, our fondest dreams and fervent hopes may not be realised in our lifetime. But that is beside the point. The knowledge that in your day you did your duty, and lived up to the expectations of your fellow men is in itself a rewarding experience and magnificent achievement. The good image which the Sash is projecting may be largely due to the wider realisation that it is fulfilling these expectations.

To speak with a firm and clear voice on major national questions, unprotected by the shield of immunity enjoyed by members of the country's organs of government, and unruffled by the countless repercussions of being ostracised by a privileged minority, is a measure of your deep concern for human rights and commitment to the principle of justice for all. In this regard your recent comments in Port Elizabeth articulating as they did, the convictions of those who strive for real progress and a new South Africa were indeed significant.

In spite of the immense difficulties against which you have to operate, your voice is heard right across the country. Even though frowned upon

*by some, it pricks the conscience of others and is warmly welcomed by
all good men and women. Those who are prepared to face problems at
eyeball range, and who embrace universal beliefs which have changed the
course of history in many societies must, in due course, command solid
support and admiration far beyond their own ranks.*

*In congratulating you on your 30th birthday, I must add that I fully
share the view that you 'can look back with pride on three decades of
endeavour which now, at least, is beginning to bear fruit'.*

*In conclusion, I must point out that I know so many of your colleagues
that if I were to name each and every one in this letter, the list would
be too long. All I can do is to assure you of my fondest regards and best
wishes.*

Sincerely,

N.R. Mandela

In 1994, in the 40th year of its existence the Black Sash had every reason
to celebrate, and we knew there was much work to be done. Our nine
advice offices were still filled every day with people seeking assistance.
Our members and staff held strong views about changes that needed
to be made to legislation and policy, as well as the introduction of a
transformed and dedicated public service, and measures to reduce levels
of inequality and poverty. Our relationship with the new government
was positive, and our proposals and comments no longer met with
closed doors. We could put our black sashes away, and we were eager
to contribute to democracy and justice.

Despite this enthusiasm, major challenges lay ahead for the Sash.
Some were external, including the funding difficulties that faced almost
all non-governmental organisations in that time of transition. Some
were internal, deriving from structural and administrative processes;
and some were prompted by changes in society in South Africa itself
and the wider world.

The structural issue had developed over the preceding ten years,
creating a division between the advice office work and other Sash

activities. Until 1985 all the financial affairs of the organisation had been managed by the national and regional office-bearers. From the beginning funds had come from membership subscriptions, from fundraising projects undertaken by members, and from donors, both local and foreign. The first major injection of funds came from the Fund for Free Expression, which crafted a legal way to support the Black Sash by purchasing the copyright to its magazine.

Several factors then led to a decision to create a trust fund, to be named the Advice Office Trust, to serve as the vehicle for raising, receiving and administering the finances of the advice offices. Legislation governing the receipt of funds from abroad had become very stringent and had been implemented so as to take action against some organisations, preventing them from receiving such funds. Furthermore, laws in other countries prohibited donors from funding political activities abroad. Through the new trust, foreign funding could be received specifically for the Sash's advice office work, though not for advocacy or protest initiatives with a political thrust.

The intention was not to split the advice office work away from the other work carried out by the members. The essence had always been that the advice offices, which encountered daily the injustices of apartheid, gave to the organisation the knowledge that underpinned the advocacy and protest campaigns. The difference between the Sash and other organisations promoting human rights lay precisely in its rootedness in the experience of those who suffered most from discrimination and injustice. That dual purpose of service and protest had characterised it ever since 1958, when the first advice office began. Furthermore, the information and training provided by the advice offices were an important part of building a civil society. Beyond simply giving advice, they gave people 'the information they need to insist on the rights they do have, and enable them to organise to establish those rights which are denied them'.[2]

The creation of the trust began a process of change that brought with it administrative problems. The number of full-time staff in the advice offices increased, and their skills and knowledge grew. Additional funds received through the trust provided for fieldworkers to carry the work beyond the confines of the offices. The need for improved management policies and practices grew accordingly. Elected office-bearers of the Sash, at national and regional levels, found themselves reluctantly becoming managers – not a task for which most of them were trained, nor their motive for joining the organisation. Management committees were established in each region, and uniform employment policies drawn up, but there were flaws inherent in a situation where professionals were being managed by volunteers.

In 1986 the position of national advice office coordinator was created, and Sheena Duncan, with her comprehensive knowledge of advice office work, took on this task in an honorary capacity. Regional advice offices, and their management committees, looked to her for guidance and leadership. Gradually, and almost imperceptibly at first, decisions relating to the advice offices and their management began to be made within that network, although always in consultation with the national elected structures of the organisation. The headquarters region had moved to Cape Town in 1986, but the majority of the trustees were based in Johannesburg.

This period, 1986 to 1990, coincided with the imposition of the nationwide state of emergency in South Africa, which brought to the Black Sash a huge increase in the tasks of monitoring and recording events, addressing a dramatic escalation in violence, and greater workloads for volunteers as well as staff. Violence monitoring, court monitoring, analysis of legislation, protest action and solidarity with other organisations all placed a heavy burden on Sash members. Distinctions between paid and unpaid workers were blurred, but some work could be funded by the trust and some could not, and eventually this started to be a cause for tensions. Members complained of a lack of clarity about where decisions were taken and about the role of the trust.

From 1990 onwards, after the lifting of the state of emergency, and the start of the process of negotiations towards a new and democratic government, it became time to look at how these tensions could be resolved. The newly elected Sash president, Jenny de Tolly, with her clarity of vision about structures, considered carefully the ways the entire organisation was managed and financed. In July 1991 she drafted an account of the 'National management of the Black Sash and all of its programmes',[3] in which she referred to the 'split persona' that was troubling it.

Further exploration followed in a series of documents, and in 1992 a small working group was mandated to consider a way forward. It came to be known as the Viljoen Commission because its proposer was Val Viljoen of East London, who had written, 'I have found that the Trust has taken upon itself more and more of a decision-making role ... It also seems to me that no-one really knows just who the final decision-making body is – the Trust or the National Executive.'[4] She herself was not available to work on the body, so the final composition of the group was Sue Power, Mary Kleinenberg, Rosemary van Wyk Smith and Rosemary Meny-Gibert.

Its report was carefully considered by national and regional committees, together with the report of a workshop with a similar objective held in Kempton Park by Johannesburg members, and recommendations were drawn up to be put to the national conference held in March 1993. They dealt with the unclear nature of the relationship between paid and volunteer workers, as well as the confusions and complexities around structures. It was clear that the dual burden of management of the trust and the regional advice offices, in addition to the national and regional elected committees, was placing a strain on the organisation.

Jenny and the national executive were convinced that in the longer term it was essential to merge the two structures, 'if we are to manage our human and financial resources effectively',[5] and that the Black Sash should work towards this. Without this, they argued, the voluntary component of the Sash would atrophy and disappear. In the short term, it was agreed that the national capacity for coordination and management should be strengthened, and in 1993 three national full-time positions were filled: a national advice office coordinator (Annemarie Hendrikz was appointed to take over from Sheena), a national financial administrator (Thisbe Clegg took on this task) and a national researcher (a position already held by Marj Brown, which was confirmed). In Cape Town, Alison Tilley was subsequently appointed as the coordinator for Legiwatch, the group which monitored parliamentary debates and followed the drafting and passing of legislation.[6]

Throughout 1993, as South Africa moved in fits and starts towards agreement at the negotiations table, the Sash continued to deliver its advice office services, its rural outreach work, and its monitoring and lobbying work. Looking towards the future, it grappled with ways of integrating all these elements, convinced that there should be ways to sustain the volunteer component.

The national executive sought to enable another region to take on the national leadership as from 1994, arguing that it was important to draw in new talents, build the capacity of the smaller regions, and share out the tasks. Jenny argued that such a move would be healthy for the organisation and would enable some of the fine and talented members in the regions to take on leadership positions. No offers to take over were forthcoming, and as the date for South Africa's national elections approached, the energies of the active members were fully engaged with preparations for voter education and for monitoring. Regular meetings were still held, but issues of management and structure were not the main focus.

It was not until the conferences of July 1994 – a national conference followed by an advice office workshop – that the organisation once again faced up to its options. In preparation for this, and in consultation with the national executive, Jenny had written a major position paper, 'Choices facing the Black Sash in 1994'. The work done by the Viljoen Commission and the responses to it had served to identify some of the key issues to be considered. These included the role of volunteers, the management of paid workers, the differences between the service work and the campaigns, funding and what aspects it could cover, and national coordination versus regional autonomy.

With regard to finding a structure which would best enable the Sash to address these needs, the national executive suggested that there were three options: the Gemini option (continuing to operate as two fairly separate structures, each with its own sources of funding and accountability systems); cutting the cords (separating the Advice Office Trust and its programmes from the Black Sash completely); and merger (uniting the volunteer body of the Black Sash with the Advice Office Trust, with a national board of elected, volunteer leadership advised by full-time employed coordinators).

Delegates came to the conferences with a variety of opinions, and there was a full debate on all aspects of these options, carried out with an independent facilitator. The decision was not unanimous, but eventually there was a substantial degree of agreement on the 'merger' option. The national executive was given the mandate to pursue this.

More turbulent waters still lay ahead, this time propelled by financial problems. Only a few months later, the Black Sash's extended national executive,[7] representing all its regions, met in Cape Town in an atmosphere of anxiety, dismay and anger. The meeting on 5 and 6 November 1994 was held in my house, and my strongest memories of it appear in flashes: tense debates; tearful groups clustered in different areas of the garden; recriminations and blame.

The written records of the meeting may not convey such strong emotions, but they do bear testimony to the urgency of the situation and the difficult decisions that had to be faced. The immediate crisis was a financial one: as Sheena Duncan explained, 'One of our major donors still owed us R200,000 from our 1993 agreement and none of the grant for 1994 had been received by October 1994 ... The second blow was that USAID, after a long and friendly partnership with us, informed us that they would not continue funding our programmes.'[8]

We were not alone among the many South African non-profit

organisations working in the field of human rights and social justice, in experiencing financial difficulties. We had all been supported in the apartheid years by generous donors from abroad, and had built strong relationships with them. We had all been aware for some time that international foundations and funding agencies were planning to divert funds to the new South African government, or else to allocate their funds to countries seen to be in greater need. For some organisations this meant that they would not survive, especially as many had also lost leadership figures to the new government and administration (a rich inheritance from civil society).

For several years, and particularly under Jenny's leadership, the Sash had been taking careful stock of its employment practices. It had always had a reputation for careful financial management, and the faithful commitment of many of its funders was testimony to this. We had anticipated a process of gradual withdrawal of some support, but the sudden loss of an important source of income was a huge shock.

The major costs of the organisation lay in the running of the advice offices, and the salaries of their staff. A portion of our funds had long been set aside to ensure that in the event of the Sash being obliged to close down (or even being banned or restricted), there would be sufficient money to afford an adequate, even generous, retrenchment package to all staff. Now it appeared that this moment had come. We were faced with the fact that we had only enough funds to survive for three or four months. It seemed that the only honourable thing to do was to give notice of retrenchment to all our staff by the beginning of December, while we were still in a position to fulfil our obligations to them. Everyone present at the meeting was deeply dedicated to the importance of the advice office work, and reaching this decision was agonising.

Many of us believed that we might still secure ongoing funding, and there were voices raised to insist that we should try our utmost to do so. Finally it was proposed that we should embark on the retrenchment process on a conditional basis, to meet legal requirements, but with the intention to reverse it if we could obtain new funding. This was reluctantly agreed, and, in addition, all regions were asked to place a moratorium on any expansion of their work, no budget increases were granted and no new projects approved.

We hoped that we might keep this decision confidential, but in the anxious climate of the time, when a number of organisations were being obliged to face the same issues, we decided it would be impossible to guarantee confidentiality. It would be wisest to make a public statement. The predictable result was a good deal of media coverage and distraught reactions from the Black Sash membership and staff.

More dreaded by me than any media or membership response was the reaction I anticipated from Jenny. She had been national president for over four years and had carefully built up structures, insisted on good management, kept a close eye on the finances, and handled many of the problems arising inevitably from making changes. She was not present at the extended national executive meeting, as she was just at that time coming to the end of a well-earned holiday abroad. I did not want her to receive this news second-hand or through the media. On the eve of her return I sent her a message, and then waited anxiously for her arrival. When she walked into the office I was overwhelmed with the tensions of the preceding days and I knew she would not be pleased with the decision taken. Rosemary Meny-Gibert said, 'I thought you were going to burst into tears,' and although indeed I had thought so too, my feelings were mostly of relief that Jenny was back.

As we could have predicted, she swung into action: the decision to issue retrenchment notices must be reversed, since no self-respecting funder would give money to an organisation that looked as if it was folding; a 'strategy team' was put in place; and urgent attention given to fundraising led by Thisbe Clegg, the national finance administrator. By the end of November some of the expected funds had been received and further aid was promised. The retrenchment process would not have to be implemented, and we were able to address staff anxieties and media perceptions, although funding difficulties remained for all non-governmental organisations.

This was an enormous relief, but the whole experience had brought us face to face with many other questions about the future of the Sash. The political and social changes which had taken place since 1990 naturally prompted discussions about our role in the new environment. Under a new government committed to a new constitution enshrining a bill of rights, what would be the nature of advice office work, or of advocacy for human rights? Surely it was no longer appropriate for an organisation made up almost entirely of white women to undertake such work? Nor would we be likely at this point to recruit women of other backgrounds, so perhaps it would be better to disband and hope that a new, truly non-racial women's organisation would come into being. The changing role of women in society, not only in South Africa but in many other countries, meant that more women were pursuing careers and were unable to dedicate themselves to full-time voluntary positions. Where would the volunteers in the advice offices, and the new leadership of the Sash, come from?

The remarkable fundraising rescue efforts by Jenny and Thisbe, which staved off the retrenchment decision, were followed by the decision of the strategy team to embark upon a major evaluation and strategic restructuring process, led by skilled consultants. Marian Nell and Janet Shapiro were briefed for this task, and Jenny was able to obtain funding for this purpose. Despite the difficulties of working over the end-of-year holiday period, they speedily engaged with all the regions, and the information and opinions they gathered contributed to a comprehensive report.

In February 1995 a three-day workshop was held at the Kirstenbosch Botanical Garden in Cape Town, where 40 representatives discussed the outcome of the evaluation. Predictably this meeting was as fraught with emotion as the one held in November, and time was set aside for feelings to be expressed. Provision was made for in-depth discussion, and for all representatives of members and staff in the regions to put forward their views and mandates, for consideration by the meeting.

The workshop was confronted with the difficulties and costs of the merger option which had been proposed. It required a daunting list of strategic planning, setting of objectives, participatory management, greater communication between all sectors, job descriptions for volunteers as well as paid staff, and proper induction and training programmes. If it had been possible to implement these, a merger might have succeeded, but this turned out to be very difficult, especially at the regional level. To be successful, additional management staff would have been needed in the regions, and the harsh reality of the funding difficulties made this seem impossible.

Nell and Shapiro ensured that all aspects of sustaining or changing the organisation were explored, and posed the question of where the future leadership would come from. Many of the delegates most strongly opposed to changing the structures were of the older generation, and unwilling or unable to take on the task. Recent attempts by the national executive to draw in office-bearers from the different regions had not met with success.

Some delegates to the workshop believed that it was time for the Black Sash to close, in the hope that a new, more broadly representative women's organisation would come into being, and expressed an eagerness to be part of such a body. Some said clearly that they did not wish to see the Black Sash in opposition to the new government.

For the three days we agonised over the choices confronting us all. Was this a question about funding, and who had the control over it? Was it about leadership and volunteer capacity? Was it about the organisation's role after 40 years, when some of its objectives had clearly been met?

In the end the decision was not about money: the mechanism we had devised to enable us to receive funds had caused us problems, but we could never have achieved all that the Black Sash did and continues to do without the financial support of generous donors. Nor was it solely about capacity to go on managing the organisation. The choice was about what the best way would be for the Sash to contribute to South Africa in this period of transition, given its skills, history and composition. The one thing we were all sure about was that the advice offices were still filled daily with people requesting assistance. This work was what South Africa still needed from us.

Agreement was reached and proposals would be taken to the last national conference for final ratification. The advice offices would be separated from the membership organisation; the membership organisation would close; the Advice Office Trust should keep the Black Sash name; the *Sash* magazine's May issue would be its last; a strategic planning team was appointed to ensure that the necessary steps were taken; and a press statement would be issued after all members had been informed by telephone of these decisions.

So we cut the umbilical cord, and set up the new structures. The Black Sash Advice Office Trust would be governed by a board of trustees according to the values bequeathed it by the Sash. A national director would head the new organisation and would be responsible for all the regional advice offices. The separation of the structures was approved by the national conference in May 1995. The closure of the membership organisation brought to an end the first 40 years of the existence of the Black Sash.

The process had been a long and painful one, characterised by argument and counter-argument, and conducted in an open and consultative manner. It is true that during its July 1994 national conference the Black Sash was taken to task by the journalist Barry Streek for having had part of its meeting in closed session. It had been important to allow members the freedom to discuss their views and feelings in private before moving on to vote on resolutions of great importance for the organisation. The entire process of revision of our structures over several years had, however, been open to scrutiny and comment.

Other organisations were facing similar issues, and one of them approached Sheena for advice. In a letter to Jenny, she wrote, 'God forbid that we should have to write the manual for the transformation process! If we ever did, whoever commissioned it would have to pay through the nose!'[9]

The tasks of disentangling the structures, appointing the staff and building the trust took time and effort over the next year or more. In March 1996 a new *Black Sash National Newsletter* reported to members on the steps taken and plans for the future. New members of staff were in place, and new additional trustees had been appointed: Phumelele Ntombela and Mpho Ndebele.

The nine advice offices and Legiwatch had developed their work plans and budgets for the year. These flowed from and reflected the national strategic plan, and all together built the national programme for 1996. As the Durban advice office commented, 'an empowering process for all those who participated in it'.

The task of ensuring that the volunteer component was not lost took longer still, and was less successful. Over the years, relationships weakened and the gap grew wider. Jenny never gave up her commitment to the value and importance of volunteer activism, and many of the documents she drafted bear witness to that view. For example, in her introduction to the showing of the film *The Early Years* to an extramural studies course at the University of Cape Town in August 1994, Jenny traced the history of the making of the film and said, 'For me the film will always also be about the women who put the film together. It was their energy, commitment and love for these veterans of the Sash and the things that they stood for that made this film a reality. This is volunteerism at its most creative and satisfying.'[10]

Many of us still wish to see a truly representative organisation of South African women, independent of any political party, pursuing the values of a strong civil society, aiming at eliminating violence, poverty, inequality and injustice, cherishing our rich heritage of different cultures while building a united country that embraces the rights of all.

In the two decades since that process of self-transformation, the Black Sash Trust has kept alive the values of its founders.[11] Though the road has not always been smooth, it has continued to aim for the goal of enabling all South Africans to obtain access to the rights which are their due. In 2014 the Black Sash Trust took the next step in its transformation by closing its one-to-one counselling service, in favour of strengthening its network of partnerships with community organisations. This was a logical progression from its support of the formation of the National Alliance for the Development of Community Advice Offices (NADCAO), which in turn led to the establishment of the Association for Community Advice Offices of South Africa (ACAOSA). These relationships have enabled the Sash to extend its reach considerably from the urban centres to more outlying areas in all nine provinces, where the need is greatest.

Since November 2006 the chair of its Board of Trustees has been Sibongile Mkhabela. She has made many significant contributions to South African society, and her discernment and dedication have been of great value to the Black Sash. It is remarkable to recall that she was the only woman of the 'Soweto Eleven' who were put on trial for sedition and terrorism after the June 1976 uprising of scholars, and who all made a powerful impression on Janet Sahli and Jill Wentzel for their 'maturity, alertness and high intelligence'.[12]

Many of the previous members have watched with pride the way in which the new structure has forged its way. Some of them have also often felt regret, saddened by the loss of the organisation they had been part of, and deprived of a channel for their voices. At times they have been tempted to don their black sashes once more, when constitutional rights have been threatened, or when there have been conflicts over poverty-related issues or violence against the most vulnerable people in society.

In December 2013, in sorrow at the death of President Nelson Mandela, and in celebration of his life, many of them did put on their black sashes and joined staff members on the steps of St George's Cathedral in Cape Town, where they had stood in protest so many times, so many years before. This time, their posters recaptured phrases quoted from and encapsulating Mandela's timeless words.

The Black Sash came into being in response to a constitutional issue. Today South Africa rejoices in a constitution that celebrates and protects democracy and human rights. Times change; people come and go; organisations grow and decline; values last longer than lifetimes.

APPENDIX
LIST OF OFFICE-BEARERS

National presidents		Vice-presidents
1956–1958	Ruth Foley	Cherry van Selm
1958–1959	Molly Petersen	Ruth Foley, Hildegarde Spottiswoode, Eulalie Stott
1960–1961	Eulalie Stott	Molly Petersen
1961–1975	Jean Sinclair	1961 Dora Hill, Jeanette Davidoff
		1963 Jeanette Davidoff, Muriel Fisher
		1964 Jeanette Davidoff, M.W. (Bobbie) Cluver
		1965 Dora Hill, Bobbie Cluver
		1966 Bobbie Cluver, Nell Green
		1967–1968 Bobbie Cluver, Jeanette Carlson
		1969 Bobbie Cluver, Joyce Harris
		1970–1972 Joyce Harris, Anna Marais
		1972–1975 R.M. (Bobbie) Johnston, Joyce Harris
1975–1978	Sheena Duncan	Gita Dyzenhaus, Joyce Harris
1978–1980	Joyce Harris	Sheena Duncan, Gita Dyzenhaus

1980–1982	Joyce Harris	Sheena Duncan, Jill Wentzel
1982–1986	Sheena Duncan	1982–1983 Joyce Harris, Jill Wentzel
		1983–1986 Joyce Harris, Ethel Walt
1986–1990	Mary Burton	1986–1987 Di Bishop, Ann Colvin, Margaret Nash
		1987–1988 Di Bishop, Margaret Nash, Rosemary Smith
		1988–1989 Di Bishop, Jenny de Tolly, Rosemary Smith
		1989–1990 Jenny de Tolly, Rosemary Smith, Sue Philcox
1990–1994	Jenny de Tolly	1990–1992 Mary Burton, Karin Chubb
		1992–1994 Sarah-Anne Raynham, Mary Burton
1994–1995	Mary Burton	Karin Chubb, Jenny de Tolly

Sash magazine editors

1955–1957	Doreen Rankin
1957–1958	Pat Causton
1958–1961	Desirée Berman
1962–1966	Dorothy Grant
1966–1973	Sheena Duncan
1973–1974	Sheena Duncan and Pat Tucker
1974–1976	Joyce Harris and Pat Tucker
1976–1978	Joyce Harris
1978–1979	Janet Sahli
1980	Gita Dyzenhaus

1980–1982   Janet Sahli

1982   Sheena Duncan

1982–1985   Jill Wentzel

1985–1986   Glenda Webster

1987–1995   During this period when the magazine was published in Cape Town, it was produced by an editorial committee, with different individuals taking responsibility for particular issues. These editors included Candy Malherbe, Sarah-Anne Raynham, Helen Zille, Di Meek, Birga Thomas, Hilary Ivory, Andrea Weiss, Martha Funk-Bridgman, Pat Tucker, Shauna Westcott and Domini Lewis. The committee included Betty Davenport, Kate McCallum, Nancy Gordon and Mary Starkey. There were representatives from each region, and Judy Chalmers and Lynette Paterson contributed to the special issue on the Eastern Cape. The very last magazine (1995) had a guest editor, Moira Levy. A masthead appeared in each issue of the magazine listing the members of the editorial committee.

Chairpersons of the Board of Trustees
Advice Office Trust, established in 1985

1985–1989   Joyce Harris

1990   Ethel Walt

1994   Sheena Duncan

2000   Di Oliver

2001–2002   Sheena Duncan

2002–2004   Jenny de Tolly

2004–2006   Di Oliver

2006–2015   Sibongile Mkhabela

NOTES

Introduction

1 Noted South African historian, founding member of Liberal Party, and his wife, a respected member of the Sash.
2 Recorded group interview, 28 April 2010. This took place at the home of Ethel Walt, and the others present included Laura Pollecutt, Jill Wentzel, Pat Tucker, Josie Adler, Jacklyn Cock, Judith Hawarden, Audrey Coleman, Julia Heaney, Mary Jankowitz and Beryl Stanton.
3 *New York Times*, 31 August 1989.
4 Eleanor Anderson, long-time Johannesburg Sash member and poet.
5 For example, Major-General Herman Stadler of the South African Police, told Kathryn Spink, 'We are interested in individuals who are part and parcel of the revolutionary onslaught and these people, most of them I believe unwittingly, are being used to further the aims and objectives of radicals.' See Kathryn Spink, *The Black Sash: The Beginning of a Bridge in South Africa*, London, 1991, p. 21.

Chapter 1

1 V.C. Malherbe, *Cape Times*, 20 October 1984.
2 Rodney Davenport and Christopher Saunders, *South Africa: A Modern History*, London, 2000, pp. 258–259.
3 Mirabel Rogers, *The Black Sash: South Africa's Fight for Democracy*, Johannesburg, 1956, p. 14.
4 Rogers, *The Black Sash*, p. 16.
5 Cherry Michelman, *The Black Sash of South Africa: A Case Study in Liberalism*, London, 1975, p. 37.
6 *Sash*, 1 (3), March 1956, p. 5. The first title of the magazine was *The Black Sash / Die Swart Serp*, until it became *Sash* in May 1969, with Volume 13 (1). In the Notes, I have referred to it consistently as *Sash*.

7   F. Bate, 'The Pretoria vigil', *Sash*, 3 (5), April 1958, p. 14.

8   D. Hacking, unpublished memoir, UCT Manuscripts and Archives, BC1065, B2.1.2. Dorothy Hacking recalls a meeting at which a story by Rudyard Kipling was cited, in which the resentful servants of an 'English sahib' contrived to place a black kitten everywhere he went, which eventually drove him to suicide. This inspired the plan for the 'haunting', in the hope that it would touch the consciences of the ministers.

9   Michelman, *The Black Sash*, p. 51.

10   Rogers, *The Black Sash*, p. iv, gives a list of the branches.

11   *The Black Sash: The Early Years* (film, 1992).

12   Rogers, *The Black Sash*, p. 176.

13   Jean Sinclair at the Bloemfontein national conference in April 1956, reported in *Sash*, 1 (5), May 1956, p. 5.

14   Rogers, *The Black Sash*, p. 133.

15   Rogers, *The Black Sash*, pp. 240–241, including photograph.

16   *Sash*, editorial, 7 (4), December 1963/January 1964, p. 2.

17   Cherryl Walker, *Women and Resistance in South Africa*, Cape Town, 1991, p. 153.

18   Helen Joseph papers, A1985, Historical Papers Research Archive, Cullen Library, University of the Witwatersrand.

19   In an SATV televised programme on 9 August 2006, and confirmed in a personal discussion.

20   Records of the Black Sash 1955–1995, Historical Papers Research Archive, Cullen Library, University of the Witwatersrand, AE862, C.1.

21   Records of the Black Sash 1955–1995, Historical Papers Research Archive, Cullen Library, University of the Witwatersrand, AE862.

22   'Geen ander doel word daardoor gedien nie, want die griewe word kunsmatig aangeblaas soos die feit ook bewys dat daar nog geen massa-steun aan die Sash-beweging gegee word nie.'

23   *Die Transvaler*, 9, 10 and 11 August 1956. My translation, except for the words in inverted commas, which appeared in English.

24   Jo MacRobert, 'The beginning 1955–1958', Anniversary Supplement, *Sash*, 17 (3), May 1995.

25   Quoted by Jo MacRobert in 'The emergence of the Black Sash advice office in Cape Town: A regional study of the Black Sash, 1956–1963', BA Honours thesis, University of Cape Town, 1988, p. 6.

26   Rogers, *The Black Sash*, pp. 133, 134.

27   MacRobert, 'The beginning', p. 2.

28   Michelman, *The Black Sash*, pp. 61–70.

29   Helen Joseph, *Side by Side*, London, 1986, p. 186.

30   Joseph, *Side by Side*, p. 167.

31   *Sash*, 3 (14), January 1959, p. 14.

32   *Sash*, 3 (6), May 1958, p. 2.

33 *Sash*, 3 (6), May 1958, p. 10.

34 *Sash*, 2 (9) (wrongly numbered 8), October 1957, p. 8.

35 *Sash*, 3 (7, 8), June/July 1958, p. 2.

36 MacRobert, 'The emergence of the Black Sash advice office in Cape Town', p. 13.

37 MacRobert, 'The emergence of the Black Sash advice office', pp. 41 and 42.

38 MacRobert, 'The emergence of the Black Sash advice office', p. 51.

39 Michelman, *The Black Sash*, pp. 10 and 11.

40 *Sash*, 4 (2), February 1960, p. 11.

Chapter 2

1 *Sash*, 11 (1), February/April 1967, p. 17. Rob Robertson's life was one of dedication to peace and justice.

2 Letters in the Jean Sinclair collection, AD1457, Historical Papers Research Archive, Cullen Library, University of the Witwatersrand, provided the basic facts from which the above account is recreated.

3 *Sash*, 18 (1), May 1975, p. 20.

4 Matrimonial Property Act of 1987, implemented in 1988.

5 Noël Robb, *The Sash and I*, Cape Town, 2006, pp. 117–118.

6 M.E. Fisher, 'Tour of Natal', *Sash*, 1 (4), April 1956, p. 13. Describing a gruelling 10-day tour, she added, 'We were rather amused to hear in one Natal town that certain leading social lights [*sic*] felt it was not quite the thing to join the Black Sash. This really tickled me, having been told in one well-known town in the Cape that no one was encouraged to join unless her blood was very blue!'

7 *Sash*, 1 (8), August 1956, p. 7.

8 *Sash*, 29 (3), November 1986, p. 29.

9 *Sash*, 13 (2), August 1969, pp. 11–14.

10 *Sash*, 26 (1), May 1983, p. 28.

11 Fleur Webb, interviewed by Mary Kleinenberg, Pietermaritzburg, 19 July 2011, for the Alan Paton Centre, University of KwaZulu-Natal, Oral History Project.

12 The Suppression of Communism Act provided for the listing of names of people suspected of being sympathetic to communism. People thus named were forbidden a number of activities.

13 Dot Cleminshaw, personal communication.

14 Myrna Blumberg, *White Madam*, London, 1962, p. 67.

15 Ruth Carneson, *Girl on the Edge*, Cape Town, 2015, p. 71.

16 Personal communication.

17 All quotations above from *Sash*, 4 (2 and 3), February and March 1960.

18 *Sash*, 3 (23), November 1959, pp. 10–11.

19 Mary Dyer, interviewed by Pat Merrett, Pietermaritzburg, 4 August 1995, for the Alan Paton Centre, Oral History Project.

20 *Sash*, 2 (8), September 1957, pp. 10–11.

21 *Sash*, 3 (10), September 1958, pp. 5–6.

NOTES

22 From documents in Jenny de Tolly's personal collection.
23 P.M. Wells, Oxford, personal communication, April 2011.
24 Personal interview.
25 'The Dean and the Sash', *Sash*, 16 (1), June 1972, pp. 7–11.
26 *Sash*, 1 (11), November 1956, p. 11.
27 *Sash*, 1 (12), December 1956/January 1957, p. 7.
28 Personal communication.
29 P. Crosoer, personal interview.
30 *Sash*, 3 (23), November 1959, p. 7.
31 A. Brown, 'Outlook in Elgin – 1971', *Sash*, 14 (4), March 1971, pp. 20–23. Also M.W. Cluver, 'Resettlement of Africans in South Africa', *Sash*, 13 (4), pp. 25–29.
32 Interview with Ann and Rachel Brown, 14 February 2013.
33 *Sash*, 37 (2), January 1995, p. 51.
34 *Sash*, 30 (1), May 1987, p. 42.
35 Black Sash national conference minutes, 1978, in Mary Burton papers, UCT Manuscripts and Archives, BC1065; also *Sash*, 20 (1), May 1978, p. 10.
36 SAIRR, *Survey of Race Relations 1970*, Johannesburg, 1971, pp. 43–46, and *Survey of Race Relations 1971*, Johannesburg, 1972, pp. 74–75.
37 *Sash*, 11 (2), May/July 1967, pp. 22–25.
38 *Sash*, 22 (1), May 1980, p. 18.
39 *Sash*, 25 (3), November 1982, pp. 12–14.
40 Title inspired by Brian Currin of Lawyers for Human Rights.
41 *Sash*, 31 (1), June 1988, pp. 5–9.
42 *Sash*, 31 (2), September 1988, p. 43.
43 Spink, *Black Sash*, p. 232.
44 Jo-Ann Bekker and Barbara Orpen, 'Death row revisited', *Sash*, 32 (1), May 1989, pp. 28–31.
45 Andrea Durbach, *Upington*, Cape Town, 1999, p. 206.
46 Durbach, *Upington*, pp. xi–xii.
47 SAIRR, *Survey of Race Relations 1997–1998*, Johannesburg, 1998, p. 25.
48 SAIRR, *Survey of Race Relations 1978*, Johannesburg, 1979, pp. 59–62: Civil Defence Act No. 67 of 1977 and Defence Amendment Act No. 49.
49 Charles Yeats, *Prisoner of Conscience*, London, 2005, pp. 8 and 91.
50 Jonathan Ancer, article in the *Mail & Guardian*, 25 August 2008.
51 Richard Luyt, Opening address to national conference, 14 May 1985, in *Sash*, 28 (1), May 1985, pp. 7–11 (includes his speech and photographs).
52 Dot Cleminshaw, 'Abortion, the campaign for the South African "Choice on Termination of Pregnancy Act No 92 of 1996"', unpublished paper, in Mary Burton papers, UCT Manuscripts and Archives.
53 June Cope, 'Abortion', *Sash*, 25 (4), February 1983, p. 15.
54 Cope, 'Abortion', p. 17. June Cope also wrote *A Matter of Choice: Abortion Law Reform in Apartheid South Africa*, Pietermaritzburg, 1993.

55 National Conference minutes, 1993, in Mary Burton papers, UCT Manuscripts and Archives.
56 D. Cleminshaw, 'Abortion', p. 8.
57 Cleminshaw, 'Abortion', p. 10.
58 Denise Ackermann, 'Liberating praxis and the Black Sash', *Sash*, 34 (2), September 1991, pp. 22–27.

Chapter 3

1 Sheena Duncan, 'The Black Sash: Starting a new advice office', September 1987, working paper, in Mary Burton papers, UCT Manuscripts and Archives.
2 MacRobert, 'The emergence of the Black Sash advice office', pp. 58–59, and personal interview with Amy Thornton.
3 The story of CATAPAW and the different perceptions of its component organisations is fascinatingly told in papers by Annette Griessel, 'CATAPAW and the anti-pass campaign in Cape Town in the Fifties', in Linda Cooper and David Kaplan (eds.), *Selected Research Papers on Aspects of Organisations in the Western Cape*, UCT, 1982; Jo MacRobert, 'Ungadinwa Nangomsa – Don't get tired tomorrow: A history of the Black Sash advice office in Cape Town', MA thesis, UCT, 1993; and Helen Scanlon, *Representation and Reality: Portraits of Women's Lives in the Western Cape 1948–1976*, Cape Town, 2007.
4 Personal interview with Lettie Malindi.
5 MacRobert, 'The emergence of the Black Sash advice office', p. 40.
6 *Sash*, 24 (4), January 1982, p. 25.
7 Personal interview with David Viti, 2012.
8 Advice Office report, October 1983, Cape Western Region, in Black Sash collection, UCT Manuscripts and Archives, BC1020, A1.
9 MacRobert, 'The emergence of the Black Sash advice office', p. 69.
10 The government struggled with appropriate terminology for the racial categories into which people were placed at birth by the Population Registration Act. Black South Africans were first defined as 'Natives', then 'Bantu', and eventually the relevant department's name was changed from 'Bantu Affairs' to 'Plural Relations', and finally 'Black'.
11 *Sash*, 12 (2), November 1968, p. 31.
12 Michelman, *The Black Sash*, p. 129
13 Athlone Advice Office Annual Report, 1966/1967 in Black Sash collection, UCT Manuscripts and Archives, BC1020.
14 *Sash*, 17 (1), May 1974.
15 *Sash*, 7 (3), October/November 1963.
16 J. Scott, 'The Black Sash: A case study on liberalism', DPhil thesis, University of Oxford, 1991.
17 Scott, 'The Black Sash', p. 165.
18 Scott, 'The Black Sash', citing Natal Coast Regional Report to national conference, 1968.

19 Scott, 'The Black Sash', p. 166. See subsequent pages of Scott's thesis for more information on the Athlone advice office and the Eiselen line and for a critical self-examination about whether the Sash's work was merely palliative.

20 Minutes of Elgin branch, in UCT Manuscripts and Archives, BC668, A4.2.

21 Jillian Nicholson, personal interview, 5 August 2014.

22 C. Pridmore, 'Albany', Sash, 16 (7), November 1973, p. 32.

23 Deena Streek, 'East London advice office report', Sash, 16 (7), November 1973, p. 34.

24 Sash, 18 (1), May 1975, p. 34.

25 Scott, 'The Black Sash', p. 217.

26 Sash, 34 (3), January 1992, p. 51.

27 Sash, 25 (2), August 1982, p. 27.

28 See further detail about TRAC in Chapter 4.

29 Sheena Duncan quoted in Time magazine, 7 September 1987, in an article by Bruce W. Nelan.

30 Sash, 34 (3), January 1992, p. 50..

Chapter 4

1 Desmond Tutu, in A. Hendrikz, Sheena Duncan, Cape Town, 2015, p. xii.

2 Sash, 5 (5), December 1961, p. 22.

3 Cape Argus, 22 August 1981.

4 Cape Times, Evening Post and Argus articles between August and September 1981.

5 Sash, 25 (2), August 1982, p. 26.

6 Sash, 5 (1), December 1960/February 1961, p. 30.

7 Sash, 3 (19), June/July 1959, p. 22. This was a special issue on the pass laws.

8 Michelman, The Black Sash, p. 110.

9 D. Dallas and V.C. Malherbe, personal communication.

10 Sash, 21 (1), May 1979, pp. 33–34.

11 Sash, 21 (1), May 1979, pp. 33–34.

12 Busi Nyide, interviewed by Mary Kleinenberg, Pietermaritzburg, 2 August 2005, for the Alan Paton Centre, Oral History Project.

13 Pessa Weinberg, interviewed by Mary Kleinenberg, Pietermaritzburg, 8 July 2010, for the Alan Paton Centre, Oral History Project.

14 Sash, 26 (1), May 1983, p. 21.

15 Sash, 25 (3), November 1982, p. 26.

16 For more detailed information, see SAIRR, Laws Affecting Race Relations in South Africa 1948–1976, Johannesburg, 1978, pp. 70ff.

17 Minister of Community Development, quoted in SAIRR, Laws Affecting Race Relations, p. 75.

18 Sash, 5 (1), December 1960/February 1961, and many other magazine articles over the next years.

19 Sash, 2 (12), January 1958.

20 M. Birt and M. Burton, 'Group Areas: Claremont-Lansdowne', *Sash*, 11 (3), November 1967, p. 28.

21 *Sash*, 9 (1), March/April 1965, pp. 7–9.

22 *Sash*, 9 (1), March/April 1965, p. 7.

23 *Sash*, 10 (1), February/April 1966, p. 2.

24 Amanda Parkyn, 'District Six is declared white', in *Skin: A Poem Sequence*, Penkridge, UK, 2011.

25 *Sash*, 17 (2), August 1974, p. 20. 'Alexandra dossier' recounts the destruction of family houses and the building of single-sex hostels for men and women in Alexandra Township and the edict that children were to be sent 'away'. On Sophiatown, 1958, see 'Catalogue of shame' by Barbara Waite, *Sash*, 17 (2), August 1974, p. 6.

26 L. Platzky and C. Walker, *The Surplus People: Forced Removals in South Africa*, Johannesburg, 1985, p. 8.

27 Tim Keegan, 'Onslaught on black farmers', *Sash*, 26 (2), August 1983, p. 22.

28 Platzky and Walker, *The Surplus People*.

29 A. Pirie, 'Life on the hillside', *Sash*, 5 (3), June 1961, p. 18. See also *Sash*, 3 (20), August 1959, p. 11.

30 *Sash*, 4 (2), February 1960, p. 8.

31 D. Patrick, 'Black spot removals in northern Natal', paper presented at national conference in 1968 and published in *Sash*, 12 (3), November 1968, pp. 17–20.

32 *Sash*, 12 (3), November 1968, pp. 17–20.

33 *Sash*, 12 (3), November 1968, p. 21.

34 *Sash*, 12 (3) November 1968, pp. 21–24.

35 P. Hall, 'Resettlement in the Ciskei', *Sash*, 25 (1), May 1982.

36 Ethel Walt, 'South Africa: A land divided', Johannesburg, 1982. (Also well reproduced in colour in C. Walker and B. Cousins (eds.), *Land Divided, Land Restored*, Cape Town, 2015.)

37 *Sash*, 25 (2), August 1982.

38 Prue Crosoer, personal interview, 11 December 2012.

39 *Sash*, 25 (4), February 1983.

40 *Sash*, 26 (4), February 1984.

41 *Sash*, 35 (1), May 1992, p. 32.

Chapter 5

1 Mary Robinson, *Everybody Matters*, London, 2012, p. 133.

2 Cherryl Walker, *Sash*, 29 (4), February 1987, p. 26.

3 *Sash*, 1 (4), April 1956.

4 Di Davis, personal interview, Cape Town, 24 March 2010 (recorded on CD).

5 Di Davis, personal interview, 24 March 2010.

6 Interviewed by Janet Cherry and Judy Chalmers, 'Lessons from aloes: Five profiles', *Sash*, 35 (3), January 1993, pp. 32–33.

7 *Report of the Truth and Reconciliation Commission*, Cape Town, 1998, Volume 3, p. 37.

8   *Sash*, 5 (1), December 1960/February 1961, p. 29.

9   *Sash*, 5 (5), December 1961, p. 30.

10 *Sash*, 5 (5), December 1961, p. 7.

11 Saleem Badat, *The Forgotten People*, Johannesburg, 2012.

12 *Bandwagon*, publication by Dot Cleminshaw, James Polley and two others (all members of the Christian Institute, but writing in their private capacity). Three of the eight issues of *Bandwagon* were banned during 1976 and the publication ceased. See Dot Cleminshaw papers, UCT Manuscripts and Archives, BC1051, MM4.1.

13 Badat, *The Forgotten People*, p. 189.

14 *Sash*, 10 (4), November 1966.

15 *Sash*, 35 (3), January 1993, p. 34. This issue had a special focus on the Eastern Cape.

16 SAIRR, *Survey of Race Relations 1978*, Johannesburg, 1979, p. 46.

17 Group interview in Port Elizabeth, 29 October 2009 (recorded), with Judy Chalmers, Valerie Hunt, Lesley Greensmith, Cathy Binell, Baa Thompson, Lindsay Woods, Viki Proudlock, June Crichton, Debbie Mattheus, Bobby Melunsky and Zoë (Riordan) Tookey.

18 SPP, *Forced Removals in South Africa: The Surplus People's Reports*, vol. 2, *The Eastern Cape*, Cape Town, 1983, pp. 197–198.

19 Personal communication, 23 July 2014.

20 HQ Circular, May 1982, in Black Sash collection, UCT Manuscripts and Archives, BC668, D1.

21 Personal communication, 3 November 2009.

22 Telephone interview, recorded, 2 August 2014.

23 See chapter 4 for a detailed account of the Sikade family's plight.

24 *Sash*, 5 (5), December 1961, p. 22.

25 *Sash*, 20 (3), November 1978, p. 25.

26 Betty Davenport, personal interview, Cape Town, 2010.

27 Betty Davenport, personal interview, Cape Town, 2010.

28 Shirley McLennan, Albany advice office report for 1973, Black Sash National Conference papers, UCT Manuscripts and Archives, BC668.

29 *Sash*, 16 (7), November 1973, p. 31.

30 *Sash*, 17 (1), May 1974, p. 29.

31 All quotations from personal interview with Val Viljoen, June 2014.

32 Interview with Val Viljoen.

33 Interview with Val Viljoen.

34 The Suppression of Communism Act of 1950 provided various mechanisms for silencing people who were 'listed' as members or supporters of communism: they could be subjected to house arrest, banned from all political or educational activities, and their words could not be quoted.

35 Joyce Harris, 'Memorandum on police conduct', *Sash*, 28 (1), May 1985, p. 27. The memorandum was available from the Johannesburg office at the time, at R2 per copy.

36 SAIRR, *Survey of Race Relations 1985*, Johannesburg, 1986, pp. 489–492.

37 SAIRR, *Survey of Race Relations 1985*, pp. 455 and 534.

38 SAIRR, *Survey of Race Relations 1985*, p. 499.

39 Cornelia Bullen-Smith and Beva Runciman, recounted in *Sash*, 28 (2), August 1985, p. 23.

40 Personal recollection.

41 For a detailed account of their work, and a vivid description of Molly's funeral, see Spink, *Black Sash*, pp. 165–185.

42 *Sash*, 28 (1), May 1985, p. 33.

43 *Sash*, 16 (2), August 1972, p. 26 (incident took place 24 March 1972).

44 S. Power, 'Sash women on trial', *Sash*, 29 (4), February 1987, p. 35.

45 S. Power, *Sash*, 37 (3), May 1995, anniversary supplement, p. 10.

46 *Sash*, 33 (1), May 1990, p. 22.

47 *The Guardian*, 9 May 1990.

48 *Sash*, 24 (4), January 1982, inside front cover.

49 *Sash*, 28 (1), May 1985, p. 31.

50 J. Chalmers, personal communication, 5 August 2014.

51 J. Chalmers, personal communication, 5 August 2014.

52 J. Chalmers, personal communication, 5 August 2014.

53 Janet Small, Fieldworker's report, 1987, Janet Small's personal collection.

54 Personal interview, 18 June 2014.

55 *Sash*, 34 (3), January 1992, pp. 11–12 and 15–16.

56 *Sash*, 29 (2), August 1986.

57 *Sash*, 29 (4), February 1987.

58 Janet Small, Fieldworker's report, July 1987.

59 Lynette Paterson, 'A poem for Janet', *Sash*, 31 (2), September 1988, p. 46. The poem was originally composed for Janet Small, but by the time it was published Janet Cherry had been redetained in Port Elizabeth on 23 September 1988. She had previously been in detention for 11 months in 1986/87.

60 P. Hall and M. Roux, 'Life after detention', *Sash*, 31 (1), June 1988, p. 44.

61 Grahamstown, Port Alfred, Kenton, Alexandria, Somerset East, Riebeeck East, Alicedale, Bedford, Fort Beaufort and Adelaide, as well as Cradock.

62 S. Middleton, J. Segar, R. Smith and G. Morgan, 'The hidden burden', *Sash*, 34 (2), September 1991, p. 39.

63 Hall and Roux, 'Life after detention', p. 45.

64 Jillian Nicholson, personal interview, Durban, 5 August 2014.

65 Robinson, *Everybody Matters*, p. 133.

Chapter 6

1 Drawing on many ideas and suggestions, the creative team that finally produced this highly successful fabric included, in addition to Patricia Davison, Sue Clarke, Sue Townsend, Andrew Putter and Roddy Davison (screenprinting).

2 *Sash*, 2 (12), January 1958, p. 3.

3 Ann van der Riet, personal communication.

4 Extract from a review of the New York exhibition, *Rise and Fall of Apartheid*, at the International Center of Photography, in *New York Times*, 21 September 2012.

5 Tonya Hays, personal correspondence with the Black Sash, 2013.

6 Philippa Taylor, *Sash*, 31 (1), June 1988, p. 59.

7 Coral Vinsen, personal communication, 2014.

8 *The Black Sash: The Early Years* (1992).

9 Jenny de Tolly, personal communication.

10 The original banners are safely stored in the Iziko National Gallery's collection, Cape Town.

11 Kassinga, or Cassinga, in Namibia, was the site of a South African air attack on a SWAPO base on 4 May 1978.

12 Sheena Duncan was a member of the Black Sash national committee at the time and had recently returned to Johannesburg after an information-sharing trip to the US.

13 There were eventually about 25 organisations involved in the CCW, and these included the Legal Status Committee (concerned with the legal status of all women); African Self Help; Cape Democrats; Union of Jewish Women; JODAC (the Johannesburg Democratic Action Committee); Communicate and Network; Association of University Women; National Council of Women; PFP (Progressive Federal Party); Women for Peace; ECC (End Conscription Campaign); NUSAS (National Union of South African Students); and Black Sash.

14 Harriet Gavshon, *The Ribbon* (1987).

15 Adele Kirsten, past ECC campaigner; Clare Verbeek, ECC; Ethel Walt; and Gille de Vlieg; all interviewed by Marj Brown in September 2004 and cited in a research paper, 'The peace ribbon: A heritage impact assessment', Marj Brown's personal collection.

16 The nationwide state of emergency had been declared on 12 June 1986, and Proclamation 109 gave the minister, or any person authorised by him, the authority to seize any publication.

17 See Appendix: List of office-bearers, for a complete list.

18 Minutes of meetings of Claremont branch of the Black Sash, in Black Sash collection, UCT Manuscripts and Archives, BC668, A4.2.

Chapter 7

1 Scott, 'The Black Sash', p. 126.

2 *Sash*, 17 (1), May 1974.

3 The Programme for Social Change was initiated by Peter Randall in early 1974, to carry forward the work done by the Study Project on Christianity in Apartheid Society (SPROCAS), of which he had been the director. See James

Moulder, 'Pale-faced peep at Spro-cas', *Sash*, 17 (3), November 1974, p. 13.

4 *Sash*, 17 (3), November 1974.

5 Jean Sinclair, Presidential address, *Sash*, 18 (1), May 1975, pp. 1–7.

6 H. Suzman, typescript, in Black Sash Cape Western region collection, UCT Manuscripts and Archives, BC668.

7 *Sash*, 18 (5), May 1976, pp. 1–4.

8 *Sash*, 19 (1), May 1977, p. 14.

9 *Sash*, 20 (1), May 1978, p. 10.

10 *Sash*, 19 (3), November 1977, pp. 14–15.

11 *The World, Weekend World*, and *Pro Veritate.*

12 SAIRR, *Survey of Race Relations 1977*, Johannesburg, 1978, pp. 31–34, 168–169. Organisations banned included SASO, BPC, BCP and the Union of Black Journalists.

13 SAIRR, *Survey of Race Relations 1977*, p. 125.

14 *Sash*, 17 (3), November 1974, p. 32.

15 Robb, *The Sash and I*, p. 104.

16 J. Seekings, *The UDF: A History of the United Democratic Front in South Africa 1983–1991*, Cape Town, 2000.

17 Joyce Harris in national circular of the Black Sash, 9, 1984, in Mary Burton papers, UCT Manuscripts and Archives, BC1065.

18 George Bizos, 2 May 1988, Delmas Treason Trial transcript (Pretoria, 1988), pp. 22654–22917, Historical Papers Research Archive, Cullen Library, University of the Witwatersrand, AK2117.

19 Day two of Sheena Duncan's evidence, 3 May 1988, Delmas Treason Trial transcript.

20 Delmas Treason Trial transcript, p. 22772.

21 SAIRR, *Survey of Race Relations 1988/1989*, Johannesburg, 1989, pp. 571–572.

22 SAIRR, *Survey of Race Relations 1989/1990*, Johannesburg, 1990, p. 201.

23 Janet Cherry, 'We were not afraid' in N. Gasa (ed.), *Women in South African History*, Cape Town, 2007, p. 283.

24 The initials used for the federation were FSAW in its early years, and changed to FEDSAW in the 1980s.

25 Karin Chubb and Rosemary van Wyk Smith, 'In praise of women: Malibongwe!', *Sash*, 33 (1), May 1990, pp. 38–39.

26 National circular, 15/3, December 1984, in Mary Burton papers, UCT Manuscripts and Archives.

27 M. Burton, letter to all regions explaining motivation and events, September 1985, in Mary Burton papers, UCT Manuscripts and Archives.

28 *Sash*, 27 (3), November 1984, pp. 10–11.

29 *Sash*, 27 (3), November 1984, pp. 10–11.

30 *Sash*, 27 (3), November 1984, pp. 10–11.

31 *Sash*, 27 (3), November 1984, p. 4.

32 J. Wentzel, *The Liberal Slideaway*, Johannesburg, 1995

33 See Circular, 1, 1985, re internal lobbying about Wentzel debate and 'Repression in a time of reform'. See also Mary Burton's letter to all members, November 1985. Both in Mary Burton papers, UCT Manuscripts and Archives, BC1065, B2.1.3.

34 Defence and Aid was originally established to provide legal defence for political trialists and support for their families. It was banned in South Africa in 1966, and in its place the Dependants' Conference was set up under the aegis of the South African Council of Churches to take on the family support.

35 *Sash*, 32 (3), January 1990, p. 57.

Chapter 8

1 At the request of Jenny de Tolly, then the Sash national president, who had received the invitation but was unable to attend.

2 Sheena Duncan, *Sash*, 36 (1), May 1993, p. 19.

3 Jenny de Tolly personal papers.

4 Letter of 12 April 1992 from V. Viljoen to J. de Tolly, copied to Sheena Duncan, in Mary Burton papers, UCT Manuscripts and Archives, BC1065.

5 Response to the Viljoen Commission Report by the national executive of the Black Sash, March 1993, in Mary Burton papers, UCT Manuscripts and Archives, BC1065.

6 The Legiwatch group included Betty Davenport, Noël Robb, Candy Malherbe, Esther Sher, Shauna Westcott, Mary Burton, Lorna Levy, Martha Bridgman and Joan Dichmont.

7 This ExNex was a body specifically put in place some time previously to provide for inclusive and participatory decision-making. It consisted of the representatives of the staff and of all the regions, together with the elected national office-bearers and the trustees of the Advice Office Trust.

8 S. Duncan, Report from the Trust chairperson to the Black Sash national conference, May 1995, in Mary Burton papers, UCT Manuscripts and Archives, BC1065, B2.2.

9 Sheena Duncan letter, in Jenny de Tolly's personal papers.

10 Jenny de Tolly, address to UCT Extramural Studies course, 11 August 1994, typescript in Jenny de Tolly's personal papers.

11 The Vision Statement (1993) and Values (1995) are published in Margie Orford (ed.), *The Golden Jubilee Report: 1955–2005*, Black Sash, 2005, pp. 110 and 19–22.

12 Janet Sahli, 'The Soweto Eleven', *Sash*, 20 (4), February 1979, p. 6.

BIBLIOGRAPHY

Badat, Saleem, *The Forgotten People*, Johannesburg, 2012

Benjamin, Eileen, 'An historical analysis of aspects of the Black Sash, 1955–2001', MA thesis, University of Stellenbosch, 2004

Black Sash, *Greenflies: Municipal Police in the Eastern Cape*, Cape Town, 1988

Black Sash, *Inside South Africa's Death Factory*, Johannesburg, 1989

Black Sash, *The Black Sash 1955–2005: The Golden Jubilee Report*, Cape Town, 2005

Blumberg, Myrna, *White Madam*, London, 1962

Catholic Institute for International Relations, *Now Everyone Is Afraid: The Changing Face of Policing in South Africa*, CIIR, London, 1988

Cleminshaw, Dot, 'Abortion: The campaign for the South African Choice on the Termination of Pregnancy Act, No. 92 of 1996', Unpublished paper, 2006

Cole, Josette, *Behind and Beyond the Eiselen Line*, Cape Town, 2012

Cooper, Linda and Dave Kaplan (eds.), *Selected Research Papers on Aspects of Organisations in the Western Cape*, Department of Econ-omic History, UCT, 1982

Davenport, Rodney and Christopher Saunders, *South Africa: A Modern History*, London, 2000

Desmond, Cosmas, *The Discarded People*, Johannesburg, undated

Durbach, Andrea, *Upington*, Cape Town, 1999

Fester, Gertrude, 'Women writing for their rights', in *Agenda*, 46, 2000

Gasa, Nomboniso (ed.), *Women in South African History: Basus' iimbokodo, Bawel' imilambo / They Remove Boulders and Cross Rivers*, Cape Town, 2007

Hassim, Shireen, *The ANC Women's League*, Johannesburg, 2014

Hendrikz, Annemarie, *Sheena Duncan*, Cape Town, 2015

Jaster, Robert Scott and Shirley Kew Jaster, *South Africa's Other Whites*, London, 1993

Joseph, Helen, *Side by Side*, London, 1986

Joseph, Helen, *Tomorrow's Sun: A Smuggled Journal from South Africa*, New York, 1967

Kleinenberg, Mary and Christopher Merrett, *Standing on Street Corners: A History of the Natal Midlands Region of the Black Sash*, Pietermaritzburg, 2015

Legal Education Action Project and Black Sash, *Working for Justice: The Role of Paralegals in South Africa*, Proceedings of July 1990 conference

MacRobert, Jo, 'The emergence of the Black Sash advice office in Cape Town: A regional study of the Black Sash, 1956–1963', Unpublished paper, UCT, January 1988

MacRobert, Jo, 'Ungadinwa Nangomso – Don't get tired tomorrow: A history of the Black Sash advice office in Cape Town', MA thesis, UCT, 1993

Michelman, Cherry, *The Black Sash of South Africa: A Case Study in Liberalism*, London, 1975

Nicholson, Christopher, *Permanent Removal: Who Killed the Cradock Four?* Johannesburg, 2001

Parkyn, Amanda, *Skin: A Poem Sequence*, Staffordshire, UK, 2011

Platzky, Laurine and Cherryl Walker, *Forced Removals in South Africa*, 5 vols., Cape Town, 1983

Platzky, Laurine and Cherryl Walker, *The Surplus People*, Johannesburg, 1985

Qunta, Christine (ed.), *Women in Southern Africa*, Johannesburg, 1987

Robb, Noël, *The Sash and I*, Cape Town, 2006

Rogers, Mirabel, *The Black Sash: South Africa's Fight for Democracy*, Johannesburg, 1956

Sash magazines, 1956 to 1995

Scott, Jennifer, 'The Black Sash: A case study of liberalism in South Africa 1955–1990', DPhil thesis, University of Oxford, 1991

Seekings, Jeremy, *The UDF: A History of the United Democratic Front in South Africa 1983–1991*, Cape Town, 2000

Smith, Rosemary, *Swimming with Cobras*, Cape Town, 2011

Spink, Kathryn, *Black Sash: The Beginning of a Bridge in South Africa*, London, Methuen, 1991

Sutherland, Carla, 'The role of whites and fundamental change in South Africa: A case study of the Black Sash', Research paper in partial fulfilment of African Studies Honours, UCT, February 1987

Walker, Cherryl, *Women and Resistance in South Africa*, London, 1982 (and Cape Town, 1991)

Wentzel, Jill, *The Liberal Slideaway*, Johannesburg, 1995

Yeats, Charles, *Prisoner of Conscience*, London, 2005

INDEX

abortion 74–5; ANC women and 76; BS's stand on 73–6; legislation 66
Abortion and Sterilisation Act (1975) 74–5
Abortion Reform Action Group (ARAG) 73–4, 76
Abortion Reform League (ARL) 73
Ackermann, Denise 77, 172
Adler, Josie 108–9, 124, 139–40
Advice Office Forum 96
advice offices 39–40, 48, 60, 79, 83, 88–93, 95–6, 104, 107, 182, 184, 196, 211–13; founding 37, 79–81; after 1990 217–19, 227–8; annual reports 191; attacks on 38; community-based 95–6; dealing with local problems 149–50; duties 83, 154; fieldworkers 94, 156, 219; finances 218, 223; focus on injustices (1990s) 97–8, 108–10, 122–3; focus on socio-economic problems 92–3, 97, 145; full-time staff 218; gathering case histories of pass laws victims 88, 98; helping squatters after shack demolition 124; identifying trends in government practice 88; in-depth knowledge gained 13, 40, 83–5, 98, 196, 211, 218–19; monitoring apartheid injustices 20, 40, 138, 142–4, 196, 219; monitoring payouts of pensions 108; recording detentions 150; reports 90; training courses 93, 96, 98, 218; volunteers 82–4, 86, 90, 94, 152, 221; voter education (1990s) 97, 221; working with organisations 93–4, 96; Athlone 80–2, 91, 190; Cape Eastern 139; Cape

Town 37, 90, 93, 190; Cookhouse 153; Crossroads 123; Durban 90–2, 228; Eastern Cape 143, 152–4; East London 44, 90, 92, 142, 145; Elgin 90–1; Grabouw 64; Grahamstown 92, 143, 150; Johannesburg 81–2, 90–1, 93, 194; Knysna 64, 94; Pietermaritzburg 92; Port Elizabeth 90, 93, 138–40, 150, 153; Uitenhage 153
Advice Office Trust 218–20, 222, 227
African National Congress (ANC) 28, 32, 192, 196–7, 200; and UDF 203; banning 38, 137; secret discussions with government 213; unbanning 69, 205, 213; Women's League (ANCWL) 29, 79–80; Youth League 134
Aitchison, Bunty 180
Alexander, Neville 193–4
Alexander, Ray 33
Amampondo 171
Ames, Frances 50
Amnesty International 67
apartheid 160, 180; laws 13, 21, 35–6, 53, 110, 125, 196; resistance to 13, 20, 145–8, 159, 180, 185–6, 189, 191–3; *see also* detentions; forced removals; pass laws
art 171–2
Artists for Human Rights Trust 172
Association for Community Advice Offices of South Africa (ACAOSA) 229
Association for Rural Advancement (AFRA) 94
Azanian People's Organisation (AZAPO) 193